THE YEARS AND THE WIND AND THE RAIN

A BIOGRAPHY OF
DOROTHY M. JOHNSON

THE YEARS AND THE WIND AND THE RAIN

A BIOGRAPHY OF DOROTHY M. JOHNSON

FOREWORD BY A.B. GUTHRIE, JR.

BY STEVE SMITH

PICTORIAL HISTORIES PUBLISHING COMPANY
MISSOULA, MONTANA

LIBRARY OF CONGRESS
CATALOG CARD NUMBER 84-61543

ISBN 0-933126-50-6

First Printing   October 1984

Book Design & Typography: Arrow Graphics
Layout: Stan Cohen
Cover Art: Monte Dolack

Also by Steve Smith

Fly the Biggest Piece Back
The Ox: Profile of a Legendary Montana Saloon

PICTORIAL HISTORIES PUBLISHING COMPANY
713 South Third West
Missoula, Montana 59801

FOREWORD

WILL ROGERS SAID OF CHARLIE RUSSELL THAT HE WAS NOT JUST A painter, he was not a just anything. So I say of Dorothy Johnson that she is not just a writer or a just anything. The person stands equal with the product, a fact certainly not true of all authors.

The product stands high, for, make no mistake, Miss Johnson is a writer. As she said to me once when her eyesight was dimming, "Writing is what I do." Amen. Her works are marked by clean prose, a fine sense of organization and contrast and a laconic wit. Edmund Gosse once said that the secret of successful fiction was a continual slight novelty. Whether in fiction or non-fiction, Miss Johnson never needed to be told that. She knew instinctively.

By turns—no by mixture—she has been newspaperwoman, editor, teacher and, first of all, writer. Her course must have been set when she was a girl in Whitefish, Montana, a place she writes of with keen memory and bright humor in the recently published *When You and I Were Young, Whitefish.*

In my hands is a bibliography of her works. It includes 17 full-length books, 52 stories, numerous poems and many other pieces, an impressive list by any writer. For years her letters to the editor have delighted readers of the *Missoulian.*

Only a reckless appraiser would venture to say which of her works is best, but when I think of her publications *The Bloody Bozeman* comes first to my mind.

Miss Johnson has persisted with courage in the face of physical difficulties that would have discouraged and defeated lesser folk.

But sympathy is not what she wants. What she wants is to write well and do it steadily.

May the gods be with her.

A. B. Guthrie, Jr.
Choteau, Montana

CONTENTS

PREFACE

DOROTHY M. JOHNSON CRACKED THE BIG-TIME FICTION MARKET IN 1930 and thought her future assured as a writer. Then, for 11 years, magazine editors ignored her. Time and again she conquered disappointment, and one day heard herself called by a critic "the most brilliant woman Western taleteller since Mary Austin." Her tools were perseverance and toil, and in the difficult and frustrating business of writing they brought her considerable fame.

For 15 years she found her way with relative ease through the maze that is New York City. Only after returning to Montana did she become lost—in the garbage dump of a town containing little more than a post office and gas pump. As she had before, and as she has since, she laughed at herself and made others laugh. Laughter was another of her tools.

Born in Iowa and reared a widow's daughter in a tough, mud-and-stump, Montana railroad town, Dorothy Johnson learned long before adulthood that optimism was better than pessimism and that to laugh at herself was better than to lament. She learned self-discipline and she learned the difference between talking and doing. She learned something about cynicism, too. In a letter written early in 1965 to the University of Montana student newspaper, the *Montana Kaimin*, she proposed a new campus organization based on these principles:

1. Although some people are absurd, life is not; life is good and we are glad to have it.

2. We retain the right to laugh (kindly if possible) at absurd people, but we will never sneer at life.

3. A member who becomes hopelessly infected with the prevalent idea that we are all worms together and nothing is any use will be encouraged to depart from our company.

4. If a member becomes convinced that he himself is an absurd worm, we will give him sympathy until he proves it. Then we will eject him from our society so that he can seek his own level.

5. We will not babble about whether this is the best of all possible worlds but will accept with grace the fact that it is the only one we have at the present time.

6. We will endeavor to live in it, and inevitably leave it, with dignity and without whimpering, believing that, although we may become food for worms, they will not be committing cannibalism.

Dorothy Johnson also learned that sacrifice was the price of achievement. Still, she went ahead undaunted—partly because she chose to and partly because her personality demanded it. A close friend, Dr. Catharine Burnham, considered her an example of dynamic equilibrium. Like an airplane in flight, Dr. Burnham once explained, Miss Johnson's equilibrium depends on her staying in motion.

Miss Johnson did, indeed, stay in motion, a fact testified to by her accomplishments in not one, but many, careers.

As a student, her potential was evident. As a secretary and stenographer—and later as an advertising copywriter and magazine editor—employers considered her a blessing. As a newspaper reporter, columnist and news editor, her work was deemed invaluable by her boss, himself a veteran editor. As a book reviewer, her services were sought by the *New York Herald Tribune, Saturday Review* and by several noted historical periodicals. As a professor of journalism, her experience and sense of humor were assets that gave to students the encouragement to try—then to try again. As secretary-manager of the Montana Press Association, her adroitness in technical matters and her masterful handling of people commanded deep loyalty and respect. As a raconteur, she was eminent.

And always—through the nights, through the weekends, through the vacations, through the years—there has been the writing. Among her lessons, she learned that perspiration, concentration and determination usually had their just rewards. She learned that one could lose many battles without losing a war. She lost many battles—like the one that lasted 11 years—but in the end she triumphed.

Time compared the best of her short stories with those of Mark Twain and Bret Harte.

The *New York Herald Tribune* placed her in the exalted company of A. B. Guthrie Jr. and Conrad Richter.

Editors of *The Outnumbered*, a 1967 anthology of stories, poems and essays about America's minority groups, thought her story "Scars of Honor" sufficiently good to be published with those of John Steinbeck, William Saroyan, Willa Cather and Stephen Vincent Benet.

Editors of *The Western Hall of Fame*, a 1984 anthology of classic Western short stories selected by the Western Writers of America, thought her stories "Lost Sister" and "A Man Called Horse" sufficiently good to be published with stories by Mark Twain, Stephen Crane, O. Henry and Zane Grey.

Richard Tyre, a Pennsylvania English professor and authority on American frontier literature, described her style as " lean, unadorned and understated," and labeled it "reminiscent of Hemingway at his best."

Jack Schaefer, author of *Shane*, described her as one of the few writers whose authenticity, integrity, sheer vigor and excitement were helping to build a body of true literature about the American West.

The National Cowboy Hall of Fame and the Western Heritage Center in Oklahoma City, Oklahoma, named her book *Buffalo Woman* the outstanding Western novel of 1978 and gave her the Western Heritage Wrangler Award.

˙ The Western Writers of America in 1976 presented her with the prestigious Levi Strauss Golden Saddleman Award for "outstanding contributions to the history and legends of the West."

The University of Montana presented her with a Distinguished Service Award as well as the school's highest honor, an honorary doctor of letters degree.

Hollywood repeatedly paid its respects.

What follows is a biography of Dorothy M. Johnson. For many hours of assistance, for much helpful advice and for encouragement in this project, I wish to thank Professor Warren J. Brier, former dean of the School of Journalism at the University of Montana. I also am indebted to Professor Nathaniel B. Blumberg, former dean of the UM journalism school, and the late Vedder M. Gilbert of the UM Department of English. Both gave generously of their time. Others whose help was especially valuable include the late Mrs. Homer Taggart of Midland, South Dakota; Mrs. A.C. (Mable) Engelter, librarian emeritus, Whitefish Public Library, Whitefish, Montana; Dr. Catharine A. Burnham, Peekskill, New York; Mel Ruder, Columbia Falls, Montana; the late Professor Harold G. Merriam, Missoula, Montana, and the late Gurnie M. Moss, Kalispell, Montana.

Finally, a word of special thanks is due my friends Richard and Ingrid Geissler. Early on in this project they gave me invaluable moral support and many memorable hours—he at the pool table and she at the dinner table.

Steve Smith
Missoula, Montana

Dorothy Johnson with her 1976 Levi Strauss Golden Saddleman Award "for bringing dignity and honor to the history and legends of the West." (*Bob Cushman photo*)

For Sandy Smith Lowmaster, who had courage

OLD MINE

Once there were men here.
The pebbled dirt roof of the cellar
Juts out from under the hill.
A pile of tin cans, so rusty
As to be almost a part of the earth, by now
Lies at the foot of the hill.
The house is gone, and the men—
God only knows where they have left their picks.
Here are only their leavings
And a gash in the earth that is almost healed.
The years and the wind and the rain
Heal everything.

Dorothy Marie Johnson

CHAPTER ONE

Iowa

R ISING IN THE NORTHERN HIGHLAND REGION of the state whose name it bears, the Wisconsin River flows south toward Illinois. The river traverses the fertile, green dairyland of the Central Plain, and near the town of Portage—70 miles north of the Illinois line and 30 miles north of Madison—cuts sharply to the southwest toward Iowa. Almost 100 miles downstream from the bend, having passed through Prairie du Sac and Sauk City, Muscoda; Boscobel and Wauzeka, it joins almost at a right angle with the wider, muddier Mississippi.

Across the Mississippi is Iowa, and in Clayton County, some two miles upstream from the rivers' meeting point, is the town of McGregor. The Father of Waters laps at its feet. Dairy farms and bountiful acres of hay, corn, oats and soybeans spread out of sight to the west, north and south. Platted in 1846, incorporated in 1857, and with a population of 5,000 in the 1860s, McGregor, by 1870, had become the main trading point for most homesteaders within a 200-mile radius. However, by 1900, its population had dwindled to 1,500, the chief reason being the westward push of the railroads, which opened western Iowa, Minnesota and the Dakotas to further settlement.

Harry and Lottie Johnson settled on a modest farm south of McGregor in 1873. Tall, stern-faced and characterized by a glass eye, he was a Pennsylvanian by birth. His wife, the former Charlotte Root, was a native of New York. They brought their son, Lester Eugene, born in Albion, New York, on December 20, 1870, and an older daughter, Grace.

A frail-looking, handsome boy with a sensitive, perceptive face,

[1]

young Lester's early education was in a country school near his parents' farm. After attending the McGregor city school, he earned a teaching certificate from Iowa State Teachers College at Cedar Falls. He taught school for five years after his graduation—four in North McGregor (now Marquette) and one in Washington state, where he acquired a lifelong love for the West. Learning that his father's health was failing, Lester resigned his teaching position

Harry and Lottie Johnson and their children, Grace and Lester.

and came home to run the family farm.

The evening of June 25, 1896, was ideal for the graduation exercises of the nine seniors of McGregor High School. Among the graduates was Mary Louisa Barlow, at 16 the class salutatorian. Known as Louisa, she was born in North McGregor on December 30, 1879, the eldest daughter of William and Carrie Barlow. William Barlow, English by birth, had come to the United States as a young man. Soon after his marriage to Carrie Hilmoe, a native of Norway, he settled in North McGregor to work in a mill. The family later moved a mile down river to McGregor, where Mr. Barlow worked for a produce company. Louisa, 13 at the time, enrolled in McGregor High School, from which she would be graduated youngest in her class and with high honors.

After her graduation, Louisa attended Teachers Institute at Elkader, Iowa, passing her examinations with high marks. Although, according to Iowa law, she was not old enough to receive a teacher's certificate, her record was so outstanding that the county superintendent sent her papers to the state superintendent requesting that she be given a certificate. She returned to North

Mary Louisa Barlow at age 16.

McGregor's streets frequently were the victim of the rampaging Mississippi River.

McGregor, where she taught at country schools for four years.

Her teaching career—at least in country schools—soon ended with the peal of a wedding bell. Box socials in Iowa at the the turn of the century were events to which young ladies brought beautifully decorated boxes of lunch to be auctioned. While young men at these affairs were enthusiastic about the food, their primary concern was who had prepared it. The auction over and the lunches eaten, each man often would escort to her home the girl whose lunch he had purchased. So it was with Lester Johnson—teacher, market gardener and potato specialist—and Louisa Barlow, teacher. Later, Lester would drive Louisa from her boarding place to her parents' home on Friday afternoons, delivering her again late Sunday for another week of school. School ended, but the buggy rides did not.

While courting, Lester and Louisa sometimes attended Chautauquas at a nearby Mississippi River summer resort called

McGregor Heights. Included in the entertainment were moon-light excursions on the steamboat "J.S.," which made regular trips, stopping at towns and presenting shows. Three stories high and offering music, dancing and dining, the vessel may have been the place where Lester proposed to Louisa. The two were married by a Methodist minister July 3, 1901, in McGregor. Lester had built a house on the farm near his parents' home, and he took his bride there.

The same frame house, white and two stories with a lean-to addition at the rear, was where Louisa Johnson, four and one-half years later, gave birth to a daughter. The date was Tuesday, December 19, 1905, the time, 6 a.m. Attending mother and child was a woman, Dr. A.M. Clark, assisted by Jessie Moody, a local nurse, and Louisa's sister, Mattie.

The Johnsons, planning to name their 6½-pound daughter Mattie after her aunt, were restrained by the aunt, herself, who

Lester Johnson and his bride, Louisa, soon after their marriage on July 3, 1901.

[5]

Dorothy Johnson was born in this house on December 19, 1905. Her father built the house, which was on a farm near McGregor, Iowa. *(Photo courtesy of Mrs. Homer Taggart)*

disliked the name. Finally christened Dorothy, the child was to go by her middle name, Marie, until her entrance into college almost 17 years later.

Sickly at first, Marie Johnson weighed 14 pounds by the time she was four months old. Within a year she was pulling herself up using chairs until her father purchased a baby walker.

As his daughter cut her first tooth, took her first steps and became accustomed to her first pair of overalls, Lester Johnson continued to operate the small farm south of McGregor. However, in 1908, a kidney ailment forced him to move with his wife and daughter to St. Paul, Minnesota, where he enrolled in a business school. The move was the first of many for the 2½-year-old Marie. Within a year, the second was planned when Mr. Johnson learned of an office position in Great Falls, Montana.

For a man trying to change jobs because of bad health, heaving freight at a railroad station was little improvement for Lester Johnson. However, that is what he was forced to do when, on his arrival in Great Falls in 1909, his resources meager, he discovered that the company that had hired him was not altogether legitimate. Lifting freight was no better for him than farming; his health remained poor.

In 1911, Mr. Johnson's business training and some brief experience as an office manager in St. Paul helped him obtain a time-keeper's job at the Montana Power dam at Rainbow Falls below Great Falls on the Missouri River. Marie Johnson, now 6, had just started school in Great Falls when her father moved the family to Rainbow.

Having to discontinue her formal education apparently did not bother Marie. As she pointed out some 40 years later in a column written for the *Great Falls Tribune*, Rainbow was "pretty close to heaven":

Dorothy Marie Johnson at age 5.

There was a little cluster of houses near the dam at Rainbow Falls, but not enough of them, so we lived in a tar-paper-covered building by the railroad track.

At six, you're still close to the ground. You can be fascinated by white pebbles the rain has washed and by the tumbling growth of prickly pear.

There were usually no children at the dam, but I had a couple of purely imaginary companions, Alice Syrup and Mabel McNamara. Mabel had a big family of brothers and sisters whom I never bothered to name. So there was always plenty of company and when we argued about what to do next, I always won.

We had a big dog named Bob—until he attacked one train too many. We also had a big yellow cat named Sputten and, for a few hours, a scared little wild rabbit that burrowed to freedom from under a box just as fast as he could manage it.

Life certainly wasn't dull at Rainbow. Trains went by our front windows. Once there was a freight wreck that couldn't have been closer. Later I watched the wreckers picking up the splinters that had been boxcars, but I slept through what must have been a magnificent crash.

Once our house caught fire when lightning came in on the railroad's telephone line. I missed that, too, although I was wide awake.

My mother heard a noise like a mouse gnawing, and when she investigated she found that the sound came from fire crackling in the wall. A couple of men happened to be out on the track picking up some freight so she called them. She was so cool about the emergency that they didn't realize there was one and took their time about getting there.

They put the fire out with water from one of our two barrels. Unfortunately, they used the drinking water, which had to be hauled by wagon all the way from Great Falls. They didn't touch the barrel of undrinkable floor-cleaning water from the Missouri River.

All kinds of wonderful things happened at Rainbow. Like the time a work train stayed on the side-track for several days. The mustached cook was one of nature's noblemen; he thought a little girl who came to call should be rewarded with at least half a pie. He was especially good with chocolate. I missed him after the work train moved on because I never got half a pie all at once at home.

Trains went by our house and I used to hurry out and hang upside down on a gymnastic bar my father had fixed up in the yard. I fancied that all the passengers stared in profound admiration. Anyway they stared.

There was one bit of excitement that I didn't miss, because I caused it. I almost got run over by a train. I was working on the tracks that day—or anyway hanging around helpfully—with the

[8]

Japanese section hands, who were our near and good neighbors. One of them was John Kimura, a six-footer, unusually big for a Japanese. He saved my life.

On this day, the men were working on the track where it went through a deep cut with a curve beyond. I climbed on their handcar and found that by pulling down hard on the pumping handle I could make it move, though very slowly. I got the handcar to inching along the track, and John Kimura looked up from his work just in time to see me on the handcar moving toward the curve, with a flag of train smoke showing above the cut.

He ran and grabbed me with one hand and threw me against the dirt wall of the cut. Then he gave a heave with his powerful shoulders and flipped the handcar off the track on its back like a turned-over turtle. After the train roared by, he carried me home. That was the only time I ever saw him look cross.

The Japanese men gave Marie the attention they couldn't give their faraway families.

"I was the only little girl around and I was the belle of the ball," she said. "They would give me such nice Christmas presents and, of course, a little girl takes that as nothing more than she's got coming."

Transportation between Rainbow and Great Falls in the early 1900s was crude. Families going to town either went by team and wagon or by handcar. The latter, pumped by two men, crossed the Missouri on a high trestle.

"I just loved it and my mother just hated it," Miss Johnson said. "We'd sit there with our feet hanging over and she'd cover up her eyes. I thought it was very exciting."

Marie Johnson's career as a writer began at Rainbow Falls. It also ended there, temporarily, a few sentences into "Jack's Lily," her first creative attempt. The trouble stemmed from some shortcomings in her education.

"My mother had taught me to read because I wanted to learn," she said. "I had also learned to write (in Great Falls) but I hadn't learned to spell. That first story didn't get too far because I thought I'd better retire until the mere mechanics were a little bit easier. There was nobody in 'Jack's Lily' named Jack and there wasn't any lily in it. I only got a couple of sentences down and it was just too hard to spell. I didn't write any more for a few years."

Miss Johnson has no idea why she started writing. She claims it was simply something she had to do.

"I didn't know then that I was always going to have to do it," she said. "This is the way it is with some writers—they just have to write. My trouble was that I just didn't have anything to write about—I didn't have anything to say."

Marie was too young at the time to realize it, but in retrospect she believes that the days at Rainbow were hard days for her parents.

"I loved every minute of it, and although my parents must have been terribly worried about a lot of things, they didn't let me know," she said.

The Johnsons were at Rainbow throughout most of 1912. Toward the end of the year they returned to Great Falls, living there for about three months. During that period, Mr. Johnson was offered a job as secretary of a commercial association. For the fifth time in as many years, the Johnsons moved. Their destination was Whitefish, Montana.

CHAPTER TWO

Whitefish

A LAKE, A SETTLEMENT, A NEW ROUTE FOR A railroad: From those elements emerged Whitefish, situated 40 miles south of the Canada border in mountainous northwestern Montana. The town was named for the scenic, 7-mile-long lake; the lake was named for the bountiful whitefish that for years had made it popular for fishing and camping.

In 1902 the area contained scattered logging camps and a dozen homesteads. Community life, such as it was, centered on the settlement of Whitefish Lake, the name given the general store and hotel situated on the lake shore west of the mouth of the Whitefish River. Mail came by buggy from Columbia Falls to the east and was distributed at the store, the hamlet's unofficial post office.

The town of Whitefish, the plat of which was filed with the Flathead County clerk and recorder on June 25, 1903, was the child of James Jerome Hill's Great Northern Railroad. Prior to a decision by Hill and other GN moguls, the railroad had angled southwest from Columbia Falls to Kalispell—15 miles— before going to Eureka, Rexford, Libby and other towns to the north and west. Disagreement still exists as to why Hill decided to remove his main line from Kalispell—a larger town—and run it through Whitefish. Some claim the strong-willed Hill, later known as the Empire Builder, was clashing with Kalispell business interests. The consensus, however, is that he was motivated by more practical reasons.

Soon after leaving the upper Flathead Valley, westbound trains on the old line encountered a substantial grade until reaching Haskell Pass—30 miles northwest of Kalispell. Eastbound trains

Not without good reason did many early residents of Whitefish refer to the settlement as "Stump Town." This photograph, taken about 1908, provides a view of the main street looking south. The area at the lower right is the approximate site of the present-day Cadillac Hotel and Hanging Tree Restaurant-Lounge. *(Photo courtesy Whitefish Public Library)*

had similar trouble. Like those going west, they required two loco-motives for the long pull. This "double-heading" slowed traffic and was expensive, two drawbacks Jim Hill would not tolerate.

Hill considered railroading a freight, rather than a passenger, enterprise. He saw his line's future in the hauling of livestock, grain, lumber and ore, and regarded Haskell Pass as an obstacle. The new line through Whitefish was some 17 miles longer than the Kalispell route, but for freight traffic it was almost a water grade. Preliminary surveys were done in the summer of 1901 and by October 1904, crews, engines and other equipment were being moved to the new terminal. Whitefish later became the railroad's division point.

With the coming of the Great Northern main line and the rug-ged railroaders whose livelihood it provided, the area's dense for-ests gave way to homesites. Whitefish still was being hacked from the woods when Lester Johnson arrived with his wife and 7-year-old daughter on a chilly March day in 1913. The girl who had loved the windswept prairie country near Rainbow was equally enchanted with the heavily timbered mountains surrounding her new home. Portions of the country had been scarred by fire, and Marie often came home covered with charcoal after playing near stumps and snags. Some of the new growth was jackpine timber scarcely taller than Marie. To her, it was wonderful to have so many of what she called "Christmas trees" so close.

"The first day I went out and looked around I found an old bird's nest," she said later. "This was something you didn't see at Rainbow, where there were two trees you walked a mile just to have a picnic under."

The Johnsons' first home in Whitefish was at 555 Kalispell Avenue. Among their first neighbors were the Millhouses, whose son, Glenn, later carried Marie Johnson's books to school and who was to become a Flathead County clerk and recorder.

Marie, who had been tutored by her mother for two hours a day at Rainbow, entered the second grade—spelling deficiencies and all—soon after arriving at Whitefish. Her return to the classroom was not without confusion, mainly because school officials were not sure whether second grade was the proper starting point.

When she first moved to Whitefish with her parents in 1913, Miss Johnson lived in this house (since remodeled) at 555 Kalispell Avenue. To the right of the house was a vacant lot where Chief of Police George Tayler, a family friend, planted a vegetable garden. Miss Johnson sold the produce door-to-door. *(Photo by the author)*

"The big question about what grade I belonged in was because my mother had been teaching me with special books she got," Miss Johnson said. "The principal, Harry Hayden, questioned me about what I knew. He asked me if I knew the multiplication tables and I said no. So they put me in the second grade. It was not until later that I found out Mr. Hayden was talking about the timeses. I knew the timeses pretty well—I had just never heard of the multiplication tables."

One of Marie's first experiences on resuming her formal education was unlike anything she had encountered under her mother's guidance. Her teacher, the late Olivia Forcum, walloped a boy with a wooden pointer, breaking it on him.

"It scared the wits out of me," Miss Johnson said. "She did have some mean boys in that class, but that was a frightful thing to have happen on my first day in a new school."

Having learned that the multiplication tables and the "timeses" were one and the same, Marie continued her education.

"The next year I was in the third grade for awhile," she said. "That teacher had both third and fourth grades, and the fourth grade was doing much more interesting things. I was kind of doing what they did anyway, so pretty soon they promoted me. This meant that all of the rest of the way through school I was two years younger than everybody else in the class. This is not good. I could do the work just fine, but I was always the little kid with the rest of them. It was especially bad in high school. It's just a shame if you don't fit socially. It was a handicap, but who was to know it was going to be?"

Early in 1914, failing health forced Lester Johnson to resign his job with the Whitefish Commercial Association. Soon afterward, he was appointed city treasurer to fill the vacancy created by the resignation of one C.H. Jennings. This was part-time work he could do in the evening, but even with the reduced work load Mrs. Johnson often was called on to help him.

During her grade-school years, Marie developed a habit that was to stay with her throughout her life—reading. She read *Ben Hur* at age 10 without much enthusiasm, then tackled *Tess of the Storm Country*, which she had been told not to read.

"I read it . . . and assumed that the reason it was forbidden was that the villain cut the warts off Tess's pet toad," she said. "The fact that Tess had an illegitimate baby escaped my infant understanding completely."

One of the marvels of the Whitefish grade school was a mysterious source of books for pupils. Where the school's library was—or what it looked like—Marie never knew. She used it to full advantage but never really got enough to read.

Poetry also began to interest Marie at about age 10. One of her first poems was about Indians:

Over the foaming river
And across the level plain
Rushed a band of Indian warriors
Thick as the pattering rain.

About the poem, Miss Johnson later commented: "Of course a

river on a level plain doesn't foam, and the simile is poor, but it does rhyme. That's all I remember of it. I had never seen any Indians except at a county fair in Kalispell and don't remember having read anything about them at age 10. Still, they were part of the tradition for children, and my mother used to call me Rain-in-the-Face to laugh me out of a spell of tears."

Lawrence (Frenchy) DeVall, who later became a Whitefish restaurateur, went through grade and high school with Marie Johnson. DeVall lived on Columbia Avenue across the alley from the Johnsons and he remembers his schoolmate as "very studious" and "always reading." She was something of a tomboy, he said, who liked being around horses and who loved the idea of the West. She had developed a lisp, was nearsighted and wore glasses almost always.

"She had a wonderful personality and was always full of fun," DeVall said. "Life seemed to mean a great deal to her."

Miss Johnson acquired her first pair of glasses in Kalispell. Later, on occasion, she was taken to Great Falls for eye examinations. During one such appointment, a doctor told the Johnsons that if their daughter's nearsightedness continued to grow worse, she would be blind at age 20. Miss Johnson's childhood reading habits are, perhaps, partly explained by that visit. She overheard some of the doctor's conversation and, misunderstanding it, decided she would have to get her reading done before her vision was gone. Thinking that reading was causing the nearsightedness, Louisa Johnson often discouraged her daughter from doing so much. Marie, however, continued reading heavily.

If there was one person Marie Johnson looked on as a hero during her formative years, it was Chief of Police George Tayler of Whitefish. A friend of her father's, it was to Tayler's memory that she later dedicated her book *Famous Lawmen of the Old West*. Somebody once wrote on the dust jackets of Miss Johnson's books that her stories were based on tales told by "old pioneers" when she was growing up in Whitefish. Although the statement is the invention of an imaginative blurb writer, it's safe to say that knowing George Tayler—his six-gun under his coat at church—provided excellent background for someone destined to write of the West.

"I just adored him," Miss Johnson said. "He was so good to us.

She started wearing glasses early.

He was the typical western hero and a marvelous man for a little girl to admire. Whitefish was a tough town with some really tough characters in it. Uncle George always had to wear a gun because there were people looking for him who would just as soon have got rid of him."

A sideline of Tayler's was blowing out stumps. He was an expert with dynamite, a skill that was handy when the time came to clear more. land for the growing Whitefish. Miss Johnson had fond memories of Tayler's stump-blowing operations:

"One time he blew up a stump right underneath one of the windows in our house. He didn't even crack the window. All the children would trail around after him. He had certain equipment that he used, including a beat-up old couch that was all metal. He'd put that on the stump and dig under it and put his explosive in the hole. Then he'd cut some trees down and cover the stump with them to keep the stump from blowing too far. When he was ready to light it, he'd yell at us to run. Believe me, we ran! We weren't afraid of the dynamite—we didn't have that much brains. We were afraid of him and what he'd say. Then there would be a grand explosion. This was a technique that not everybody had perfected. I can still remember the wonderful smell of the pieces of wood that came raining down."

Among other friends of the Johnsons were the Lockridges, the two families having become acquainted through Methodist Church activities. Considered an accomplished ball player and marble shooter, Marie occasionally stopped by the Lockridge home to see if the boys of the family—John and Leon—could go gopher shooting. The two families sometimes exchanged holiday dinners, with Thanksgiving at the Johnson home and Christmas at the Lockridge home. Once, Mrs. Lockridge—having asked Marie if she cared for a second helping of anything—was told, "Yes, a little of everything, please."

Lester Johnson never regained his health. He died of chronic nephritis, with complications of the heart, in Whitefish on December 13, 1915, seven days before his 45th birthday, six days before his daughter's tenth. Active in Methodist Church circles and a member of the Oddfellows, Mr. Johnson gained considerable respect during the brief time he lived in Whitefish. Miss Johnson later described the winter of her father's death:

"It was an awfully bleak Christmas. I remember asking my mother, 'What should I send to Uncle Billy?' Billy Seibert had been a good friend of ours at Rainbow Falls. He was a young bachelor who dressed very sharply according to the styles of the day. He was so good to me when I was a little kid at Rainbow, and a good friend of my folks. I told my mother that maybe I'd make him a pen wiper and then she had to tell me that Billy was dead. He had been electrocuted in an accident at the Rainbow power plant. My father was dead and Uncle Billy was gone. It was an awful shock."

Louisa Johnson took over her husband's job as city treasurer. The following June she and Marie returned to St. Paul, Mrs. Johnson to attend business college and Marie to have an operation on her nose. They lived with Mrs. Johnson's sister, Mattie, and her husband. In the fall of 1916, Louisa Johnson, still working on her business course, enrolled her daughter in the seventh grade of a St. Paul school.

Returning to Whitefish in November, Louisa Johnson resumed her duties as city treasurer, undertook the teaching of a Sunday school class at the town's Methodist Church and became an assistant to the city water commissioner. She subsequently was fired from the latter job because of a political upheaval in the city administration. However, she soon was hired as a cashier for the Mountain States Power Co., a job she held for 10 years.

Her daughter, meanwhile, happy to be back in Whitefish's seventh grade and apparently a better speller, renewed her writing career.

"I started to write poetry," she said. "It was terrible stuff but I had to do it anyway."

School, however, could no longer be Marie's only pursuit. Although her mother provided living expenses, little money remained for spending. Also, there was college to consider. The responsibility of providing spending cash and a college fund fell to Marie:

> "I worked at any little odd jobs I could get. A nickel was pretty good pay for running an errand and a dime was generous pay. For 15 cents you'd almost sell your soul. I used to go over and wash dishes for a woman who didn't like to do it. I think she paid me 15 cents an hour. She never got her dishes rinsed and so the food would all be stuck on them. It was perfectly horrible but I worked at it willingly."

George Tayler, besides being good with explosives, also was an expert gardener. He planted a garden on the Johnson family's two extra lots and launched Marie into the produce business:

> "I would take the stuff around town in a market basket and peddle it. I hated every minute of it, but all the money that came from it I could have. I couldn't spend it but I could have it to put away for college. I had peas and lettuce and all kinds of stuff. I

hated it because I was so timid. It just killed me to go up on somebody's porch and rap on the door.

"My opening gambit, standing on one foot, scratching my mosquito bites and lisping, was, 'You wouldn't want any nithe ripe peath, would you?'

"Sometimes I'd walk by four or five houses because I could just tell by the color of the paint that they weren't going to buy anything. I think many people bought stuff just because it was such a sad-looking little girl selling it. Or maybe they wanted it—you didn't get those things in stores at that time.

"Two little boys, with a bigger garden as their source of supply, cut in on my territory. Worse than that, they peddled from a coaster wagon while I lugged a market basket. They were big dealers.

"I was shocked; I was mad; I wept. Somebody should thtop them, I proclaimed. But there was no way to thtop them, and nobody but me seemed to think they should be thtopped. As a matter of fact, there was a bigger market around town than they and I together could supply. Not many people had gardens and very little produce was shipped in. Prices (set by our parents) brought no complaints from customers.

"Competition had no effect except that we were more careful about the quality of our merchandise and we got going with it earlier in the day."

Selling horseradish was another way to make money. The horseradish grew in the Johnsons' yard and had only to be dug, scraped, chopped up, mixed with vinegar and put in jelly glasses before being marketed at a local restaurant.

"Scraping the peeling made me cry like everything," Miss Johnson said. "You can't breathe." She came to detest the pungent root.

Another fund-raising method was to participate in Whitefish's annual cleanup campaigns:

"Everybody just threw his old tin cans out in the back yard, so the city government decided to pay children to clean up at a rate of a nickel for each 100 cans. The Presbyterian and Episcopal churches of Whitefish were built on a solid fill of old tin cans, faithfully delivered by money-grubbing children, of whom I was one. The children earned small fortunes, the citizens got their back yards and alleys cleaned up, and the valleys downtown were filled up so they were level with the hills."

Selling subscriptions to *Youth's Companion* provided Miss

Johnson with experience and an occasional prize:

> "I never was meant to be a salesman. I just hated to sell anything, but that was about the only way a kid could make any money. Babysitting had never been heard of. With each subscription you sold, you had the privilege of sending in a little money—not very much—and getting something awfully nice. If you sold five, you got something really nice. Once I got a gray sweater and cap I needed pretty bad. This was not because I was a salesman. It was because the people who subscribed were just nice."

In one sense, Marie grew up in offices. At least she spent considerable time in them. With her mother working at city hall, she often went there for lunch. Mrs. Johnson would heat soup on a wood stove and they would have it with sandwiches. When the town built a new city hall, Mrs. Johnson had to keep her treasurer's books in a vault in the police station. She did bookwork there at night, joined by Marie, who preferred to have company while she did her schoolwork.

The arrangement was not altogether satisfactory. Occasionally, a night policeman would come in and give the city treasurer and her daughter sour looks, presumably because he thought police stations were for police business, not bookkeeping and reading. One policeman, a particularly disagreeable sort, kept a tub of mash near a wall where Mrs. Johnson worked. He had taken it from a local moonshiner and was holding it for evidence. Mrs. Johnson disapproved violently of alcoholic beverages of any description and the tub of mash—periodically going "blub"— offended her. The policeman refused to move the tub, however, and for many nights Marie and her mother were subjected to the gurgling batch of prunes and bran.

As Marie grew, she became more interested in the outlying area of Whitefish. Dressed either in tweed knickers or bib overalls, a broad-rimmed hat firmly on her head, she often could be found hiking Lion Mountain west of Whitefish or even on an occasional fishing trip. She frequently carried a .22-caliber Savage rifle, more for protection from tramps than wild animals.

> "I fished in a boat on Whitefish Lake and once caught two fish that my companions indelicately called blue bellies. The people with me remarked scornfully that the fish were really biting that day.

[22]

"Once, on the shore of Whitefish Lake, without a hunting license but with my .22 rifle, I shot something that I fondly believed was a duck. The waves brought it in, and I hid it under my jacket and sneaked home. With much effort I got the feathers off. Then I boiled the corpse for hours and it smelled worse and worse—fishier than fish. Finally I gave it to the chickens for a treat, but they thought even less of it than I did. Chickens will eat almost anything, but those chickens refused my hell diver."

There were other types of outings:

"Once, with a girl friend, I went swimming in Beaver Lake, five miles west of Whitefish. After we got into the water we hung our suits on the end of a log and swam without them, like a fish. It was a very private place; nobody ever came there except us . . . We were having a lovely time when we were startled by the sound of maniac laughter across the lake and coming closer.

"That was no situation for a couple of . . . girls to be caught in, so we hastened to get back into our swimming suits. You can hang yourself that way. Getting into a swimming suit under water is quite a trick even if you have solid lake bottom to stand on. We didn't because the bottom was quicksand. Try sometime to get into a swimming suit under water while treading water and worrying because you can hear approaching laughter that you assume is somebody in a rowboat . . . . It turned out to be only a confounded bird."

"Whitefish on the main line, rah, rah, rah!
Kalispell on the branch line, yah, yah, yah!"

Such was the rallying cry at athletic events in September 1918 as Marie Johnson began her freshman year at Central High School in Whitefish. Her way with words was becoming increasingly evident and theme writing became a specialty. Latin, in contrast, proved difficult:

"Latin was gruesome. My freshman year there were only three in our class and we had a perfectly delightful teacher who, unfortunately, didn't teach us very much Latin. The second year there were only two of us. We had a good teacher but we didn't have any foundation. Consequently, if my friend was sick and stayed home, I stayed home, too. Who wants to be the only one in a Latin class when you don't know any Latin and the teacher is cross about it? We plugged along and got through Caesar and that's about all. My mother assumed I would be studying Cicero the next year and Virgil the year after that, but, fortunately, a class of one is not very sensible. I was sorry my girl friend moved away at the end of our sophomore year, but that was what saved me from having to take any more Latin."

At 14, still anticipating college expenses, Marie became relief operator at the telephone office in Whitefish. She worked every Sunday and every other Friday night, receiving $1.65 for an eight-hour shift.

While she continued to refine her theme-writing ability, Marie used her sophomore year to dabble in poetry, playwriting and even politics.

Marie Johnson as relief switchboard operator in Whitefish.

One of her poems, contributed voluntarily, was "The Moon Queen," published in *The Alforja*, the school's yearbook for 1920:

The full, bright moon from her heavenly throne
Looks down with calm, cold countenance
Upon the lake, which, smooth and clear,
Encircled by snow-capped mountains, lies.
The dark pines on the distant shore,
Gloomy and sad, are sentinels
To guard the treasures that Nature keeps.
A few clouds scarcely visible
In the light of the queenly moon,
Drift toward the western sky;
Mere wisps are they, and their edges
Are softly touched with gold.
The stillness is unbroken
And the moon shines, queen of all.

In addition to serving as "personal editor" of *The Alforja* her sophomore year, Marie was named class president. On the debate team for two years, she learned "an appalling number of affirmative and negative arguments about compulsory arbitration of labor disputes and the advisability of permitting immigration from Japan."

She even tried dramatics, winning the role of Mademoiselle Zenobie in the freshman-sophomore presentation of the French comedy *A Scrap of Paper.*

"For obvious reasons, I always got a comic role," she said.

Despite her numerous extra-curricular activities, Marie continued to read.

If the lively arts were Marie's forte in high school, science was not. All she gleaned from her physics and chemistry courses were enough memories for a column written years later for the *Great Falls Tribune*:

Some day the grave and learned men of science will come to their senses and vote me an impressive award. (Keep the medals, boys; make mine cash.) A good many years ago I did a great thing for science. I deserted it and its various branches have been making spectacular progress ever since.

Nowadays, high school pupils in physics classes probably practice atom splitting at recess. When I dropped the physics course at

Whitefish High School after two weeks to take typing, we were coating a block of wood with paraffin. I never knew why.

In high school chemistry we learned to make an evil-smelling concoction known as hydrogen sulphide. Our class gave the teacher some of it in a small perfume bottle, gift wrapped, and she thanked us graciously by not opening the bottle. We concluded that she had run up against hellions like us before.

Another thing I learned in chemistry was that you can't believe everything you read. I read somewhere that chlorine gas will cure a cold, so I sneaked into the laboratory and made some chlorine and took a deep breath. When I regained consciousness, I still had the cold.

The typing course Marie enrolled in at the expense of physics was a necessity, particularly since she had decided to fill her mother's shoes as Whitefish stringer for the Kalispell *Inter Lake*.

"I was a very bad reporter because I was too scared to ask strangers questions," she said.

While she wasn't the most prolific correspondent, her experiences were to provide the basis for "First Date," a 1949 short story published in *Collier's* magazine. In addition to being an excellent example of how Miss Johnson learned to write fiction using fact as a starting point, the story provides an insight into Marie Johnson as news gatherer. It begins:

> I went into journalism when I was fourteen, not because I had any aptitude for it but because O'Leary's Hardware Store had a twenty-two rifle for sale, and my parents weren't in sympathy with my burning desire to own it. I sent news of Whitefish, Montana, to the *Daily Inter Lake*, published in Kalispell, a few miles away. The *Inter Lake* editor paid me for it at the rate of a dollar a column foot.
>
> He didn't know I was fourteen, or even that I was his reporter. He thought my Aunt Tillie was still his Whitefish correspondent.

If the reader acquainted with Marie failed to guess that "First Date" was based on her experiences, he knew for sure when Loretta, the story's narrator, spoke of her "Aunt Tillie's" job in the city water office.

Latin and science were not enough to keep Marie Johnson from being graduated second in her class with a high school honor scholarship. She thrived on hard work and busy schedules and her high school days were fruitful and enjoyable. She remembered them with fondness three decades later in a column exhorting young people to make the most of the experience:

There were 14 of us in the class of '22 in Whitefish High School. (And I want it clearly understood that this means 1922, not 1822. Appearances are deceiving.)

One member of our class was a boy. The others were, naturally girls. A giggling lot we were, as I recall, except along toward the last when we realized how important we were. Then we began to act pretty solemn, not to say downright snooty toward the poor worms in the bumbling class of '23 and the even lower life forms farther on down the scale.

There were no fashion magazines to tell high school girls what was the latest thing to wear, or at least the latest thing to yearn for, so we wore middy blouses—white cotton in warm weather, red or green flannel in cold weather—and about the only variation in style was whether you pinned your middy to fit snugly around your waist or let it hang like a sack. I let mine hang, being built along the general shape of a middy blouse in the first place.

We wore high-laced shoes, having been warned that low shoes made your ankles big. Don't ask me what use it was to have nice ankles when your shoes covered them up anyway.

Senior year, we cut loose from the high shoes and decided to get some good out of our ankles by exposing them. For commencement we wore low-heeled pumps with two or three straps—very risque. Even more daring were our stockings. We peeled off the black cotton-ribbed jobs and went into silk in a light tan shade, new that year, called nude. Nude was a naughty word in 1922. And nobody wore perfume named My Sin, either.

The class of 1922 may sound pretty dowdy . . . but we were considered dangerous rebels. Our class was the first one in Whitefish to break with the tradition that sweet girl graduates wore white dresses.

"We are modern!" we proclaimed. "We are the Latest Thing. Let us be gay and gaudy!"

So we wore pastels and got ourselves talked about. I was a dainty dish in pale green organdy with a flutter of hemstitched panels and a shash. If there is anything more impractical than an organdy dress with floating panels of the same, I don't want to hear about it.

We spent a lot of time doing our hair. Part of the performance involved making cootie cages. These were puffs that covered the ears, and the bigger they were, the more fascinating we felt.

To make them, we held a strand of hair in our teeth while snarling a larger chunk by combing it briskly in the wrong direction. This style went from bad to worse: it developed into something spectacular that we called . . . a bushel basket. When you did your hair, your head looked swollen to immense proportions.

And I might point out . . . that no girl with a bushel hair-do ever looked so peculiar as a boy with a crew cut, even when she was losing her rats.

Somebody in our class went mad with red paint and put a great big "22" on the sidewalk in front of the school so that future generations would remember us. The school authorities proclaimed that the numerals must be eradicated—or else. So a handful of timid souls, including milk-toast me, tried to scrub the paint off . . . . We couldn't even dim it.

I have always regretted being such a panty-waist about the paint. I had nothing to do with putting it on there, the main reason being I didn't know it was going to be done.

We didn't have band or physical education or art or football or skiing or imported talent for assembly programs. We almost didn't have a co-educational school, because the boys quit school to go to work for the railroad as soon as they were big enough to lie about their ages. We also didn't have school dances, because the school board didn't approve of dancing.

We did have a glee club (which I ignored because I couldn't carry a tune) and ghastly performances called assembly programs, with strictly local talent if you could call it that.

To lend counterfeit zip to assemblies, the whole high school was divided into "literary societies" called, I think, Alpha and Theta. A semblance of competition was developed thereby, but believe me when one of us quaked up to the front of the room to give a recitation or read a paper or play the piano, it wasn't for the honor of good old Alpha or Theta but simply because we couldn't get our required English credits if we didn't.

We went through this agony semi-annually, and the only way to get out of it was to die or go out for debate, which amounted to about the same thing . . . .

Central High School's Class of '22 assembled for commencement in a "thin, brave" row across the stage of the Whitefish Masonic Temple. Directly in the center was the group's lone male, whom the speaker of the evening referred to as "a rose among thorns." Sixteen-year-old Marie Johnson—her nickname "Oui Oui"; her talent, writing themes; her ambition, "poet or something," and her favorite expression, "Gee gosh!"—did not remember another thing the man said as he ushered the group out of high school and into the world.

Dorothy Marie Johnson at her high-school
graduation in 1922.

High school actress.

As a girl, Dorothy Johnson spent many hours hiking the mountain surrounding Whitefish. At the far left, the Great Northern's tracks be seen skirting Whitefish Lake. At the upper right is Big Mountain world-famous ski area. *(Photo by Lacy Studio, Whitefish)*

Feeding chickens and splitting wood were but two tasks that Dorothy Johnson took on as a girl after the death of her father. By age 13, she had developed "impressive arm muscles" and also was adept at house-painting. She remarked in later years, "Feeding the chickens wasn't hard, but did you ever clean under the perches of a hen house?"

CHAPTER THREE

College

I N T H E F A L L OF 1922, IGNORING THE WRITING talent that had begun to emerge during high school, Marie Johnson enrolled as a freshman in pre-med at Montana State University in Bozeman, Montana. Her decision, she said, was based entirely on literary romanticism brought on by her reading at age 12 of B.M. Bower's *Chip of the Flying U*. Having learned that a woman doctor won Chip's heart, and having heard from friends in Choteau that Chip was really cowboy artist Charles M. Russell, Marie promptly decided medicine was for her.

Nursing the dream through her freshman year, she concluded in June 1923 that writing—not mathematics and science—was her calling:

> "I didn't have anything that a doctor ought to have. I just wasn't the scientific type and I found it out at the end of the freshman year. I wasn't doing very well in qualitative analysis and I didn't have the faintest idea where the money was going to come from for medical school. Besides, the cat course was coming up the next year. I couldn't see myself cutting up a cat, especially when you had to get the cat. Bozeman people were awfully suspicious of people who became interested in their cats. There was great demand for cats by sophomores. I didn't mind cutting up frogs or those big worms that come out about a foot long, but I liked cats."

With these thoughts, she came to the University of Montana in Missoula in the fall of 1923. In following Bozeman's registration instructions by including her first, middle and last names on all forms, she had come to be known as Dorothy rather than Marie. The name carried over when she transferred.

During college, Miss Johnson and her roommate lived on the second floor of this house (since remodeled) at 422 Ford Street in Missoula. (*Photo by the author*)

Her major was English, her prime interest poetry, both of which soon brought her into contact with Professor Harold G. Merriam and his campus literary magazine, *The Frontier*. Begun in 1920 and published three times a year, *The Frontier*'s purpose was to serve as a vehicle for student literary endeavors. Occasionally it contained creative contributions from professors. Considerable material was in the form of essays from faculty and students alike who wanted to make observations while abroad. In an essay, "Endlessly the Covered Wagon," Professor Merriam eloquently stated the goals of *The Frontier*. The essay indicates the magazine could not have been a more appropriate outlet for the emerging talents of Dorothy Johnson and some of her contemporaries in Professor Merriam's creative-writing class:

> The Northwest is industrially alive and agriculturally alive; it needs to show itself spiritually alive. Culturally it has too long either turned for nourishment toward the east or accepted uncourageous, unindigenous "literary" expression of writers too spiritually imitative and too uninspired. We in this territory need to realize that literature, and all art, is, if it is worth anything at all, sincere expression of real life. And the roots for literature among us should be in our own rocky ground, not in Greenwich Village dirt or Mid-west loam or European mold, or least of all, in the hothouse sifted, fertilized soil of anywhere.
>
> Out of our soil we grow, and out of our soil should come expression of ourselves, living, hating, struggling, failing, succeeding, desponding, aspiring, playing, working—being alive.
>
> *The Frontier* is pioneer endeavor to gather indigenous Northwest material. It offers itself to readers and writers as a non-commercial channel for expression. It desires hardy writers; it will need hardy readers. Living is active. Literature is not only escape from life. Literature is a vigorous dive into it. Literature plunges into the joy and the sorrow of it, into the ugliness and the beauty of it with equal energy and with understanding and sympathy. Literature has its eyes both on the ground and on the sky; and it persistently pours its searching glances into the . . . depths of the human soul. It can dally, work, play; sing, groan; despair, aspire; shout, purr; cajole, chastise, cheer, delight; throw light and absorb light, lift a spirit and cast it down—make men of its lovers. This it does for readers through imaginative pictures of life.
>
> This region, from Colorado to Washington, has vast store of materials in experience of the pioneer warring against physical nature, of the exploiter who trailed the ways of the discoverer and

pioneer, of the settler who, finding conditions made by the pioneers and exploiters, devoted himself in uncritical spirit to making a living. The present generation, restless in the settled physical and social conditions, finds also the spiritual conditions irksome. "The frontiers are wherever a man fronts a fact"—these younger generations are turning their gaze upon the world that makes comparison of near and far-off matters and conditions. Out of their critical attitude it is to be hoped will come spiritual growth. Truly, materials for true expression lie at hand lavishly strewn. The early day, the present day; the ranch, the mine; the lumber camp, the range; the city, the village, these have not yielded their treasure of the comedy and tragedy of human life.

It is not cleverness or sophistication or sheer brawn or realism or romanticism or pessimism or sentiment that we want; it is all these—life honestly seen and felt, and passed through a healthy imagination.

What is the state of civilization in this Northwest region of the United States? We hope that *The Frontier* will furnish some joyous and provocative material toward an answer.

Professor Merriam set high standards for material submitted to *The Frontier*. His creative-writing students—usually four to 12 persons—served as a board of editors. Contributions were read before the class, discussed and voted on. Acceptance required not merely a majority vote, but a substantial majority vote. In a class with eight persons (Merriam's vote making nine), a five-four vote on a contribution meant rejection. At least a six-three, and preferably seven-two, vote was needed. Students who made *The Frontier* had cause to be happy.

Dorothy Johnson joined the select group in March 1924 with a poem entitled "Marjory." In May she published three poems— "Old Mine," "From a Train Window" and "The Breed." She had submitted them midway through winter quarter and soon after had suffered a nervous breakdown. Caused by a seemingly incurable cold, various social pressures she believes stemmed from being younger than her classmates, and financial worries (she was washing dishes part-time in a tea room near the campus), the illness forced her out of school for almost a year and a half. It also resulted in the tremor that was to trouble her throughout her life.

A reading of those first poems in *The Frontier* lends credence to Merriam's evaluation of Dorothy Johnson's early verse.

"Her poetry was more in the nature of statements," Merriam said. "It was symbolic, not highly imaginative, but a response to things she had seen, like a lost mine or a ghost town. It was a little nostalgic."

OLD MINE

Once there were men here.
The pebbled dirt roof of the cellar
Juts out from under the hill.
A pile of tin cans, so rusty
As to be almost a part of the earth, by now,
Lies at the foot of the hill.
The house is gone, and the men—
God only knows where they have left their picks.
Here are only their leavings
And a gash in the earth that is almost healed.
The years and the wind and the rain
Heal everything

THE BREED

Down by the Post Office there slouched a tall boy,
A dark, slim, insolent half-breed
With a floppy black hat and a loud checked shirt.
He wore perilous, high heeled boots
And he hooked his thumbs into a brass-studded belt.

I took all that in at a glance and a half—
It would not do to stare. Then I went and bought
A stunning Spring hat
Which I will blossom with at Easter.
But how I shall wish when I wear it
That I had a loud checked shirt and
A brass-studded belt to hook my thumbs into!

FROM A TRAIN WINDOW

Fine twigged white birches lean
Out over the river
Like carven things of ancient ivory.
They wade knee-deep in scarlet, leafless brush.

Crumbled, crumbling rainbow rocks
And yellow grass
All sliding down hill to the creek.

Tall brown rocks stand silent by the river
Forgotten of God and living things,
Except one twisted cedar, half-way up.

A furry colt who tosses his mane,
Sideways glancing, and gallops off to the hills.

Why are there circus posters
On every battered gray building
That leans before the wind, on these prairies,
Showing light through its uneven cracks?

A faded green house among the weary hills,
With blank windows and dead vines upon the walls.

Bright yellow, misty weeds
Upjutting through the snow,
And naked brown rocks, weirdly sculptured rocks,
Leering above them.

And
A slow, mauve, curling plume suspended
From the smelter tower, hanging in the mist.

Recuperating in Whitefish the spring and summer of 1924, Dorothy helped her mother in the power company office and worked as a telephone operator. She also decided to earn her teaching credentials.

In September, she enrolled at Western Montana College of Education at Dillon. She described her brief stay in one word—horrible. She realized within a month she had charted the wrong course and when her mother became ill and asked her to return home, she did so without reluctance, not completing the quarter.

Soon after returning to Whitefish—unsure whether she ever wanted to go back to college—she decided to attend Spokane's Kinman Business College. She did so, moving on to Seattle in late November to look for work:

"I was possessed by a terrible wanderlust. I just had to go somewhere. About the first day I was there, somebody in the YWCA stole my purse with all my money in it. It wasn't very much but it was all I had. So I borrowed a dollar from somebody and wired home. My mother sent me some money but she was awfully mad. She hadn't wanted me to go to Seattle at the age of 18 anyhow. She was quite right.

"I got into a funny situation. I answered an ad in the paper in which a man wanted a stenographer with literary abilities. I thought, 'Well, I'm a stenographer and maybe I have literary ability if he doesn't want too much.' It was an old prospector who had made his pile in the 1898 gold rush in Alaska. He wanted somebody to write the story of his life. Well, I wouldn't have been able to if he had hired me. I don't know who he hired, but he had all kinds of girls coming into this funny, beat-up, old hotel to be interviewed. He gave me a long poem about how he carried the mail from some place to some place with a dog team. It was one of those bumpity-bumpity-bump poems and he wanted me to rewrite it for him. I thought, 'Oh, no, this is just not for me.' I was not able to rewrite somebody else's jingles."

Dorothy passed up the prospector's offer and found a position that offered in security what it lacked in color—stamping dates on bills for the gas company.

"It made my roommate so mad!" she said. "She told me I was rubber-stamping all night long and that she couldn't sleep."

In Seattle slightly more than three months, Dorothy saw some of the sights and missed others:

"I didn't know until after I came home and read about them that there were mountains visible from Seattle. I never saw any mountains because it rained all the time I was there. Mount Rainier is right out there but I didn't see it. It was an exciting experience, though. I used to go down and walk along the waterfront, which was probably not a good thing to do. But it was so glamorous. I saw ships with Japanese names on them and I'd never seen ships before. I lived on 50 cents a day. Eating in a cafeteria, that would buy one meal and part of another one if you were careful."

Early in 1925, Dorothy left the coast and returned to Whitefish. Hired as a stenographer by the city attorney, she became involved in a salary dispute and was fired. It was the only job in her life she ever left on those terms:

"He started me out at $20 a month. Then I was to get $25 and then $30. He led me to believe that when I got up to $50 that was all the riches I could possibly expect to have. Well, I didn't get up to $50. He decided that since I could take shorthand so handily that I should attend all the city council meetings. I worked eight hours a day for him with nothing much to do. Then I had to go to the city council meetings and listen for hours to fights between the mayor and the council. This was keeping me away from home at least one night a week.

[39]

"Whitefish was in political turmoil at the time—the mayor had one councilman on his side and the rest against him. Neither faction could accomplish anything. They fought constantly. So I had the nerve to innocently ask my boss one day in the presence of the mayor whether I couldn't get extra pay for going to the council meetings. He let me know as soon as the mayor left that he had never been so insulted in his life, that he was deeply offended, and that he didn't need me anymore. I went home in a terrible state. I thought I would never be able to get another job. It was a dreadful blow."

To provide herself with an income, Dorothy got a job demonstrating washing machines for the Mountain States Power Co. She received a $10 commission for each machine sold.

Being away from the campus did not influence her creativity; while still in Whitefish she sent three poems to *The Frontier*, all of which were accepted. One of them, "Confession," was inspired by a man with whom she had become infatuated one summer at Whitefish Lake. Named Jack, he was older than she, very knowledgeable in the ways of the world, and widely traveled:

CONFESSION

I try to forget you and all you mean to me
And tell myself I hate you, but I lie.
If I should hear your call upon the wind tonight,
I could not even stop to close the door behind me.

SHAMS

Why should you begrudge me happiness?
For seven dollars and a half
I bought a big revolver with a barrel
Half as long as my arm;
for the sum of eighty-one cents
I got a cartridge belt from Sears Roebuck.

If for this paltry sum I buy
Ashes of Romance to bring back to me
Wild days I never saw, then why
Should you begrudge me happiness?

QUESTION

I thought that I would care for you
Perhaps, when you had done all things
That other men have feared or failed to do.

But something's happened. You have feared or failed
To do all things that other men have done,
And still I care for you.

What mockery is this?

Dorothy returned to Missoula and the University of Montana
in the fall of 1925. Still a sophomore, she was to see many of her
former classmates graduate the following spring. She lived off campus, sharing with Grace Baldwin, a graduate student in English, a
$15-a-month, second-floor apartment at 422 Ford Street. Their
landlord's daughter, the former Ruth Muchmore and later Mrs.
L.E. Noel of Missoula, remembered Grace as "prim and proper"
and Dorothy as very liberal.

"I admired Dorothy because she had a mind of her own," Mrs.
Noel said. "She smoked then, and not one girl in 10 did that in
those days."

Another acquaintance, later a close friend, was Cyrile Van
Duser, circulation manager for *The Frontier*. Miss Van Duser,
who became student union publicity director and adviser to the
university yearbook, *The Sentinel*, remembered Dorothy as a
conscientious, determined person who appeared to have little
time for frivolities.

"I think she made up her mind to be a writer before she came
here," Miss Van Duser said. "Consequently she worked hard at it."

By late 1926, Dorothy still was devoting her energies to poetry.
In March *The Frontier* published "Bread and Hyacinths":

When I left the Port of Seattle
I thought to throw some pennies in the bay,
And shut my eyes, and hope some day
To come again, and see the gulls dipping
Down to green water, and the dirty shipping,
And the rain, and the dim, far line
Of mountains in their pale sunshine—
But I saved my pennies, and dropped them instead
In a box at the depot to buy children bread.

In the November 1926 issue appeared "I Was Never a River":

I was never a river,
I was spring water
Flowing from dark to darkness.

I shall never be a lake nor an ocean,
I am a little pool in the midst of a meadow
And you may never catch me
Not glinting at the sun.

There has been tumult,
There will be disaster,
But where was once swift beauty
Must it not come again?

Was it a swallow that skimmed over me
And made these ripples
That still try to catch the sun?

Miss Johnson never knew why, but her interest began to turn toward prose near the end of 1926. Possibly she was influenced, directly or indirectly, by Professor Merriam, who in later years commented that, as her instructor, he could see her real talent lay in stories rather than verse.

"What she wrote always had vigor, and that, of course, is a good thing," Merriam said. "Her writing was not self-conscious, as so much of the writing of undergraduates is. As a writer, she seemed to be involved in her material rather than thinking of herself."

Miss Johnson said of her shift in interest:

"I suddenly became *not* a poet. I began to think differently; I began to think in terms of short stories. It all had to do with emotion or the expression of emotion. Somehow the channeling of my emotion changed to short stories.

"At that time, in the 1920s, there was a great writing movement on the campus here. I must say that the writers who were getting published in *Frontier* were a bunch of snobs. I was one of them. We had a little group that met every Saturday night to read each others stuff and comment on it. Just the idea of knowing other people who were writing was fine. It was a creative climate that was good for us all."

Another man who contributed to the campus' creative climate was Sidney Cox, an assistant professor in the English department. During the 1925-26 school year, Cox assumed several of Professor Merriam's tasks while the latter was at Columbia on leave of absence. Dorothy considered him one of her better professors:

"He was a wonderful teacher and was the first person who got the idea across to me that there need not be a dividing line between what you might like to read and what you ought to read. There had been in high school. Sidney Cox opened up a whole new world to everybody in the general literature class. The Coxes had a wonderful institution—it took place on Friday night, by invitation only. Certain selected students went over to their house and he would read from various books or from something he had written. Most of us sat on the floor. It was a great honor to be in on this; it was intellectually stimulating."

During that period, Dorothy and Grace Baldwin began a similar session at their apartment:

"We had a smaller group over on Saturday night. The boys had to bring wood up from the wood shed and, as at the Cox home, everybody sat on the floor. The next year, when I lived alone, I continued it for awhile. The main trouble was not in getting people to come but in providing refreshments. We were so darn poor. Once I boasted that the cake I was serving was butterless and eggless and that those were its only virtues. Somebody remarked that the raisins were good."

In the spring of 1926, *The Frontier*, under Cox's supervision, published a short article in which the phrase "son of a bitch" was used in three different ways—the damning way, the friendly way and the habitual way. Reminiscent of similar incidents in subsequent years, the piece was seen by several Montana newspaper editors and used as the basis for demands that Cox resign. At almost the same time, Cox received an attractive offer from Dartmouth College. He resigned from the university, was hired by Dartmouth and became one of the institution's most valued professors until his death in 1952. Merriam referred to Cox as "one of the finest teachers we ever had."

Among students who showed promise in the English classes of the period were Helen Addison Howard, Ernest Erkkila, Elsie McDowell, Grace Baldwin and John K. Hutchens. Hutchens, who became a literary critic for *The New York Herald Tribune*, later favorably reviewed several of Miss Johnson's stories.

In affirming the goals of *The Frontier* in his essay "Endlessly the Covered Wagon," Professor Merriam wrote that "the early day, the present day, the ranch, the mine, the lumber camp, the range, the city, the village had not yielded their treasure of the comedy and tragedy of human life." In speculating as to the state of civilization in the Northwest region of the United States, he expressed hope that his magazine would provide some "joyous and provocative material toward an answer."

To what extent the magazine succeeded is a matter for conjecture. Nevertheless, it cannot be denied that *The Frontier* sought to maintain the flavor of the West and Northwest in its pages.

Although it also is only a matter for speculation, one wonders whether her association with *The Frontier* and Professor Merriam influenced Dorothy Johnson's choice of subject matter. Indeed, though she brought to the university a fondness for the West and its traditions, it seems likely that H.G. Merriam—with his interest in regional literature—nurtured that fondness and helped it thrive. Unquestionably he had some influence on the fledgling writer, because some 25 years later she dedicated her short story collection *Indian Country* to him.

Among Dorothy's first short stories published in *The Frontier* were "Happy Valley" and "He'll Make a Good Sheriff," both in 1927. The latter tells of a young deputy who captures a moonshiner, then is bribed into releasing him to buy his fiancee a wedding ring. The same year she wrote "And One Came Back," a story of three men on a trapping expedition. Two of the men, staked by the third, plot to leave him behind to die in the wilderness. Fate intervenes, however, and the man conspired against is the only one who returns.

While the story is based on too many coincidences, is structurally weak in places and exhibits exaggerated dialogue, it was good enough to win first place in competition with 10 manuscripts entered in the annual Annie Joyce Memorial contest. Hearing she had won, Dorothy faced a dilemma:

> "You had your choice of a gold medal or $20 and I went up to Main Hall to tell them what I wanted. I was so embarrassed, but I needed the $20 awfully bad. I told them that and thought, 'I'm just going to look like a heel,' because, obviously, a rightminded person would prefer to have a gold medal.
> "I . . . apologized when I talked to whoever it was and he said, 'If you'd wanted a gold medal, I don't know where we'd have got it. Nobody ever wanted one yet.' "

Looking back to her first short stories, Miss Johnson expresses embarrassment. To her, the stories—including "And One Came

Back"—seem childish:

"I was a little uneasy about 'And One Came Back' because we were constantly told that we ought to write about what we knew. In that story, I didn't know. I was using my imagination and I didn't know whether this was right. The preaching on the subject was that you were to write about what you knew. I don't think the meaning of that was quite clear to us. I am sure nobody meant that you couldn't use imagination. What they meant was that you shouldn't describe something going on in Westminster Abbey when you had no idea what the inside of Westminster Abbey looked like or what went on there. You should stick close to what you could realize. I thought that maybe writers should write about events that they had experienced."

Later she would reject this philosophy, backing up her rejection by writing capably about the frontier West of the 1800s, which, obviously, she neither lived in nor experienced. Her security came from the realization that as long as an incident or event seemed real to her—real enough to evoke an emotion—she did not have to experience it.

Another thing that disturbed her about "And One Came Back" was its structure—always important to her. A youth, rowing a girl across a lake, casually mentions the legend of the man who survived the devious trapping expedition.

"Oh, isn't that thrilling?" the girl asks. "Wouldn't you *love* to know what happened?"

From there the story proceeds through a flashback, a technique Miss Johnson learned to use sparingly:

"Why not just tell the story? Why fool around with this flash-back type of framework? This part about the young man rowing boats isn't part of the story at all. It was hard for me—and I think hard for many beginning writers—to get going. I felt I had to have an excuse so I put in a framework to give me a reason for telling the story. Many, many writers did the same thing. I used to adore Kipling stories; he was a cracker-jack storyteller. I got a whole set of Kipling books for Christmas when I was in my teens and I read it over and over. He did the same thing and I think that even when Kipling did it, it was weak. If you notice, there is a series of short stories told by a bunch of men at their club. Well what of it? The story ought to be strong enough to stand by itself without having this excuse for telling it."

Professor Merriam's evaluation differed from Miss Johnson's.

[45]

He described her first attempts at short-story writing as "slightly immature" but said they could not be called childish.

"One must realize that she was not a professional writer then," Merriam said. "You couldn't expect the stories to be very advanced because students that age are still learning how."

The winning entry in the 1927 Joyce Memorial contest bore the byline "Dorothy M. Johnson Peterkin." Dorothy was 21 and scarcely a senior when she met George William Peterkin, a soldier at Fort Missoula, on a blind date. Peterkin, according to Miss Johnson, strongly resembled Jack, the man she had been so fond of earlier. The two were married secretly in Missoula on April 5, 1927, an event that greatly upset Dorothy's mother.

Known as "Red," Peterkin proved to be hot-tempered, an inveterate gambler and footloose. The couple moved into an apartment on the corner of Higgins Avenue and Ford Street and Dorothy continued to work for her degree.

At about the same time, she suffered a serious financial setback. Sneaks, days on which students deliberately cut classes, had become traditional at the university. The administration's decision to end the tradition, poorly received by the students, resulted in still another sneak. Dorothy was among the participants.

The administration stood firm. Professors, who took roll anyway, penalizing for unexcused absences, were directed to penalize double those who had snuck. The resulting loss of grade points was particularly painful for Dorothy; she lost her high school honor scholarship.

"I felt very bad about it because I never was really the rebellious type," she said.

The first piece of free-lance writing for which Dorothy received pay was a poem submitted to *Weird Tales* magazine her senior year. The magazine, specializing in ghost, vampire and werewolf stories, informed her the poem was acceptable and that payment of 25 cents a line would be made on publication. The magazine cost 25 cents a copy, and in the months that followed Dorothy bought several while searching for her poem. When it appeared, along with her check for $2, the money had long since been spent.

"It did my morale a lot of good for awhile," she said. "I needed something to boost it. These little things were all the encouragement I had to keep me going for a good many years."

Among requirements for the bachelor's degree in English in 1928 was seminar, usually conducted by Professor Merriam in the evenings in the library. Cyrile Van Duser described the class as "a tough one," adding that when she went to Northwestern University, she was told she had done more for a bachelor's degree than that school was requiring for a master's.

In addition to an oral examination and a comprehensive written test, prospective graduates were required to complete a major paper similar to a short thesis. Prior to her orals, Dorothy became so tense that she had to seek chiropractic treatment. Then, for her test, she was asked only one question—why she disliked the poet Wordsworth. She was so stunned that she not only forgot why she disliked him, but whether she did.

Many students—Dorothy Peterkin among them—were concerned about a topic for their senior paper. On Professor Merriam's suggestion, Dorothy selected a book by George Gissing, *The House of Cobwebs.*

> "I thought, 'Ah, a mystery. Merriam must have flipped his lid.' *The House of Cobwebs* turned out to be the most gruesome, melancholy set of little essays and short stories ever written. Every one of them was dismal, but I was stuck with it. I read everything I could get hold of that Gissing wrote. He never smiled in his life."

Dorothy labored through the project, building her paper by classifying each of Gissing's offerings as to form—short story or sketch.

Professor Merriam, showing little enthusiasm for the paper, gave it a C grade. While that did not please Dorothy, she still believed she had learned something about short stories, which had become her preoccupation.

Although Harold Merriam did not care for Dorothy's approach to George Gissing, he saw great potential in her:

> "She wrote prodigiously—story after story. I felt from the beginning that she had a real talent for them. I think the reason for her success was that she kept right at it—she didn't let up. Most students who take creative writing give up if they don't succeed in the first eight or ten stories. Dorothy kept right at it. I imagine she has a trunkful of stories that have never been published and materials that were never used. She was determined to write.

Many of her contemporaries also were determined to write, but when they left college they became involved in business or housewifery or whatever and stopped."

Dorothy Peterkin completed her bachelor's requirements in March 1928, the end of winter quarter. Not waiting for commencement exercises in June, she left for Whitefish, the first stop in a search for work. Her husband remained in Missoula where, that summer, he "bought out" of the Army. Meanwhile, Dorothy had left Whitefish and was in Spokane seeking a job.

CHAPTER FOUR

Bonnie George Campbell

DESPITE HER COLLEGE EDUCATION AND though the gloom of the Depression was yet to settle, Dorothy Peterkin found jobs scarce in Spokane. The problem was that "everybody from three states was doing the same thing at the same time." However, she eventually found part-time secretarial work with a private detective who was furtively investigating a Spokane bank.

"After I typed for him each time, he would collect all the carbon paper and waste paper I had used and take it with him in his brief case," she said. "His investigation was so quiet that he wasn't even going to leave that around."

Next, she became a typist for a gold-mine promoter. The man had sold mining stock in Spokane and through repeated assessments and encouragement was convincing shareholders to ante additional funds to keep the mine open. The promoter's chief inducement—that shareholders would lose their investment and miss out on the main strike (due any week)—was the subject of numerous letters typed by Dorothy Peterkin for a modest fee. She did not know then, but suspected later, that something was amiss.

A *Spokesman Review* classified ad provided her with another memory of her Spokane job-hunting days. The ad, seeking girls who knew typing and who were willing to travel, sounded ideal. Dorothy arranged for an interview, but it was short-lived:

"I went over and talked to a man in a hotel room. He sort of leered and told me that this would involve typing reports quite late at night in one city or another, wherever they had a crew working. He said I should expect to have their salesmen dropping in at almost any time. Then he cozied up and put an arm around me and I left. I went over to the newspaper office and told the classified man what kind of ad it was they were running. He was quite excited but the ad kept running. I didn't worry him enough to get it canceled."

Dorothy had registered with almost every employment agency in Spokane, many of which were operated by typewriter companies. Soon after her encounter in the hotel room, she received a message to call a man in a place she could not pronounce, a small town some 110 miles northwest of Spokane.

Spelling the town's name—Okanogan—to an operator who apparently never had heard of it, she returned the call. The man seeking her was C.E. Blackwell, owner of Okanogan's C.E. Blackwell & Co. department store. Blackwell had received her application from one of the typewriter company employment agencies and wanted her in Okanogan for a stenographic position.

The offer worried her; she could not understand why a store in tiny Okanogan needed a stenographer. More distressing to her, however, was her critical financial situation. She was "scared to death" and still uneasy about Blackwell's call when she boarded the train. With $10 cash and two dresses, she arrived in Okanogan just before the 1928 apple harvest.

Dorothy's anxieties were unwarranted. C.E. Blackwell & Co. was the largest store in Okanogan, a prosperous, well-stocked establishment serving the entire Okanogan Valley from the Canada border, the Colville Indian Reservation to the east and the area as far south as Brewster. Its owner and founder had barged his goods up the Okanogan River and had built a small merchandising empire. Miss Johnson later remembered her job and her boss:

"It was a big job, but after awhile we got another stenographer. We had a bustling and busy office. Mr. Blackwell was a bear to work for. He used to come out and stand and look over my shoulder and he had a habit of pushing up his glasses so you knew he was glaring at you. He was forever pulling up his pants, even though he wore both a belt and suspenders. He would come and flip through the unfinished work on my desk, and I would cringe and explain I was doing it just as fast as I could. He would not let anybody put any work away, and that is how I got into a bad habit I've never been able to break. I've never been able to put unfinished work anywhere. I have to keep it out where I'm going to work on it next time or else I lose it. Other people can be the clean-desk type but I can't. Charley Blackwell wouldn't stand for it."

Dorothy persevered in her creative writing but found she missed the encouraging atmosphere of the university and her English classes.

"It was really lonesome business because hardly anybody else in Okanogan was a writer,"she said. "The only other one I knew of was the boss' sister-in-law, who wrote and . . . got paid for stories for Sunday school magazines. I was really envious of her because she got $100 apiece for them."

She realized, however, that Sunday school magazines were not her market.

"I grew up on that kind of literature and had a pretty low opinion of it even when I was small," she said.

She decided to start near the bottom with confession stories and proceed to better things as she gained experience and ability. That approach failed.

"I tried writing confession stories, and I just couldn't stand them," she said. "I certainly couldn't sell them! I thought they were horrible and didn't sell one. I didn't really ever finish any."

Had she not yearned to write, Okanogan might well have been the end of her literary career.

"I was awfully lost then because I didn't have people around who wanted to write," she said. "Nobody cared whether I did or not. I had a typewriter and as long as I didn't use it too late at night nobody was interested."

George Peterkin had not joined his wife on mustering out of the Army in Missoula the summer of 1928. Where he went she never learned, even when, in late 1928, he arrived in Okanogan. Peterkin went to work but, nevertheless, accumulated several sizable debts. In April 1929 he told his wife he was going to California. She asked him not to, but he left. She never saw him again, although 15 years later, during World War II, he called her in New York City.

Some six months after Peterkin's departure, Dorothy obtained an interlocutory divorce decree. The divorce became final in April 1930, whereupon she resumed use of her maiden name. She spent the year from April 1929 to April 1930 paying Peterkin's debts. Then, wanting a new start, she set out to save enough money to get herself out of Okanogan.

In the fall of 1928, Harold Merriam had expanded his magazine, *The Frontier*. While students still could contribute to it, they no longer had any editorial authority. The magazine received contributions from, and circulated into, almost every state. It boasted a handful of subscribers in Europe, was taken on a regular basis by a library in Moscow, and even was ordered by Al Capone, a resident of Alcatraz, who apparently had thought it was a periodical of western pulp fiction. By early 1930, *The Frontier* was receiving more than 800 story contributions a year and printing fewer than 50.

One that made the January 1930 issue was "The Fruit Tramps," the story of a young couple who earn a living following the West Coast fruit harvests. In the magazine's preface, a section called "Aboard the Covered Wagon," Merriam wrote the following about the story: " 'The Fruit Tramps' comes from Okanogan, Washington. Its author, Dorothy Marie Johnson, formerly lived in Whitefish, Montana. We have never published a story truer to its background."

Unquestionably, Miss Johnson had begun to find herself as a writer. She had simplified her story structure—writing as though she no longer had to furnish an excuse for what she was saying—and had severely tightened her narrative style. The last paragraph of "The Fruit Tramps" is illustrative:

> Washington to Oregon to California, from season to season, from apple harvest to orange harvest, they follow the fruit. Homeless, despised, from rich to penniless. Living in tourist parks, or paying high rent for a bare room. Buying a cot, eating off a packing box. No green curtains, no yellow table. A suitcase and a nail stripper, roll of blankets and some tin plates jolting in the back seat. Working and wandering. They follow a luscious harvest.

In the March 1930 issue appeared "Fear," a chilling, 373-word description of a woman's feelings as she comes home alone to her apartment at night. It begins:

> Long ago you locked the other door and threw the knob away. Then you moved the dresser against that door, because, you said, it was handier that way.

Now there is only one door to open when you come up the stairs at night. Quietly you climb, but not too quietly, for after all, there has never yet been anyone waiting for you there. Quietly you walk down the hall—slowly, because, of course, the stairs have tired you. You take out your key before you reach that door, because, you say, it saves time.

And ends:

You drop into a chair for a moment, and your breath is sharp and quick. The stairs, of course, tired you. When you can breathe slowly again, you put the frying-pan on the electric plate and wind the phonograph. "I'd Rather Be Blue Over You" will drive silence from the corners. And you learned long ago that it was no use to banish heartbreak.

But as you walk quietly to this home of yours in the evening, carrying your loaf of bread and a dime's worth of hamburger, the loafers in front of the pool hall would never think to stare and realize, "There goes a woman who fears for her life."

Miss Johnson liked Okanogan and its people. While renting an apartment in the Shaller Building, she met Opal Colbert, a woman who not only became a good friend but who provided the young writer with the situation from which her first big-time story would come. Mrs. Colbert later said of Dorothy Johnson:

"She typed all day at her office job . . . . Evenings and most weekends she typed out reams of her own copy. She worked very hard at her writing in those days and she enjoyed it. At that time she was interested in making her story situations as authentic as possible. Many of her characters' traits were taken from actual people she knew. Dorothy had an infectious laugh. It was a rather loud laugh but not unpleasant. She would get so amused over something that everyone around her laughed, too. She was lots of fun and a pleasant companion to be with."

While in downtown Okanogan one summer day in 1930, Mrs. Colbert met Ed Peasley, a friend from the reservation. Peasley, who had established himself as a capable bronc rider, asked Mrs. Colbert if she would like to attend a Sunday afternoon community rodeo at the Leo Moomaw ranch near Monse, south of Okanogan. Thinking some of her relatives might be there, Mrs. Colbert accepted. When she asked Miss Johnson to come, Miss Johnson immediately agreed.

Staged frequently in the Okanogan area, the impromptu

rodeos produced some of the finest bucking stock available for the region's fair and major rodeos. Cowboys participated for the fun and received no pay. Many of the horses were straight from the range and those with genuine bucking talent became part of Moomaw's rodeo string.

During the Sunday gathering at Moomaw's—Miss Johnson's first experience with cattle ranches—one of the riders was thrown and knocked unconscious. Miss Johnson was not prepared for it:

> "For all I knew he was dead. The way everybody treated him so casually shocked me terribly. Some men picked him up and took him into the house and nobody made any fuss. His wife came out of the crowd carrying a baby and wandered into the house. She wasn't making any fuss either. I asked Opal, 'Doesn't the woman care? Maybe her husband is dead.' Opal said, 'They just don't do that. You're not supposed to get excited about it.' And I said, 'Well, what a strange tradition.' You did not change. There were no hysterics."

Mrs. Colbert also recalled the rodeo: "Dorothy sat on the fence taking pictures with both her camera and mine. It kept me busy changing exposed rolls of film for fresh rolls. She must have taken a dozen rolls of pictures that day."

The rodeo at the Moomaw ranch made a distinct impression on Miss Johnson, an impression that still was with her a few weeks later when she left Okanogan for Wisconsin to find a new job. Also included in her plans was a visit with her mother and the man her mother had recently married, a Waukau beekeeper named Fred Alger.

Alger somehow had thought his stepdaughter was a child. With that in mind, he purchased a large bag of fireworks with which to welcome her to Waukau. The only fireworks that interested Miss Johnson were those in her mind as the idea for a story began to materialize. The elements were the bronc-riding she had witnessed at Moomaw's and some impressions from an old English ballad she had read. The ballad was titled "Bonnie George Campbell."

"I had been in Waukau just a couple of days when this thing suddenly came to full flower in my mind," she said. "The things tied up—the rodeo and the ballad—so the story, itself, is called 'Bonnie George Campbell.' "

In the sweltering heat of the Algers' attic, Miss Johnson, in one day, wrote, "Bonnie George Campbell," a story of a cowboy and his girl. Letting it jell overnight, she rewrote and polished it in one more day, dropped it into an envelope and mailed it to the Curtis Publishing Company's *Country Gentleman.*

"I had had *so* many rejections from *so* many magazines by that time," she said.

She chose *Country Gentleman* on the basis of a letter received a year earlier from one of the magazine's editors suggesting that perhaps she had something the magazine could use. The editor had seen one of her stories in *The Frontier* and had been impressed.

Early in September, a letter arrived at the Alger home in Waukau. It was not from *Country Gentleman*, however, but *The Saturday Evening Post*, also a Curtis publication. The *Post* said the story was fine and that a check for $400 was forthcoming. Miss Johnson was highly surprised.

"Somehow a letter from *Country Gentleman* caught up with me saying that 'Bonnie George Campbell' wasn't for them but that they had handed it on to the *Post*," she said. "This was all very queer, but utterly wonderful, because $400 was four months pay in the job I'd had in Okanogan."

Along with three illustrations, "Bonnie George Campbell" appeared in the October 18, 1930, issue of the *Post.*

"Okanogan Girl's Story of Rodeo Published in Post!" said the *Wenatchee* (Wash.) *World* in a two-column, three-line headline. "Former Employee of Blackwell Store Breaks Into 'Big Time' Publication," said the deck. The news story said in part:

> An impromptu rodeo at the Moomaw ranch near Monse is the basis of a story appearing in this week's issue of the *Saturday Evening Post*. It was written by Dorothy Marie Johnson, a former employee of the Blackwell store at Okanogan. Miss Johnson left Okanogan a few weeks ago to live with her parents in the Middle West.
>
> The characters and scene are easily recognized by anyone familiar with the region. Although the names are slightly changed, Phil Bedard, senior, and Phil, junior, both appear in the story. So do the Moomaw boys, Johnny Patterson, Bert Evans and a number of other well-known Okanogan riders . . . .
>
> Illustrations for the story are not as accurate as the word pictures . . . . Miss Johnson gives a very accurate picture of the reservation region and its life.

She had been writing short stories and poems for six years.

Now, at age 24, Dorothy Johnson thought her future assured as a writer. *The Berlin* (Wis.) *Evening Journal* said she had "come to the notice of those who count" and that she was "sure to continue her good success." She had no way of knowing that for the next 11 years she would not sell a single story.

For good reason, Miss Johnson was to remember "Bonnie George Campbell" as the only thing that kept her "warm" during the years of trying and failing from 1930 to 1941. From the standpoint of her creative-writing career, those years were to be the most dismal in her life.

CHAPTER FIVE

Poultry or Paper,
She Could Sell It

PERHAPS HER SUCCESS WITH "BONNIE GEORGE Campbell" convinced the women of the Waukau Church that Miss Johnson could write a flier promoting their annual chicken supper and bazaar. Miss Johnson accepted the task, but later wondered why. Her 23 ebullient lines oversold the affair, and long before the people stopped coming the chicken was gone. The ensuing confusion, and the unhappiness of those who had done the work but had to go hungry, did not help matters. Many people said they were attracted by the mimeographed flier, which read, in part:

> The frost is about to descend upon the pumpkin, and corn shocks march along by the fence-rows. In a hundred farm houses, women are stealing half-hours from their fall canning to sew for the bazaar. Plump chickens stroll in farmyards, not knowing that they're soon to be cut off in the flower of youth and tenderness to grace the chicken supper at Waukau Church. Farmers' daughters are practicing for the cake-baking contest—and can those girls cook!

Soon after arriving in Waukau, Miss Johnson went to nearby Oshkosh to register with employment agencies. Through one of them, she learned of an opening at the Menasha Products Company, manufacturers of paper products ranging from napkins to ice-cream cartons. The company, formerly based in Chicago, had just moved its headquarters to Menasha, some 25 miles northeast of Waukau.

Menasha Products needed a secretary for its advertising manager; the previous one had decided that she wanted to live in Chicago, not Menasha. On the basis of her application letter, Miss Johnson was asked to Menasha for an interview. The trip meant a bus ride and an overnight stay, but when it was over she had the job to which she was to devote five years.

Starting work in November 1930, Miss Johnson found the Menasha Products advertising department stimulating. Reading her boss's trade magazines prompted her to enroll in an evening course in printing. What she gleaned from that course later proved useful.

Until Menasha Products began a new era in waxed paper, Miss Johnson's creative writing was limited to evenings and weekends. Other than two college poems published in *Northwest Verse*, an anthology edited by Harold Merriam, her only contribution to reach print in the early 30s was "Highways are Happy Ways," a short story about fruit harvesters. It appeared in *The Frontier*.

A combination of events allowed Miss Johnson to put her creativity to work for Menasha. First, the company developed a new line of printed waxed paper. Second, her boss, who was supposed to write the advertising copy for it, was busy with other projects. He suggested Miss Johnson write the copy.

"It had pretty little green and yellow flowers and nobody had ever had waxed paper like that to wrap sandwiches in," she said. "Here was my first big opportunity."

She made the most of it, showing as much enthusiasm for waxed paper as she had for the bazaar supper:

> Just as fresh as the flowers in the spring is food wrapped in De Luxe Waxtex. Glossy, velvety waxed paper decorated with modernistic posies protects food from air, and with an air. It dresses sandwiches and all manner of other dainties as the jolly Prince of Wales dresses a ball. To the fingers, De Luxe Waxtex, extra heavy in weight, is as pleasant as banknotes; and to the eye, as sweet as a field of buttercups. Waxed paper is in every modern home and how women will welcome this new household waxed paper that's always on dress parade! A clever idea, to be sure.

Except for adding one adjective, the company used Miss Johnson's copy exactly as submitted.

"How I prized that," she said. "Of course, it didn't do anything for me except help my morale."

As time passed, she began writing direct-mail advertising. One of her first assignments was a letter to jobbers in Texas explaining a pool-car shipment of paper headed their way.

"I found out what a pool car was and wrote the Texans a perfectly ecstatic letter about the wonderful opportunity for them to save on their freight rates," she said. "I don't think I ever wrote about anything I wasn't enthusiastic about; I could work myself up to it."

Although Miss Johnson was interested in the company's goals, her enthusiasm, by 1934, also was sparked by personal motives. She was tired of Menasha and wanted to leave.

"It's hard to go from the Far West to the Middle West where everybody is related to everybody," she said. "I was a minority in that town; I wasn't related to anybody. Furthermore, I was neither German, Polish nor Irish and I was a Protestant. That was just not good in Menasha."

By 1934, Harold Merriam had combined his magazine with *The Midland*, a regional periodical that had been published since 1915 at the University of Iowa and later Chicago. In addition to publishing quarterly, *Frontier and Midland* became a magazine of the West rather than just the Northwest.

Miss Johnson's last contribution to her former English professor's magazine was a poem, "If You Know War Again," in the March 1934 edition. She enclosed a note with it, saying, "There's been too much heroic war poetry; here's a different kind . . . .":

When you breathe deep, clean moving air
Into ecstatic lungs, recall
The fallen ones of wars, who breathe
No more at all.

And when the green of living vibrant trees
And movement of all things are sweet,
Remember blind eyes under sod, who see
The last defeat.

Whether yours is compassionate, high God
Or jeering laughter in the skies,
Shudder to dream your punishment
If these should rise!

This be your curse, if you know war again:

The quivering flesh that shrieked and fell
Shall cheat you of your Paradise,
Mock you through hell.

Yours was a ruthless victory, empty pride.
Forget they died for glory—recall: They Died.

At Menasha Products, Miss Johnson continued to write advertising copy, particularly for direct mailing:

> Linen-like and practical, Colonial paper table napkins make life easier for home-makers. They're kept clean and white in sparkling Cellophane, in a generous package that takes care of many a meal. Colonial napkins are pleasant to handle, attractive to look at—and they never add to Monday's washing woes! Colonial napkins save tempers, laundry bills and time; they keep trousseau linens for really big occasions.

In a memo to her boss, she proposed a verse about toilet paper for some promotional blotters:

How about a picture of Tiffany and this,
on the blotters:

Van Puyster's seventh bathroom is wonderfully done
In chromium and marble and three kinds of jade;
The Sultan's palace glistens 'neath an Oriental sun,
And the Perkins' neat white cottage is somewhat in the shade,

But a little touch of luxury can make the whole world kin—
The tissue in those bathrooms is fit for baby's skin.
Mrs. Perkins buys her tissue with considerable care—
And Tiffany will still be it when Bill's a millionaire.

Dorothy Johnson

P.S.—Please note the admirable way in which I restrained my baser impulses, which sometimes overpower me.

A letter promoting ice-cream cartons brought this response from a Menasha salesman on the West Coast:

Roy Gute to Dorothy Johnson:

> Please thank the proper party for the wonderful letter . . . sent out to my ice cream trade . . . . It was "wonderfully" written in good pulling language. *Dam good* in any man's language, say I.

A professional magazine called *Printed Salesmanship* was one Miss Johnson found especially intriguing. Each month, a national authority on commercial correspondence named L.E. Frailey conducted a contest in business-letter writing. Miss Johnson and her new boss began to enter.

"Both times we entered we placed," she said. "It was embarrassing because each time we got our names in the magazine, I was one notch higher than my boss. This is not good."

Her entry in the September 1934 contest ultimately got Miss Johnson out of Menasha. The problem called for an application letter from a young man recently out of college. Assuming the name James Birch, Miss Johnson took first honorable mention with this letter:

Dear Sir:

Out here we don't believe in Santa Claus any more, and if there are any soft jobs left in the world, I wouldn't know what to do with one. Getting through four years at the University of Montana in these times fits a man for work. (My B.A. in Business Administration was granted in June 1934. My senior thesis did not attempt to cure the Depression.) We're used to working by the time we finish school. Summer of 1931 I worked in the harvest fields; summer of 1932 I sold washing machines (second paragraph from the last tells more about that), and in 1933 a crew of us picked spotted-fever ticks for the government and good wages. Spotted-fever ticks are nobody's pets.

Here is a transcript of my completed courses and grades received. A High School Honor Scholarship paid my fees all four years; you lose them if your grades get down to C average.

"Active in a leadership way," your advertisement reads. So: Bearpaw (honorary sophomore men's organization), M Club (varsity basketball two years), Duniway prize books in 1933.

I couldn't afford a fraternity, but two years spent managing the barb house helped out the social graces. My freshman year was spent in the men's dormitory; they're used to rubbing the rough edges off aspiring business men in South Hall. I can still get by with the boys in the Butte mines, too.

Salesmanship?—I sold twelve washing machines in two weeks in a railroad town of 4,000 one summer, when half the men in town were cut off the board.

I would like to sell you the services of one James Birch, who could do more good in your organization than he could as a deputy sheriff. But he has to earn a living, and while he is ambitious, he isn't fussy. Would you like to ask questions about this merchandise, and look it over?

Sincerely yours,

In congratulating winners for their letters, Frailey wrote:

> I rather imagine the ghost of idleness would never follow you long. Yours is the power of originality—you know how to fashion your story in a way that is different than the average.

The next year, Clyde Blanchard, general editor of the Gregg Publishing Company in New York, was preparing a chapter on effective letter-writing for a Gregg textbook, *The English of Business*. While looking for examples, he discovered Miss Johnson's letter. He wrote her for permission to use it.

Miss Johnson was delighted. She immediately wrote Blanchard, using the opportunity to ask him "as casually as possible" if he knew of any jobs in New York City. Blanchard wrote her again, asking if she would be interested in working for Gregg Publishing:

> "I went down to Chicago to meet Mr. Blanchard and his wife. Chicago was 200 miles and I didn't really have enough money to be wasting it on a trip there. By this time my pay had been cut. I had had a couple of raises and then we all got three cuts. But I took a chance and went to Chicago to meet him. I never knew when that man was interviewing me. It all seemed like just a pleasant social conversation. He happened to be in Chicago because he was teaching at Gregg's school there during the summer. He and his wife were so nice. When I went back to Wisconsin I didn't know whether he liked me or not."

Blanchard liked her. As managing editor for Gregg's magazine, *Business Education World*, he decided he wanted her as an assistant editor. His only problem was that the magazine's editor-in-chief, John Robert Gregg, was cruising the Mediterranean. Gregg retained final say in all hirings.

For what seemed to Miss Johnson an interminable period, she heard nothing. She had begun to lose hope when, one July day, she came home to prepare for a picnic and found a telegram. Blanchard wanted to know how soon she could come to New York.

"I nearly lost my mind," she said. "I went on the picnic but I certainly didn't have my thoughts on anything but this marvelous thing that had happened. I was going to get $150 a month, twice what I was getting in Menasha. Everything in New York cost twice as much, but, just the same, it was my big break."

Those who knew Miss Johnson might have wondered why,

with her interest in fiction, she joined a business-education magazine. They could have argued that a newspaper or general-circulation magazine would provide her with the best experience for creative work. Miss Johnson did not think so:

"I got all the newspapering I wanted as a stringer for the Kalispell *Inter Lake*. That is exactly why I didn't take journalism at the university. At that time, journalism on our campus was nothing but newspaper work. Radio had been invented but it wasn't anything you went to work in. I didn't want to work on a newspaper. I really hadn't had enough contact with papers to know what they were like. I knew what *The Whitefish Pilot* was like since my mother worked there for awhile. But it didn't seem to me this was the kind of place you wanted to be in if you wanted to write stories. How would you ever get them in? I didn't see newspapering as a training ground. You have no idea what dull stuff I used to write for the *Inter Lake*—you know, 'Somebody came from Polson for Sunday dinner with his sister.' It's still the bread of life for small-town papers; it's terribly important but it's not creative. I didn't have the faintest idea what people did on newspapers. There was nobody to tell me about how maybe journalism would be good for me. It would have been in this respect: I was so scared of people. I was very timid. In the English department in college, you never had to interview anybody. This proved to be a dreadful handicap. I never did any serious interviewing until I went to New York and had to interview a vice president of CBS. Talking to a big shot like that is a terrible way to start learning how to interview. I was so afraid to talk to anybody and ask snoopy questions."

In terms of her development as a writer, Miss Johnson could not have made a better job choice than the Gregg Publishing Company. Her nine years with the company provided a thorough education in writing discipline, something that had never been stressed to her.

Soon after Blanchard's telegram arrived, Miss Johnson received a letter from L.E. Frailey, the letter-writing authority:

July 22, 1935

Dear Miss Johnson:

I was happy . . . to hear from Mr. Blanchard that he had selected you as his personal assistant. I had a conference with him in Chicago and the news came out in rather amusing fashion.

During our chat, we happened to talk about the folks who had answered my letter problems, and I made the remark that if I were ever the head of a big advertising agency, there were three women I would want to hire—Mae Weishampel in Baltimore, Virginia Young in Denver, and Dorothy Marie Johnson in Menasha.

You can imagine my surprise when he said, "But you can't hire Miss Johnson—she belongs to me."

Congratulations, Dorothy Marie! I know that you will be very successful in your new position.

L.E. Frailey

Frailey had been perceptive when he wrote of Miss Johnson: "Yours is the power of originality." Her originality and enthusiasm, teamed with the mechanics she would learn at Gregg, would demonstrate their worth.

CHAPTER SIX

Beulah Bunny

L E. F R A I L E Y WAS AS PROPHETIC AS HE WAS perceptive. By October 1935 Miss Johnson was at work at 270 Madison Avenue, home of Gregg Publishing and its magazine, *Business Education World* (*B.E.W.*). Her college training had emphasized creativity, not mechanics, and soon she was compelled to memorize the rules of punctuation, spelling and composition.

"These things had never seemed important before, but at Gregg they really had high standards," she said. "If there was one possible error in a textbook or in one of our magazines, they'd hear from 40 teachers who maybe knew nothing else except that 'there shouldn't be a comma there.' "

She began with minor writing and editing tasks, among them the preparation of biographical sketches of business teachers who had articles in each month's *B.E.W.* Soon she was editing the articles, many of which she found extremely dull:

"It was terrible stuff. Some of those people couldn't write for beans, but we had to make the magazine come out looking as though they were all geniuses. I did a great deal of rewriting and every now and then somebody would sit on me really hard because I had let something go through in a manuscript that should have been changed. They were tough, but kind, and it was wonderful training."

Miss Johnson shared bathroom and kitchen facilities with other tenants of the West 94th Street apartment building that was her home for two years. She disliked cooking (and always would) and usually ate at cafes.

"Nobody did much cooking there," she said. "You couldn't

Miss Johnson in 1942. She was in New York City with Gregg Publishing
Company at the time.

keep stuff in the refrigerator because somebody would swipe your butter."

Miss Johnson soon learned how to select eating places. If an establishment did not have its menu clearly printed in the window, she knew immediately it was too expensive. She considered a 75-cent Sunday dinner a "pretty high-priced treat."

She still read voraciously but thought the New York City Public Library an "awful flop" because of its lending practices. She discovered private lending libraries, which allowed books to circulate more freely, and came to depend on them.

With little success, she continued her outside writing, publishing no stories and only three articles from 1935 to 1940. Despite much effort, writing and rewriting, rejection slips of every description continued to accumulate. (She never got used to rejection slips and always became dejected at getting them.)

"I went on writing endlessly and not selling a thing," she said. "I was reading writers' magazines and most of them were awfully poor. They told you how to sharpen pencils and how to keep track of your rejection slips."

Miss Johnson had little trouble adjusting to New York City. She found the pace and people exhilarating and offset any loneliness by frequently attending plays and museums. She found it difficult, however, to establish personal contact with New Yorkers.

"You don't make casual friendships in New York," she explained. "When you meet people you have to write down their names and addresses and make luncheon and shopping dates to see them. The friendships you do make, however, are apt to be more solid because you have to go to so much trouble to establish them."

Miss Johnson became acquainted with New York City through her own efforts and through those of the Yosians, an informal organization that provided inexpensive Sunday excursions sponsored by the *New York World-Telegram*. On her own, she often took buses or subways to the end of the line, then explored what she found. Once, on the Manhattan waterfront, she left a bus and followed a small crowd onto what she assumed was an observation pier. She had put her nickel into a slot and was preparing to enjoy the view when the "pier" weighed anchor for New Jersey.

"I had never been on a ferry before," she said. "I had never even seen one!"

Each Friday the *World-Telegram* published a guide to Sunday activities planned by the Yosians. Readers could check the columns to learn what different groups were doing. Persons with the Yosian excursions were asked to carry a copy of the *World-Telegram* for identification, and on many Sundays Miss Johnson, clutching her paper, could be found on a Yosian walk, picnic or bus tour.

By late 1936, in addition to her editing responsibilities, Miss Johnson was writing subscription promotions for *Business Education World*. They, too, exhibited her lively, original approach.

In 1937, Miss Johnson moved from West 94th Street to Grove Street in Greenwich Village. Her first and second homes in the Village were furnished rooms, and in the second—"a charming room with a fireplace"—she set out in 1939 to write a novel:

> "The room had windows that looked out into a garden with trees in it. It was a marvelous place to write—I had never had such a good place before. I didn't think I had enough stick-to-itiveness to write anything as big as a novel, but I thought to myself, 'All right, let's see if I have what it takes—other people write novels; I don't know why I can't.'
>
> I resolved to write a thousand words a day and I did. In those days I was still reading all the writers' magazines and believing everything in them because I hadn't learned otherwise. One of the things they all said was that the art of writing was the art of applying the seat of your pants to the seat of a chair. This is not true, although you have to do this to get any writing done.
>
> If I missed my thousand words a day by going to the theater or something, I would catch up the next weekend. I wrote for three months and that was 90,000 words. Then nobody ever published it. That was before I had an agent, but not even an agent could have sold it. I wracked my brain for a title for that thing—I had a whole string of them . . . . Anyway, I found out I could do it."

If Miss Johnson's career as a fiction writer appeared finished by 1940, her career with Gregg Publishing seemed to be just starting. In addition to editing articles for *B.E.W.* and writing the magazine's promotional material, she became director of the divisions of business personality and business-letter writing. In each capacity she designed and wrote manuals containing numerous hypothetical problems.

She became responsible for a monthly letter-writing contest in B.E.W. and not only had to pose the problems each issue, but had to read and evaluate the hundreds of entries. B.E.W. awarded cash prizes for winning letters. The number of entries grew steadily and Miss Johnson began taking them home at night. Her results with the contest were excellent.

As she was to solve the problems of many fictitious characters, a warm-hearted, incurably romantic, spinster school teacher named Beulah Bunny was to solve several of Dorothy Johnson's in 1941. In July of that year, Miss Johnson returned to Wisconsin to vacation with her mother and stepfather. A story idea had occurred to her in New York, and during her stay in Waukau she wrote "Fellow Has to Get Away Sometime," relating how Beulah Bunny changes the life of one Walter (Strawberry) Rowan. Strawberry is a pathetic lad who works on a ranch for almost nothing. He possesses remarkable musical ability, which the subtle and determined Miss Bunny encourages.

Narrated by Miss Bunny, the story takes place in Okanasket, Washington, a town Miss Johnson invented by combining Okanogan (where she had lived after college) and Tonasket, a small town north of Okanogan. Miss Johnson described what happened:

> "After I wrote 'Fellow Has to Get Away Sometime,' there seemed to be a lot more to be said. Not long after getting back to New York, I had four Beulah Bunny stories written. I never meant to write a series but these were interesting people. I knew that if I sent one of them to a magazine and it came back, as it certainly would, I would be too crushed to go ahead with any more for a long time. That's why I finished four before I sent them anywhere.
>
> "When I was done, I shipped them off to The Saturday Evening Post. Next day I read in a writers' magazine that you should never send more than one story to a magazine at a time because they would take it for granted you had been cleaning out your desk drawers and wouldn't pay any attention. That was a terrible time to find that out. So I said, 'I always do everything wrong; they weren't going to take them anyway.'
>
> "A few weeks later I got a brown envelope in the mail. But it wasn't as heavy as it should have been. It didn't have the four stories but, instead, quite a long letter from the editors saying they

were buying three of the stories and the fourth if I wouldn't mind making a few changes. I almost fainted. I got this at my office at Gregg . . . and got the whole place excited. I kept looking through this letter and I couldn't believe what it seemed to say, which was that *Post's* check for $1,700 for the three stories would be along soon. They bought all four of them for $2,100 after I did some fast rewriting on the last one. $2,100 was an awful lot of money and this was simply unbelievable. My boss was so happy he rushed in with the letter to show Dr. Gregg. Everybody was upset and excited."

In a telegram dated August 29, 1941, Miss Johnson wired her mother the good news: *"Post* bought four stories. What do you want for Christmas?"

The three stories purchased by the *Post* in addition to "Fellow Has to Get Away Sometime" were "This Will Be Mine," "Going to Whittingham Fair" and "Cruel Barbara Ellen." On the title page of its October 25, 1941, edition, *The Post*, in re-acquainting its readers with Miss Johnson, said:

"In 1930 a young writer sold us a short story about a boy, a girl and a ballad. Then Dorothy M. Johnson disappeared from our ken. Several weeks ago—and eleven years later—she popped up in the mails with four stories. We bought them all. Here's the first."

Selling the four stories was the biggest stimulus Miss Johnson had received in 11 years:

"I thought, 'These apparently are pretty interesting characters.' So I went ahead and wrote several more stories about some of the same people, always with Beulah Bunny as narrator . . . . Then I found out in conversation with some of the editors that what they liked was Beulah Bunny herself. To me, she was only the vehicle to get the story across."

Inspiration for several Beulah Bunny stories came from Miss Johnson's longstanding interest in traditional English ballads and folk songs. (Her first story, "Bonnie George Campbell," also had been prompted by an old ballad.) She wrote of folk songs:

"I recommend folk-song study. It's a scholarly pursuit; some of the songs still extant trace from the sixteenth century, and some are offshoots from ancestors at least 300 years older.

"The people who loved these songs and passed them along through the generations were not scholars; they were, for the most part, illiterate, and they simply wanted entertainment or vicarious romance and adventure or to pass the time while they worked. Some of them were rich and royal; most of them were poor. The songs they sang, passed along through oral tradition, seem to bring those past generations closer to us than what was written down about them."

Soon after the good tidings, Miss Johnson received a second letter inviting her to Philadelphia for lunch with some of *Post's* editors. Suspecting a joke, she wrote a humorous reply declining the invitation. The *Post* wrote back: The invitation was no joke; they wanted to discuss some matters concerning future stories.

This time Miss Johnson did not hesitate. Taking a day off, she boarded a train for Philadelphia:

"I had lunch with several of the editors and I was scared of the whole bunch of them. I still didn't believe this was really happening. I think the main reason they wanted me to come was to take a look and also to get the idea across that they wanted first crack at my stuff from then on. They let me know, and not very subtly, that they would be offended if I gave first look to any other magazine. I was too naive to know that first look is what big magazines pay for. They would rather not see something that has been rejected by somebody else. At this time I didn't have an agent. I didn't need one—I was getting along just fine . . . . "

Elated, Miss Johnson wrote and sold several more Beulah Bunny stories to the *Post* in late 1941 and early 1942. Among them were "Miss Bunny Goes to Jail," "Blanket Squaw," "She's Gone With Gypsy Davey" and "Beulah Bunny and the Lethal Blade." (For Gregg Publishing she wrote two radio scripts—"Training for Careers" and "A Girl and Her Shadow"—for distribution and production in high school business classes.)

Miss Johnson earned enough from her *Post* stories to enroll in a short-story course at New York University. Her instructor, a novelist, requested each member of the class to write a story a week. At least one student—Miss Johnson—complied:

"When I told the *Post* what I was doing, they almost collapsed. They thought it was the most horrible idea they had ever heard of. I wasn't doing anything except working eight hours a day and writing in the evening. I would eat a meal once in awhile but I didn't get much sleep."

The year 1941 changed Miss Johnson's life in several ways, as it did the lives of millions of Americans. On December 16, nine days after Japan attacked Pearl Harbor, she enrolled in the Air Warden Service, United States Citizens Defense Corps, City of New York. She was hesitant at first:

"I searched my soul before deciding. I fully expected to be bombed out of existence any minute. Of course, I did everything wrong. I read the paper and got a little mixed up, then went over to the nearest fire station to enlist. The fireman I talked to was very sweet about it when he told me that what they were looking for was good sturdy men who worked on the docks. He told me to go over to the police station, which I did. From then on, the police station was almost my second home. It was awfully hard on the police to suddenly have this bunch of civilians to order around and educate, but they got used to it."

"Date With a Soldier," Miss Johnson's first big-time story since "Bonnie George Campbell" not to involve Beulah Bunny, concerned an air warden who felt that what she was doing was silly:

"We had all been pushed around enough by the general population by that time that we were feeling abused. It took character to stay in that outfit. Everybody thought we were crazy and we did, too. We had to pay our own expenses and we were always getting orders from on high that made us simply furious. I remember the time the city had a bad blizzard. *The New York Times* came out with a nasty editorial about all the air wardens sitting around eating their heads off at great public expense. They wanted to know why we didn't get out and shovel the walks and streets. Well, we blew our tops, because whoever wrote the editorial didn't realize that no tax money was being appropriated."

Miss Johnson took time to write the editor of *The Times*. (She would write many letters to many editors in subsequent years):

TO THE EDITOR OF THE NEW YORK TIMES:

Considerable publicity has been given to a double-header baseball game held on April 14 for the benefit of the CDVO. I'd like to express a hope that equal publicity will be given to the allocation of whatever money is raised. I do not suggest that someone is going to make off with it; I only want to know whether the Air Warden Service is going to get some of it.

I have never been told what the CDVO is or does, but I know what air wardens do, because I am one. One of the things we do is pay our own expenses. We pay for the entire upkeep of our sector organizations—rent, light, telephone, paint, printing bills, stationery, postage. We buy stretchers and first-aid equipment for a placid public.

Long ago $100,000 was allotted to civilian defense here. Where it went I never heard, but the air wardens have been paying their own way ever since the service was organized, so I know we didn't get any of it for necessary office expenses.

Most people assume that the expenses of the Air Warden Service are paid out of taxes. Those who know better agree that it is not fair that people who are voluntarily doing a necessary, time-consuming, patriotic job should pay for the privilege of doing it.

Now that money is being raised by and for the CDVO, is this extra burden of ours going to be lifted?

BLUE ALERT

For organizational purposes, the Air Warden Service divided New York City into precincts. Precincts were divided into zones, zones into sectors and sectors into posts. As a resident of Grove Street in Greenwich Village (AWS Precinct 6, Zone A, Sector 2), Miss Johnson was headquartered in a deserted, rent-free store.

"I spent a lot of my life there between 1941 and 1945," she said. "We were supposed to spend 30 hours a month doing something—patrolling the streets during blackouts or talking to people to see if they had any invalids who would have to be evacuated in an emergency."

Sector 2 started a small, mimeographed newspaper for servicemen. Its name was *The Neighborhood News* and its editor was Miss Johnson, whom a Greenwich Village paper referred to as "a forceful, young woman in slacks."

Miss Johnson had found that living in Greenwich Village made getting acquainted considerably easier than it had been on West 94th Street. Through the Air Warden Service she made even more friends:

> "I got to know some of the tenement people who had very much mistrusted and despised us. The white-collar people and the blue-collar people all lived on the same street, but there was a big gap. They scorned us because we weren't permanent. We might live in an apartment for a couple years and then disappear. They'd been living in their flats for two generations and they knew who belonged there and who didn't."

In a column written in 1951 for the *Great Falls* (Mont.) *Tribune*,

Miss Johnson described her New Year's Eve of 1941 as an air warden:

I was watching for saboteurs, without knowing what they looked like or how they would act or what I would do if I caught one . . . .

The orders didn't come until early New Year's Eve. A man who said his name was Kenneth Hamon telephoned to say he was squad leader of the post I was assigned to, and we were supposed to patrol the streets of the neighborhood all night. Members of our post were meeting at his apartment on Barrow street, he said.

Barrow street, to my surprise, turned out to be right next to the street I'd been living on for over a year, which shows you how well acquainted residents of large cities are with their own surroundings.

But before another year had passed, I could find any house for blocks around in the dark, and also fire hydrants. Fire hydrants are easy to find in a blackout. You just fall over them.

The other members of Post 9 assembled at Hamon's place looked normal and not excessively heroic. I felt relieved. The men would take the patrol job from midnight on, he said, and I pulled a two-hour shift from 10 to midnight, with three blocks to cover and an official armband to wear, and a police whistle.

When we got out on the street, I still didn't know what to do. Walk along, sure, but what else? Under the circumstances would one blow the whistle? What would people be doing that they shouldn't be doing, and how was I supposed to stop them?

The questions stopped Hamon, poor man. The cops hadn't given him much information to go on. . . . He was quick-witted, though. He said sternly, "Watch out for sabotage."

I looked at the small apartment houses and rundown little stores and demanded, "Who's going to sabotage what?" He was equal to the challenge. "Watch that corner street light," he advised.

And so, for two hours, I watched that street light. No street light was ever more closely guarded. If falling snow seemed for a moment to make it flicker, I went tense, prepared to kick, scream and blow the whistle if the situation got beyond me. I grimly scrutinized the few pedestrians who passed, especially if they got within six feet of that street light. I memorized a description of each one of them, in case I had to identify him before the Supreme Court. . . .

The night was cold and so were my feet. To keep in condition to defend the street light, I had to walk around. Besides, the three blocks to be patrolled weren't all in a string. I had to get a block away from the street light to see what was going on in one of them. . . .

I never walked more than 10 steps without making a quick turn

Deputy Sector Commander Dorothy M. Johnson of New York City's
Air Warden Service in 1945.

to see that all was well with my street light. In the next block, I had a chat with a large, cold policeman, who for some reason unknown to him had orders not to stir from an intersection. He confided that his feet were killing him. While we were talking, I watched my street light.

Along toward midnight, my big moment arrived. Two men came out of a building and stood talking together, looking toward the street light.

They were Orientals, no doubt about it, and probably Japanese. If they were Japanese, I concluded, they were potential saboteurs. And if they were saboteurs, they'd make a pass at my street light. I watched them like a hawk.

After a while, apparently discouraged by my surveillance, they went back into the building. A few minutes later, Hamon arrived to relieve me of my arduous duties. I told him about the dangerous-looking characters.

"Where did they come from?" he demanded.

"That door right over there. And they went back in the same one."

He heaved a sigh. "That's a Chinese restaurant," he said, "and they're Chinese waiters and they've worked there for 20 years."

CHAPTER SEVEN

From Writer to Author

THE BEULAH BUNNY SERIES WAS MORE popular than Miss Johnson had anticipated. In the spring of 1942, she received a call from William Morrow, president of the New York publishing house William Morrow & Company. He had been following the Bunny stories in the *Post* and invited Miss Johnson to lunch to discuss the possibility of publishing them as a collection. Miss Johnson was astonished.

"I just didn't believe it," she said. "I was so ignorant that when he asked me how much of an advance I would need, I told him I didn't need an advance, that I had a job and was getting along fine."

The book came out in September 1942 as *Beulah Bunny Tells All.* Miss Johnson went to Morrow's offices and autographed several copies in green ink. She was elated when presented with the first one for her own. Putting the book into a briefcase she had recently purchased, she left Morrow's and jubilantly boarded a bus for Greenwich Village. Not until she was again on foot and walking toward her apartment did she miss anything. The bus, her briefcase aboard it, had disappeared.

Miss Johnson rushed home and telephoned the transit company, reaching the firm's lost-and-found desk only after several exasperating conversations with various employees. By the time she was connected, the briefcase had been turned in. She wasted little time in retrieving it and its precious contents.

Miss Johnson dedicated *Beulah Bunny Tells All* to her mother, who by that time had come to live with her in New York following the death of Fred Alger. In a prefatory inscription, Miss Johnson noted that "All the characters in this book are purely imaginary.

The author regrets this because she would like to meet some of them."

After the release of the book, which brought its 36-year-old author considerable publicity, Miss Johnson discovered something peculiar. She discussed it in an article several years later:

> A writer is not an author until he has produced a book. What the book is doesn't matter much. *Beulah Bunny* contained 10 or 12 short stories that had already appeared in the *Saturday Evening Post*. Any one of them brought a bigger check from the *Post* than the total royalties on the book. They were the same stories, no better in hard covers than they had been singly, and in book form they were not read by nearly so many people.
>
> But there was a noticeable increase in prestige. My friends began to act respectful. With a book, I had become an author. Magazines are transitory. A book is permanent—anyway in theory. . . .

Beulah Bunny as a character was well received by readers and critics alike. In a review of *Beulah Bunny Tells All* in the *New York Herald Tribune*, Page Cooper said of Miss Bunny:

> Beulah Bunny, school teacher by accident, gambler by intention, is one of the most lovably ruthless meddlers-in-other-people's-affairs that you will find between covers. Perhaps you have met her in *The Saturday Evening Post* and know how she took up fencing, sacrificed her comfort, endangered her creaking bones and won a courtly and chronically hungry suitor, all because she gambled that the pretty new school teacher didn't know her own mind about the dentist. Of course Miss Bunny won. She always does because she is always on the side of true love and doesn't hesitate to use unorthodox—not to say, unethical—means of furthering romance . . .

In a review broadcast over WDNC, Durham, N.C., J.B. Clark said:

> "Remember Will Rogers—how plain and much like homespun garments he was? How human and philosophical and kind and understanding? Remember how Will could take the problems of the world and in a jiffy show you how to solve them—always with that twinkle in his eye and that sane, level head of his working trigger-quick? Sure, you remember Will Rogers. He's an American institution, even in death. This isn't about Will Rogers. It's about a female counterpart of Will—not even a real woman, but a creation of fiction so vividly alive on the pages of print that

you feel you have known her for years.

"I'm referring to Beulah Bunny. . . Dorothy M. Johnson, her creator, has had many of the famous Beulah Bunny stories published in *The Saturday Evening Post* and Beulah . . . has become . . . as much a part of the American home scene as Will Rogers was in life."

Understandably, Miss Johnson, by 1941, had lost all confidence in her ability to write fiction. Later, in analyzing her 11 years of rejection slips, she concluded that her use of first person was one factor that helped her get back into print:

"I had a story to tell and it had to be told in the first person because it just did. By the time a narrator evolved who had all the qualifications to tell it, she turned out to be a school teacher named Beulah Bunny. She is not anybody but herself, and she is definitely not me."

In a 1943 article for *The Writer*, she speculated further as to the causes of her years of failure:

For one thing, most of the stories were pretty tragic. If I came out with nobody completely ruined, I thought I was doing pretty well by the reading public—which never got to appreciate my efforts, however. There was some block in my mind that turned plots into dismal ways. Don't ask me why. I like to laugh better than any other two people, and heaven knows I like to laugh at my own jokes. But there was something that kept me from making fiction that could be laughed at or even endured by anyone except me.

Maybe the trouble was this: Boiled down, there are two kinds of writing, expression and communication. I insisted on expressing myself, ignoring the possible reader. Finally, I learned to communicate. It's a lot of fun.

Expression often precludes communication, but a story that lets the reader in by no means keeps the writer from enjoying himself through expression. Pure expression is often hard for the reader to translate into his own terms; if it's hard, he won't do it; if he won't do it, editors won't require him to try.

Whether you express or communicate depends, perhaps, on your attitude toward people. Writers who insist on saying what they want to say without considering the difficulty that busy people may have in getting something out of it may go on doing it for a couple of unrecognized reasons.

Either they don't like people very well and aren't going to do any favors or they are avoiding hard work by refusing to be bound by the technical requirements of plotting and characterization.

If you like people in general, you want to let them in on the enjoyment you get from writing. You put in more drama, because people like to be kept on edge in reading. You get your characters into bad fixes so that the reader can worry about somebody other than himself. You get them out again so that the reader can return to his own problems without extra burdens. You supply good reasons for everything that happens, so the reader won't be puzzled and get the idea that he is stupid or that you are haughty. You see to it that something really happens.

All this is involved in communicative fiction. Communication is *not* condescension. It involves understanding, skill, good will, and a lot of work.

Expression is easier—and less fruitful. You assume that the reader is going to do much of the work for you. You say things in ways that require the reader to stop and translate into his own terms. You are subtle. You beckon the reader austerely with one hand and fend him off with the other. You don't have to bother much with a plot, because a couple of incidents will do. You assure yourself, "This is life." You say, "I am retaining my literary integrity." And if you really think you can do that in no other way, you must follow your convictions.

But communicative writing includes expression, too! It is harder work, but it's more satisfying to everybody, including the writer. The things you want to tell the world about your own thoughts come out in this kind of writing as subtle propaganda. You don't simply say that a character does a certain thing; you know and sometimes tell why he does it. That's where the work comes in—there, and in making your plot. Expression doesn't require a plot. Communication does. If you like people and want to let them in on the enjoyment you get from writing, you will sweat over a plot. Maybe some people get them direct from heaven, but I have to dig for one and then smelt it down.

When I used to insist on pure expression, I avoided dramatic situations. I led up to them, all right, but then I went onto a siding and got back on the main line later, where nothing disturbing was happening. But readers like disturbances—if you quell them later. Now I look for them—a friction here and there, in addition to the main struggle theme, and perhaps a couple of laughs. In rewriting, I go over the whole thing coldbloodedly (and many times), trying to find places where another little joke wouldn't do us any harm.

The situation has got a little out of control. My chief character, Beulah Bunny, has developed a personality stronger than mine. Her wise cracks are better than mine, too, because I polish hers. Sometimes people seem to think I am stealing her lines. Sometimes I suspect they're right about it. Still, in the beginning she had no personality. She was only a technical necessity that would permit me to tell stories in the first person and thereby get in more jokes.

Hasn't the writer's attitude toward other people got a lot to do with their attitude toward him? If he seems distant, what reason is there for readers to pursue him? If he puts his thoughts before them haughtily, why should they accept? If he condescends, they will notice. But if he opens his mind and heart and says, "Let's enjoy this together," he achieves a double purpose—communication and expression.

In July 1942, two months before *Beulah Bunny* was published, Miss Johnson returned to the Pacific Northwest for a vacation and to gather more fiction material. Her mother, who had retained her property in Waukau, spent the summer there. Miss Johnson visited Portland and Seattle and then, in the locomotive of a Great Northern train, rode through the Cascade tunnel to Wenatchee, Washington, to do some research for a magazine article. Later, she traveled north to the Okanogan Valley.

Back in the region that had been her home for two years, she was warmly greeted by people who had followed the adventures of Beulah Bunny from the start. Miss Johnson's fears that residents of the Okanogan Valley might not like her stories proved unwarranted. Beulah Bunny had been so well received that Okanogan, Tonasket and even Omak all were claiming to be the setting for the series. At a rodeo in Omak, Miss Johnson was guest of honor. Later, for research purposes, she visited the Pilot Wheel ranch near Tonasket. Her hosts, rancher Bob Fancher and his daughter, Roberta, invited her along as they moved a small herd of cows and calves over a mountain. She later described the experience in a column:

> Before the first half of the first inning, I knew I was in the wrong league.
> When we reached the foot of the mountain, the Fanchers saw they had enough of a problem with all that peripatetic beef, so they gave me the lead rope of the pack horse and said why didn't I go down yonder and wait by the creek in the woods.
> The pack horse kept trying to tie me up with the lead rope, and the saddle horse kept turning around to stare at me, which was disconcerting. So when we got to the creek I figured we all needed a drink and a fresh approach to the situation.

The cowhand: Miss
Johnson at Birney,
Montana.

Some people assumed
that Miss Johnson
was a skilled
horsewoman because
of her interest in, and
knowledge of, the
West. In truth, she
was more at home out
of the saddle than in
it, and often made
light of her limited
riding experience. In
this photograph, one
of her favorites, a dog
shows his disapproval
for her mounting
technique by turning
his back and skulking
away.

At Birney shortly after World War II, Miss Johnson stands ready to toss a loop over anything that comes close enough and stands still long enough.

I kindly tied the reins to the horn so the saddle horse wouldn't step on them and was sloshing around in the creek when I felt a great loneliness.

Both horses were beating feet gladly down the road. I had read in western stories that western horses would do that if you didn't let the reins dangle. How was I to know the Fanchers' horses read the same stuff I did?

I chased them, panting, lurching along with the burden of bat-wing leather chaps, which were never built for fast footwork. The only reason I ever caught up was that the horses had to stop for a fence.

After a couple of weeks, I could walk without limping very much.

Later, back in New York City, Miss Johnson took up riding again. She later wrote:

Most of the horses you can rent at a suburban riding stable have serious personality defects. There was one big bay named Major that I thought liked me. He had an affectionate way of reaching around and rubbing his nose on my left boot.

It was very touching and I called him pet names until a more experienced rider informed me that Major's whole aim in life was to bite somebody's foot off. When he nibbled my boot, he was only getting the range.

My riding partner was a Kansas girl named Frances Smith. Once when I got into trouble in the woods of Forest Park, on Long Island, she carried the bad news from Aix to Ghent, or anyway back to the riding stable.

That time I drew a bony black horse with a persecution complex, and Frances got a gray one about the size you see on a merry-go-round.

The black tried to dodge out from under me, but, of course, I had found out what a saddle horn is good for . . . . He showed his real character a couple of miles from his home stall. He folded his knees and lay quietly down on his right side.

I rolled off and grabbed the reins, because stable owners tend to speak sharply to riders who walk back horseless, and got back on again. I can get on a horse fine if he stands still beside a nice big log.

Three minutes later he lay down again, this time on his left side, and we did it all over . . . . I walked him back and forth to keep him from collapsing again while Frances made like Paul Revere back to the stable for professional advice about the way to treat a folding horse.

The man from the stable came in a hurry, but Frances wasn't with him. She was unavoidably detained at the stable by her pint-sized horse, which was putting on a solo rodeo, trying to buck her off.

Anyway, even if I couldn't make that black horse stand up, I proved I was versatile enough to get off him on either the port or starboard side, and while he was in a reclining position.

Another time, in another park, a chestnut named Popcorn tried to get me arrested. He wouldn't budge out of a walk except when another horse came up behind him. Then he'd bust into a run until the other horse got past and around a bend. There was a rule in that park against galloping, but Popcorn could not read signs.

One of the horses that came up behind us happened to be ridden by a uniformed policeman whose duty it was to see that nobody galloped a horse. Popcorn and I raced him for a quarter mile. The cop won. He didn't say anything, though. He must have guessed that I wasn't galloping Popcorn. Popcorn was galloping me.

"Date With a Soldier," with its New York setting, marked the beginning of the end for Beulah Bunny. The fadeout was deliberate, Miss Johnson having realized that when the *Post* rejected a story from the series—as it had on occasion—there was no other market for it.

"It was all very nice to have a magazine buying a series, but I had to get away from the limitations involved and start writing individual stories," she said.

Beulah's departure was gradual: The last of the stories included "Beulah Bunny Barters Bonds" (July 3, 1943), "Beulah Bunny and the Boy Called Joe" (October 9, 1943), and "The Lost Musician" (January 8, 1944). "The Gay Desperado," published in the March 17, 1945, issue of the *Post*, ended the series. About "The Gay Desperado," the *Post* had the following to say:

In case anybody thinks that doing a short story is a brief and facile occupation, it might be well to record that Miss Johnson's folder on this story alone is now packed with about one hundred pages of discarded manuscript and revised plot outlines.

Miss Johnson said about "The Gay Desperado":

"It was an awful lot of work. I had no great message to put over; I just hadn't done a Miss Bunny for a long time and I missed her. 'The Gay Desperado' was all nicely typed and ready to mail in September, but before I could mail it it started to smell, so I did it over twice more.

"The *Post* bought it just when my mother was having an operation. At the same time, another story of mine, 'The Snow Is on the Grass Again,' was broadcast on The Listening Post, so I didn't have to cash any War Bonds to get Mom out of hock with the medical profession."

At Gregg Publishing, Miss Johnson was busier than ever. In addition to editing a section on school journalism in *Business Education World* and writing regularly for the *Gregg Writer* and the *Gregg News Letter*, she continued to produce scripts for business school dramatizations. Among these were "Poor Mr. Hill" and "The Army That Doesn't Wear a Uniform." The latter was a patriotic, inspirational assembly program explaining why students needed to finish their education before leaving school.

Although Miss Johnson's job and fiction writing were time-consuming, she still found time to write the *Whitefish Pilot* inviting Whitefish servicemen and women traveling through the New York area to visit her and her mother. She wrote:

26 Grove Street
New York-14-N.Y.
November 20, 1943

Dear Whitefish Pilot:

My mother and I want to issue a cordial invitation to service men and women from Whitefish to look us up when they come to New York. Will you tell them . . . ?

If the boys and girls can't remember our address, maybe they can remember Gregg Shorthand—I work for the Gregg Publishing Co. and can be reached there.

The honor roll of Whitefish boys and girls is impressive. I'd like to send particular regards to Billy DeVall. He used to come over to our house when he was very small because he liked my little rocking chair. He usually rocked himself over backward, but that never kept him from getting right back into it and starting all over again . . . .

In 1943, Gregg management decided to publish a college-level textbook in secretarial practice. Asked to write it, Miss Johnson agreed. She was given a year off from her duties on the *Business Education World*, assigned to a walnut-paneled office and told what was required. Said Miss Johnson:

"A textbook has to be pretty competitive. It either has to be on a subject so unusual that there isn't any competition in the field or else it has to be better than all the current competition. The job sounded like a . . . good idea—at least it was something new and different.

"I began by reading all the competitive books, studying them and deciding how our book could be better. The book came out as *The Private Secretary*, a college text by John Robert Gregg. That was no surprise to me; I knew my name wasn't going to be on it. Dr. Gregg was a very old man by then—too old to be writing his own books. But if they had his name on them, they sold like hotcakes.

"Writing the book was . . . good for me. It improved my standing in the company . . . and I learned self-discipline. Writing a text-book isn't the most exciting thing in the world, but I learned a lot.

"I did get some credit in the book, but for a very funny reason. Part of the book dealt with business-letter writing. Our editors were supposed to make all our published writing come out about the same way—all sort of on the level and pretty dull. But when they got to this part about business letters, they had to give up. They were able to edit a good deal of the life out of the rest of it since it was Dr. Gregg's thinking and he was not a funny man. The part on letter writing sounded so much like me that they couldn't make it sound like Gregg."

Named Gregg's advertising manager soon after *The Private Secretary* came out, Miss Johnson's future, by 1944, was unquestionably secure. Still, she was growing restless, "thinking about getting out into the wide world where something more exciting was going on." Her friend, Frances Smith, had worked at Gregg for a time, had signed on with a confession magazine and was then with J. Walter Thompson in public relations. Said Miss Johnson:

"I kept thinking about getting out. I started watching the ads in the newspapers. Finally, I spotted one in the *New York Herald Tribune* that sounded ridiculous. They wanted a managing editor for a magazine for women. I thought, 'This just can't be—jobs like that are not advertised in the paper. . . .' It sounded phony but I had nothing to lose. I wrote a rather flip letter applying for the job. In effect, it said that if you are interested in me you can telephone me during office hours at the Gregg Publishing Co.

"I told them to be a little diplomatic because I'd be where I could be overheard. Then I forgot about it.

"Awhile later I got a phone call from a man who said he was being diplomatic. I thought, 'Who is this? He's crazy.' Then it dawned on me what it was about. The man was the magazine's editorial director, William Kofoed. We made an appointment. It wasn't a phony ad at all—they really did have an opening."

The magazine was *The Woman*, a digest owned by Farrell

Publishing Corp. Miss Johnson discussed the job with several of the editors and was interviewed by the company's president, Tom Farrell. Farrell told her that if she was hired, she would have to stop her outside writing.

"It didn't take me five minutes to consider that proposition," Miss Johnson said. "I told him I was sorry but that I wouldn't be able to accept the job because I had spent years and years getting to the point where the *Post* wanted my stories."

Miss Johnson went back to watching newspaper ads, thinking the managing editor's job was lost. Within the week, however, Farrell Publishing underwent a change in its thinking. No objections would be raised to the new managing editor's contributing to the *Post*.

When Miss Johnson resigned from the Gregg Publishing Company in 1944 to the join *The Woman*, Clyde Blanchard, the man who had recruited her nine years earlier, realized the loss. Later he wrote:

> One of my luckiest days was the day I read a prize-winning letter in a national magazine contest. That letter was written by a Dorothy Johnson, an employee of a Wisconsin manufacturing concern . . . .
>
> Editors, faced with daily deadlines, mountains of manuscripts and never-ending conferences with authors and printers, count as one of their rare blessings a talented, imaginative, yet dedicated assistant always ready to help.
>
> Dorothy Johnson was that assistant from the day she joined us. After the first year she was given more and more freedom to develop her own creative ideas. I attribute much of the success of the magazine to her editorial ability.
>
> They say that the highest compliment that can be paid a boss is to point to the success of those under his supervision. If this is true, and I believe that it is, then I have received the highest compliment because of the small part I played in giving Dorothy the opportunity to use her talents to the maximum while with our company.
>
> When Dorothy left us to enter a larger field of writing, our loss was the public's gain.
>
> I wonder if she realizes how fortunate she has been. So many talented persons never realize their potential. They are too concerned with security and fringe benefits and fear to go it on their own. Dorothy never gave this kind of false security a thought. She is one of the best examples that I know of in following her first love to a fruition, both financially and in a full life.

CHAPTER EIGHT

Homecoming

OROTHY JOHNSON ENTERED A NEW WORLD when she entered New York City's Graybar Building at 420 Lexington Avenue to begin her job with *The Woman*. It was a world of considerably more freedom than she had known at Gregg Publishing, a world in which those in executive positions did, for the most part, as they pleased. Miss Johnson found this startling.

"At Gregg, everybody came to work at 9 o'clock and worked until five and there was no fooling about it," she said. "At *The Woman*, when I got in at 9 o'clock, or even a little before, there was nobody there but the switchboard operator and three or four stenographers. The editors didn't start drifting in until about 10 o'clock."

Miss Johnson found herself under some suspicion; other staff members could not understand why she was always there when they arrived. Informed by a fellow editor that it was not necessary to arrive at nine, she tried—without success—to adjust. She had developed the habit of getting to work on time, a habit that proved hard to break. Finally, she stopped trying and went back to arriving at nine.

Miss Johnson enjoyed some of the job's advantages, one of which was having a "second breakfast" sent in midway through the morning. It occurred to her, however, that office hours at *The Woman* were not especially conducive to accomplishment, particularly since the middle of the day often was taken up by lengthy press luncheons.

Miss Johnson did not approve of the laxity she found at *The Woman*, but decided that as a newcomer it was not her place to try to change traditions.

Among the first tasks Miss Johnson assumed was styling manuscripts, something rarely done at the magazine.

"Nobody bothered to improve the punctuation or check the spelling or do any rewriting on manuscripts that really needed it," she said. "This is what I had been doing at Gregg. Some of the staff members thought it was unnecessary and probably even silly, but they didn't say much about it."

As a digest, *The Woman* gleaned about half its contents from other magazines. When *Woman* editors decided they wanted an article, a secretary was instructed to call the magazine in which it appeared, relay a predetermined offer and make the preliminary legal arrangements to permit a condensed version to be reprinted.

Working on the staff of *The Woman* had a certain glamor. In the six years Miss Johnson was to spend there, she learned that considerable business is done over lunch tables on expense accounts. As she put it, "I hadn't known how much freeloading could be done in New York until I got into that job." She explained:

"If you were conscientious, you were under tension all day at the office. If somebody had the bright idea he wanted to talk to you about promoting one of his products in a perfectly legitimate way, the best way to do it was to invite you to lunch.

"Maybe you took more than an hour for lunch but you got a lot of talking done and you could make decisions then. This was fine. I started eating lunch in places I'd never been in before. And then there were big press parties. Sometimes they would be elegant luncheons where the public-relations people for a product put on a show and gave free samples. You could decide later whether you had any use for the information in your magazine.

"A lot of business was done this way, too. And, of course, there were cocktail parties. Pretty soon, things got so congested that one PR man got the idea of having press breakfasts. I don't know whether it's gone any further than that—I don't know where else, it could go. Practically nobody ever set up a press dinner because almost everybody wanted to go home at night and most of them lived in the suburbs.

"The press breakfasts started at 10 o'clock in the morning and they were pretty good. And, of course, if you didn't go to work until 10 o'clock, you just didn't stop in at the office at all. You went to the press breakfast. That would last at least until 11:30. Then you might drop in to look at the mail. Then it would be time for lunch. I'm sure it wasn't this way on all magazines, but, as editors, we did have quite a lot of freedom, which I enjoyed. But there was altogether too much liberty at the Farrell Publishing Corporation and I never did really approve of it."

Beneath the glamour, however, was much hard work. As her career at *The Woman* developed, Miss Johnson found herself in an exacting job calling for astute planning and extensive reading and editing of manuscripts. The initials "D.M.J." became familiar to many writers and would-be writers on accepted and rejected articles.

With almost 15 published short stories and a dozen articles to her credit, Dorothy Johnson might well have decided to slow her pace and enjoy the security and relative luxury at *The Woman*. If the temptation ever occurred to her, she overcame it. Her short story "Letter from Bessie" had appeared in the March 25, 1944, edition of *The Saturday Evening Post*. On July 1, the *Post* ran "Home Coming." Next came "The Snow Is on the Grass Again," published October 14. (The same story was reprinted nine months later in *Australian Women's Weekly*.)

By March 1945, Miss Johnson's former employer, *Business Education World*, had carried two more of her articles—"Ten Commandments for Practical Punctuation" and "How Many Jobs Are There?" Following "The Gay Desperado" in the March 17 *Post* came—in the same magazine—"Widow's Walk" (August 18) and "Wild Kitten" (November 2). Two articles—"The Dead Language That Won't Lie Down" and "The Feud of the Fur-Bearing Fish"—appeared in *The Woman* that year.

V-E Day found Miss Johnson and several fellow editors and friends high above Fifth Avenue watching the victory parade.

"It was tremendously moving," she said. "There was no great amount of glee, only great satisfaction."

A few months later, Miss Johnson again was among thousands of New Yorkers who joyously hurled tons of confetti from the city's skyscrapers following the surrender of Japan. The end of the war brought the end of the Air Warden Service, which Miss Johnson had faithfully served since just after Pearl Harbor. (She rose from squad leader to deputy sector commander.) The war's end also brought the fifty-first and final issue of *The Neighborhood*

News. In what she called the "Good-by Edition" of *The News*, Editor Johnson wrote:

> Our job of getting your neighborhood gossip to you is finished with this issue, after more than three years of publication. Reasons: So many addresses have changed that the mailing list has become positively puny, and we just don't get enough news to keep on anyway. This is all to the good—it means that most of our Village boys are home or coming home, where they can get the news fresh off the griddle where it happens. Maybe we should have signed off while we were still more or less in demand, instead of fading out this way, but this ending is in line with almost everything else your neighborhood Air Wardens did. None of it was very dramatic; we just plugged along until we weren't necessary any more. We're glad we did it. Somebody had to.

By autumn 1946, although her production of short stories had decreased, Dorothy Johnson's by-line had begun to appear in a wider variety of publications. The late Joseph Kinsey Howard, a widely known Montana historian, author and newspaperman, used her story "The Fruit Tramps" (from *Frontier*) in his anthology *Montana Margins*. *Seventeen* magazine published "Greenwich Village Block Party" in September. For *The Woman* Miss Johnson wrote articles entitled "Emergency Unlimited: The Story of Express" and "Shorthand Through the Ages."[1]

Miss Johnson wrote only one short story in 1947, "Family Legend," which appeared in the January *Seventeen*. For *The Woman* she wrote "Study Folk-Songs and Like 'em" (January) and "The Case of Frank Sinatra" (December). Another article, "Wanted: One Typist," appeared in the October issue of *Business Education World*.

Perhaps the most significant project in 1947 was the start of a second novel. Tentatively entitled *The Prisoner at Skull Creek*, it was to be a story of goldrush days on the frontier. A decade later, reduced from its original 65,000 words to a 39,000-word novelette called *The Hanging Tree*, it would provide the backbone of its author's third book and, two years later, her first movie.

---

[1] The editor-in-chief of *The Woman* did not think it would look well to readers to have the magazine's managing editor writing articles. Therefore, Miss Johnson frequently wrote under pseudonyms, two of which were Libby Root and Helena Kuo.

A neighbor and friend of Miss Johnson's, Catharine Burnham, was to play a key role in the development of *The Hanging Tree*. Miss Burnham, who became a clinical psychologist, met Dorothy Johnson through a friend named Mary Hale. Miss Burnham and Miss Hale shared an apartment until the latter left New York and returned to California. The apartment was in Greenwich Village's Grove Court, almost under the back windows of the 2 Grove Street apartment Miss Johnson shared with her mother. Miss Burnham's recollections offer insight into Miss Johnson's later years in New York City:

"We'd get together to cook meals—this mostly when Mrs. Alger was away during the summer—or sew for an evening, or see a movie or a Broadway show. Dorothy and her mother didn't entertain very much and the cocktail-party life was never part of their picture at all. Mrs. Alger was involved somewhat with church activities but was quite dependent on Dorothy's companionship. She had to limit her activities somewhat for health reasons. I remember Mrs. Alger as a strong-minded lady, small in stature, white-haired and very pretty.

"She was Dorothy's number-one fan and an avid scrapbook keeper. You could see that Dorothy must have been somewhat isolated by unconsciously made parental demands (an only child has a *lot* of responsibility) and yet encouraged to be a law unto herself in many ways all of her life. They lived in a three-room apartment and Dorothy did her writing mostly in the bedroom. Actually, it was in whichever room her mother wasn't in at the time. They were very experienced in living together. The only outright complaint I recall Dorothy making was about interruptions: 'She thinks if she just whispers or speaks softly it doesn't really count. But if I'm miles away in the middle of a big gunfight I sometimes feel as if I'd been shot. Dulcet tones don't help it a bit. I have an awful time getting back there where I was.' "

Comparing 1948, when the *Post* published her stories "Beyond the Frontier" and "Difficult Courtship," with the work she had done previously, one might conclude that Dorothy Johnson had suddenly decided to write about the frontier West. That conclusion, erroneous, seems even more plausible when her two 1948 stories are compared with those she wrote in the seven years after 1941, most of which were contemporary and several of which were set in New York. Miss Johnson began writing about the frontier West in college with stories such as "And One Came Back" and "Happy Valley." Her interest in the West and those who settled it had been aroused when she was a child; it was an interest that grew more intense with the years. The frontier West had always seemed to her to be the natural place about which to write.

"To write about the West wasn't just some decision I sat down and made," Miss Johnson said. "It was just what I happened to want to know about. Anytime I write anything that isn't the West of the 19th century I'm sort of off my track."

So 1948 marked Miss Johnson's return to the subject matter and historical period she preferred. Although she continued to write contemporary stories and articles, most of her fiction began dealing with the old West. In 1949, *Cosmopolitan* published "The Man Who Shot Liberty Valance." Then, a contemporary story, "Hold That Bull," appeared in *Argosy* under the by-line L.R. Gustafson. She ended 1949 with two articles in *Steelways* magazine—"The Obstreperous Factory" and "Mark Nance: Maker of Beef"—and another short story, "First Date," published in the December *Collier's*.

What might have been Miss Johnson's greatest challenge in 1949 never came to fruition. Her agent asked if she was interested in ghost writing actress Mary Pickford's autobiography. He told her Miss Pickford had considered several writers she knew in Hollywood and had discussed them with him. He said he was afraid they would be inconsiderate of Miss Pickford's feelings and that he wanted Miss Johnson because she was gentle. Miss Johnson told what happened:

"Nobody had ever told me I was gentle before, but I think my agent was right about the Hollywood writers. Mary Pickford was sensitive because she had had a terribly exciting and tragic life.

"Anyway, the prospect thrilled me. My agent took us to lunch at a place where I remember the main course of fish was four dollars. Of course I had rushed out the day before and bought a new dress and coat because I wasn't accustomed to having lunch with Mary Pickford or having lunch at a restaurant like that either. During lunch, they got to talking about how much rent they paid. My agent paid $300 a month. Mary Pickford had sublet a duplex on Park Avenue and my agent asked her outright how much she paid. She told him outright $1,500 a month. He said,

'Oh, very reasonable.' And out of three there was one who didn't say a word about how much rent she paid.

"Later I went over to this $1,500 apartment and got myself past the doorman and past the elevator man and past another man whom I never did figure out. Up at Miss Pickford's door I came to the butler. I handed him my coat because the only other butler I had ever met in my life had done nothing but yearn to put my coat somewhere. I don't know what Miss Pickford's butler did because he looked as though he had never had a coat in his hands before in his life. He put it down on the back of a chair and when I came out it was still on the back of the chair.

"I met Miss Pickford's husband—he was an orchestra leader (Buddy Rodgers)—and her adopted little girl, who was running around playing cowboys on the terrace. We talked about what might be in this book. By that time I had done quite a lot of homework at the public library. She was having a man install a tape recorder into which she could talk. We kind of got things squared around and then I left.

"I never heard anything more from her. I was too timid to be lighting a fire under anybody as famous as Mary Pickford. Somebody else ghost wrote the autobiography . . . . The woman who did it had written a lot of books very well and I think it must have been Miss Pickford's distaste for digging up skeletons that made the book pretty dull. Of course I read it with great interest but the things I wanted to tell—that I am sure the woman who finally wrote it would have wanted to tell—she didn't want to discuss. Some things she had told me, herself, very frankly, she didn't want in the book. My agent had said I was gentle and wouldn't scare her. Obviously I was too gentle. I couldn't scare her into doing anything."

The year 1950 was a banner year in which *The Woman's* 44-year-old executive editor (she had been promoted) seemingly could not miss. *Collier's* carried "A Man Called Horse" in January. The same month, *Cosmopolitan* published "Prairie Kid." In May *The Woman* published "Rancher's Wife" under the pseudonym Libby Root. "War Shirt" appeared in *Collier's* in July, while "Scars of Honor" was published by *Argosy* in October. "Sensible Marriage" appeared in *The Saturday Evening Post* in November, while "Flame on the Frontier" was included in the December *Argosy*.

Long before 1950, Dorothy Johnson had come to dislike New York and had begun looking for a job that would allow her to leave.

"People there had such bad manners," she said. "I thought for the first few years they'd change or I'd get used to them. But by 1950 I knew neither of these things was going to happen. New Yorkers just didn't act like the kind of human beings I was raised among in Montana. I knew I wasn't going to be able to stand it much longer."

With those thoughts, it's little wonder that by late 1950 Miss Johnson and her mother no longer were residents of New York. They had abandoned the East to return to Whitefish and a log house at 836 Columbia Avenue. The idea grew out of a Montana vacation trip the two took in the summer of 1950—a trip during which they visited Whitefish. In an article for *Ford Times*, Miss Johnson described the welcome they received on the trip:

Miss Johnson and her mother lived in this log house from 1950 to 1952. Miss Johnson was news editor of the *Pilot* at the time. *(Photo by the author)*

Beth and Leonard Moore, who got engaged when they were members of Mom's Sunday School class, were waiting at the airport with Ralph Stacey. We were introduced to C.I. Moulton, the mayor; Ray Steiner, secretary of the chamber of commerce, and Les Scott, president of Rotary. We shook hands, pretty bewildered because we were half deaf from the plane trip and starved for breakfast.

Then we like to died of joy at being so much honored—why, those men had left their regular work on purpose to drive nine miles and welcome us home! And they were so tactful about it that they didn't even tell us what they were there for because it might embarrass us. That's Whitefish people for you. They make you happy without making a fuss. They let you relax.

From the time "Bonnie George Campbell" had appeared in the *Post*, Whitefish had been conscious of Dorothy Johnson as a distinguished former citizen. Each time she had published another story the event had been hailed in *The Whitefish Pilot*. It is no surprise, then, that following the airport welcome, Miss Johnson was made a life member of the chamber of commerce and an honorary police chief. She also was permitted to ride to a fire on a fire truck, a memory she considered one of the high points of her career. Whitefish went all out to honor her and she discovered the town was just as exhilarating a place in which to live as it had been when she was a school girl:

> "We came out here and I saw how people lived. They work hard but they have different kinds of pressures. For one thing, they don't have to ride long distances to get to work . . . . Just getting from one place to another in New York is time consuming and it wears you down. To me, the way people in Whitefish lived looked like heaven."

While Mrs. Alger went to Oregon to visit her sister, Miss Johnson went to Virginia City and Yellowstone Park, places she had never seen. Then she flew back to New York, using her flying time to write some notes for a short story.

The idea for the story came from a book about outlaws and hangings she had read in Virginia City. Soon after arriving in New York she wrote "Last Boast," published by *Cosmopolitan* in January 1951.

While writing "Last Boast," Miss Johnson's thoughts continued to return to Montana. Finally, she made a decision. She wrote to her mother in Oregon, told her she thought Montana was a wonderful place and asked how she would feel about returning there. Mrs. Alger replied quickly—she thought it was a fine idea.

Soon after hearing from her mother, Miss Johnson resigned from *The Woman*. The Labor Day weekend found her in Whitefish again, this time to buy a house.

"I had 40 hours there because I had to get back to work on time," she said. "In that time I bought a house and a second-hand Oldsmobile."

Miss Johnson flew back to New York and was joined by her mother. They remained until the latter part of October, then, for the last time, headed for the West and their new home. They arrived in Whitefish on Halloween day, 1950, a day that marked the end of 15 years as an easterner for Miss Johnson.

"Quitting a job and coming back here just because we wanted to was a wild thing to do," she said. "Nevertheless, it was the most brilliant idea I ever had. I'm so glad I did it."

Excerpts from Miss Johnson's *Ford Times* article indicated her happiness about being back in Whitefish:

> This is a love story. The main characters in it are me and my home town. We have been carrying on a long-distance affair for twenty years . . .
> Of course, Whitefish isn't quite Paradise. I'm trying not to be prejudiced. It's a nuisance keeping deer off the golf course, Roy Arnold admitted last summer. Some villain shocked the town by shooting a doe on the fourth green, but Archie Emerson adopted her fawn, and everybody's glad it has a good home.
> It's inconvenient, too, to have moose amble down the main drag; a moose is bigger than a horse and nobody's pet. Three of them invaded the town last winter, and the game warden had to shoot one over by the old Lakeside School. Last June when I was in the City Hall talking to George Good, the police chief, Brad Seeley came in, looking embarrassed, and said he was sorry but there was a moose at his lake resort. The reason he was embarrassed was that this was his second loose moose. Anybody is entitled to report *one*, but he felt he was getting into the habit . . . .

Although her first two years back in Whitefish occasionally would cause Miss Johnson to question her judgment, the decision, if for no other reason than what was happening at *The Woman*, was the right one:

"*The Woman* was going from bad to worse. Before I left, the management already was getting the idea of selling its soul for the sake of sweet publicity. Because of this, we had Anna Roosevelt on our masthead as editor for awhile. Anna Roosevelt had a program on the radio and the idea was that she would promote our magazine and we would promote her radio program. This is very bad, indeed, and it didn't do us a bit of good. But the Roosevelt name was good in those days.

"When the management started this, they were hoping to get her mother, Eleanor, involved in it too. But somehow she stayed out—she had her own radio program. So we had to make do with Anna . . . . She had some family photographs and she wrote some long articles about life with her father. We had to be extremely careful in editing them for fear we might offend her. We couldn't publish them the way they were because they were infernally dull. The experiences that woman had had would have made such good stuff if she could have realized what people wanted to know about and if she could have put it down on paper . . . .

"After I left they sold their souls to Kate Smith. This was really a bad situation, and I was awfully glad to be out of it. Somebody who was still there told me in a letter that Kate Smith got the idea she was really going to run the magazine. Anna Roosevelt had never tried to do that. But Kate Smith was going to decide what went in it. She had a manager who was well known as the most dreadful man to get along with. Nobody could get along with him. In fact, the vice president of our company used to speak of him as 'that bastard' and you always knew who he meant. I got out of there just in time . . ."

Returning to Whitefish had, indeed, brought some favorable changes in Miss Johnson's life, including elimination of two chronic ailments—sinusitis and colitis—that had been aggravated by the pressures of city life. Still, there was trouble ahead.

Miss Johnson and friend enjoy a picnic lunch. *(Photo by Cyrile Van Duser)*

CHAPTER NINE

Whitefish Revisited

THE IDEA OF A SUCCESSFUL FICTION WRITER and New York magazine editor working on his weekly newspaper apparently had not occurred to Publisher Gurnie Moss of *The Whitefish Pilot* in northwestern Montana. He remembers that when Dorothy Johnson suggested it to him during her visit in the summer of 1950, he "thought she was joshing."

After Miss Johnson had returned to New York, Moss began to suspect that she was serious about returning to Whitefish.

"I really wasn't too surprised to see her," he said. "She had told me during the summer that she had lost all her ambition and inspiration and that she didn't see how she could accomplish much more in New York."

Whitefish proved good for Miss Johnson and Miss Johnson proved good for the *Pilot*. Officially she was the news editor, although her primary responsibilities were reporting and photography. In time, she took over the society desk. She also began writing editorials and finding other ways to help. One week when Moss was gone, she sold several advertisements. She discovered that many potential advertisers never had been approached and were pleased to be asked.

"That week we had a lot of ads but we didn't have any news to speak of," she said. "You can't do two things at once."

Moss was gone the following week and Miss Johnson again decided to try selling ads. She mentioned her intentions to another staff member and was told, in effect, "It's no use, they all advertised last week." From then on, she confined herself to news-gathering.

Miss Johnson's salary at the *Pilot* was a fraction of what it had been at *The Woman.* From a financial standpoint, the success of her return to Whitefish depended on her ability to sell fiction to magazines. However, the year 1951 gave indications that the ability was waning. Her only sales were "Last Boast," published in *Cosmopolitan* in January, and "Warrior's Exile," in the September *Argosy.*

"It was a frightful thing to have to worry about," she said. "I didn't have anywhere near the income that I had counted on to support my mother and me."

Miss Johnson faced another problem when she discovered that her agent was selling her older stories without telling her and without paying her. She began receiving fan mail concerning a story whose title she had never heard of. One letter mentioned the magazine in which the story had appeared; it was a grocer's magazine she had not sold to previously. Writing to the editor, she received a cautious reply explaining when the story had been purchased and the price—$400. Miss Johnson wrote her agent immediately and demanded an explanation:

> "I really laid it on the line because by that time I could prove that he had sold a story and hadn't told me about it.
> "Later, after I got the money from him with an apology that just didn't hold water at all, I wrote and told him we weren't going to do any more business. He phoned from New York and put in a great plea about how this was just a dreadful mistake that had occurred in his office. I still didn't do any more business with him."[1]

Miss Johnson had not been at the *Pilot* more than a few weeks when she began a weekly column called "Here We Lie."

"It involved the mythical return to Big Mountain of the mythical Paul Bunyan," she explained. "That was good, clean fun until one day somebody asked why I wrote all that nonsense. So I stopped lying—except occasionally about my cat, Lucy—and

---

[1] Soon after this misfortune, Miss Johnson acquired her present agent—the New York firm of McIntosh & Otis—by writing to the Authors' League for recommendations. Miss Johnson's troubles with her former agent still were not over. Several years later she came across an anthology containing one of her stories. The agent was connected with this, too. Later, Miss Johnson learned that the same agent was selling reprint rights to her stories to British publishers without paying her. Again she wrote the man an angry letter asking for reimbursement. Finally he sent the money but at a reduced rate of exchange.

changed the title."

The column, changed to "This Is No Lie," was a potpourri of comment on everything from chuckholes to ice harvests, storm sewers to baseball.

Though disappointed at her slump in fiction sales, Miss Johnson continued to write in her spare time. The remainder of her output in 1951 included seven features in the *Great Falls Tribune's Montana Parade* and an article for the *American Ski Annual and Skiing Journal* entitled "The Mighty Axe of Toni Matt." Those sales, while providing some encouragement, were not enough to offset the disheartening arrivals of rejection slips from fiction editors. Miss Johnson would remember the early 1950s as "grim years."

Foresight and perseverance seem to have had much to do with her comeback in 1952. Before leaving New York, she had visited several editors to learn what Montana subjects would interest them for articles. The *Steelways* editor told her his magazine rarely got so much as a postcard from west of the Mississippi and that he would be happy to hear from her. As a result, she sold "Hungry Horse Eats Steel" and "Uncle Sam's Snowmen" to the magazine. Both were published in January. The former concerned the construction of Hungry Horse Dam while the latter—written under the pseudonym Miriam Zwerin—told of snow-removal operations in Glacier National Park.

The man who took Miss Johnson to Glacier to watch giant plows also was in the weekly newspaper business. His name was Melvin Ruder and he published *The Hungry Horse News*, a paper in nearby Columbia Falls he had started in 1946 on the advice of Miss Johnson's employer. Ruder and Miss Johnson had met and become friends soon after her return from New York. Neither knew then that a rampaging river, Ruder's talent and energy and Miss Johnson's letter-writing ability would combine 13 years later to bring a Pulitzer Prize to *The Hungry Horse News* and its publisher.

Among other articles Miss Johnson sold in 1952 were "The Wonderful If" to *The Writer* and "Hungry Horse Dam in Montana" to the *Great Northern Goat*. An additional 40 features in *Montana Parade*—written "strictly from hunger"—brought about $10 apiece.

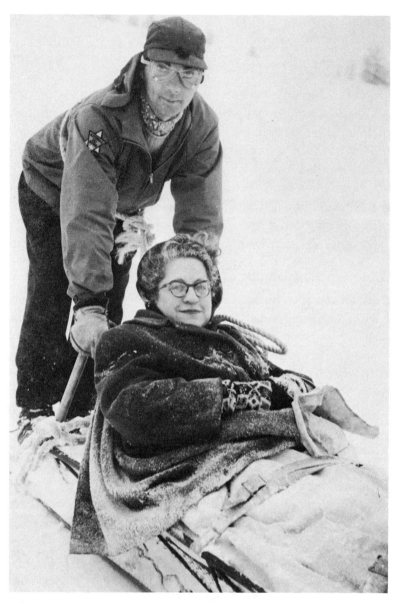

An unidentified ski patrolman helps Miss Johnson down Hell Roaring Ridge on Big Mountain following some research for an article. Throughout the descent, the manager of the area—ever conscious of public relations—kept skiers informed by loudspeaker that the woman strapped to the toboggan was a writer, not a casualty.

Miss Johnson in the early 1950s.

Miss Johnson's first short story in seven months appeared in the April 4, 1952, *Collier's*. Entitled "Journey to the Fort," it represented, in her words, a "crack in the dam." The crack widened during a trip to Glacier National Park; returning to the Lake McDonald Hotel after a hike, Miss Johnson found a telegram from her mother saying *Collier's* had bought another story, "The Unbeliever." She later described her feelings:

> "Was *that* ever great news. It took a terrible burden off me. I would never have dared moved to Whitefish if I hadn't assumed that I would be selling several stories a year. The strange thing was that 'The Unbeliever' had drifted around ever since we moved to Whitefish. It was a darn good story and I couldn't understand why nobody would buy it. One time *Atlantic* even lost the manuscript. I retyped it and sent another copy to my agent. The *Atlantic* didn't buy it. It had been to *Collier's* four times. They were changing fiction editors so fast nobody knew what was going on. Finally they got one who thought it was a good story.
>
> "I could have used that money quite awhile before that. They did want some changes on the story. They offered several suggestions, all of which I was perfectly willing to take. By that time I was so discouraged that out of a kind of superstition I had invented, I hadn't made a carbon of the manuscript. I was just desperate. There had been no reason for not making a carbon except that I thought maybe if I changed my system my luck would be better. So here was this embarrassing situation in which I couldn't tell what paragraph 4 on page 3 was. This, of course, made me look like the rankest amateur. When they learned this, they wouldn't even trust me with the manuscript they had. They had photocopies made of the necessary pages, assuming I would lose it if I got my hands on it."

"The Unbeliever," the story of a fading Army scout who tempts fate once too often, appeared in the August 16, 1952, *Collier's*. The same month, *Better Living* published "Laugh in the Face of Danger." *Collier's* then published "The Deer Hunter" in September and "Gallagher's Wife" in November.

Miss Johnson had displayed an aptitude for editorials, and by the latter part of 1952 was writing them regularly for the *Pilot*. Her long-standing interest in books and libraries was evident in two December editorials. An anonymous Whitefish man had offered the city $2,500 cash toward construction of a public library building. His stipulations were that the money be used for building purposes only and that the city council accept or reject his offer before the end of 1952. When Miss Johnson learned of the offer—and that conservative elements of the city administration were reluctant to commit the city—she went to work. Her first editorial was "Christmas Gift for Our Town":

A man who wishes to remain anonymous has offered Whitefish a splendid gift—$2,500 cash on the barrelhead toward the construction of a public library building. It must be used for building purposes only, and the city council must accept or reject it before the end of 1952.

Two committees of the council were assigned by the Mayor to study the offer. Decision will be made at a special council meeting Monday, Dec. 29.

That we need larger quarters for our cramped library there is no doubt. It has no place to stretch. Books take up space, and so do the hundreds of people who come in to borrow them.

The Whitefish man who is offering us this gift realizes, of course, that it won't pay the whole cost of a library building. But it is $2,500 more than we had before. It will get us off to a fine, encouraging start.

For many years our public library received scant support, if any, from taxes. It was carried along through the years by the patient and devoted work of the Whitefish Women's Club.

Civic and service organizations will, we think, be interested in raising more money toward a library building fund. It seems unlikely that the city fathers will refuse so splendid a gift. They may worry about the possibility of increasing taxes slightly to help pay for a building.

The opinions of taxpayers and of local organizations will probably interest members of the council when they meet December 29 to decide whether to accept the gift or not. It would be a good idea for a lot of people to attend that council meeting and express their opinions. . . .

The following week she followed with "Who Can We Blame?":

Whose fault will it be if Whitefish doesn't get a public library building? Yours, maybe, if you don't say you want one.

Next Monday night the city council is going to decide whether to accept or reject a gift of $2,500 toward a library building fund. Some councilmen may be doubtful or lukewarm.

It's your city council. The six men in it represent you in conducting local government, levying taxes, doing what you want done in the public interest. How will they know you want a library building unless you say so?

Whitefish has progressed a long way since the first axe rang out in the forest that has been replaced by a town. Every bit of progress was costly in effort or money or both. Nothing we have here was free except the scenery and climate.

A public library building won't be free, either—but $2,500 of it will be unless the city council turns down the gift. They might do it unless the people who want one say so.

The council will meet at 7 p.m., Monday, December 29. Council meetings are public. Every Whitefish organization should be represented there even if it's snowing. And every individual who favors a library building should tell his aldermen about it . . . .

The city council unanimously accepted the gift. In subsequent editorials, Miss Johnson outlined the work ahead in forming a library committee. She urged citizens to participate, then followed her own advice by accepting, on February 3, 1953, the job of recording secretary for the Whitefish Library Association.

A month later, Miss Johnson received a letter from Ken Byerly, president of the Montana Press Association, concerning an opening for a secretary-manager. W.L. "Din" Alcorn, a former Wyoming publisher who had held the position for seven years, was leaving for Seaside, California, to become co-owner of a weekly.

Miss Johnson, who had scarcely heard of the association, had been recommended by President Carl McFarland of the University of Montana. McFarland, Miss Johnson thinks, remembered her from a 1952 banquet on the university campus at which Phi Chi Theta, a professional business sorority, had named her Montana's outstanding professional woman of the year. As guest speaker, she had told many anecdotes. McFarland remembered the speech and, knowing something of her background, suggested her to Byerly.

When Miss Johnson expressed interest in the job, Byerly, publisher of the *Lewistown Daily News*, drove to Whitefish to discuss it with her. He told her that, as secretary-manager, she would need a supplementary job, since the association could afford only a modest salary. He explained that Alcorn had been teaching some courses in the University's School of Journalism (where the MPA had its office) and that perhaps President McFarland eventually could offer her a similar arrangement. In the meantime, Byerly said, the University probably could find her part-time work. She would have to take a chance on when the work would be available and how much it would pay.

Miss Johnson gave Byerly's proposal considerable thought. She drove to Missoula to talk with President McFarland. Finally, she decided that despite the risk, the position held more promise and challenge than did her job with the *Pilot*.

Gurnie Moss was unhappy at losing his news editor. Nevertheless, he told Miss Johnson he thought the new post was a fine opportunity and encouraged her to take it.

Miss Johnson, writing her final "This Is No Lie" column for the March 27, 1953, *Pilot*, said farewell to the place she always would regard as her home town:

> Good-by folks, it's been nice knowing you and it still is. The day this *Pilot* comes out, I'll be on the streamliner headed for a quick business trip to New York, and right after coming back on Easter I'll start to work in a new job in Missoula.
>
> Mom will move down, with Lucy the cat and the furniture, when I find living quarters. One hopeful real estate agent down there said he had a mighty nice house for sale at $90,000. The gray coat I was wearing, half price at Woodward's, must have looked as if it had a solid gold lining. As far as we are concerned, he will have his $90,000 house for a long time. We will look for accommodations more in keeping with our station in life. Like an unoccupied two-car garage . . . .
>
> Mom and I don't like to leave Whitefish; it is our favorite town. But the new job is a challenge, and Missoula is a nice place, too.
>
> The job is secretary-manager of the Montana State Press Association, to which the newspaper publishers of the state belong. It's something like a chamber of commerce, you might say. The office is in the Journalism Building on the University campus, with elegant parking space out front.

Miss Johnson had been having eye trouble. The trip to New York was to see the oculist who had treated her during her years with *The Woman*. She was unaware that good news awaited her:

> "Jack Schaefer, the author of *Shane*, and I had been corresponding once in awhile, writing mutual fan letters. Jack was living in Connecticut and happened to be in New York talking to Ian Ballantine, who had just organized Ballantine Books. Jack had told him about me and had suggested that Ballantine come out

with a collection of my westerns. We went up to Schaefer's place for dinner—the Ballantines, Jack, my agent and I—and Ian Ballantine somehow had got hold just that day of practically everything I'd ever published.

"He had sent somebody to a shop where they specialized in old magazines. It was all so miraculous that I never was sure just how he did it. We didn't get back to New York until almost midnight. This was great stuff for the country kid. I was thrilled at meeting the great Jack Schaefer and also a publisher who was so pleasant."

Miss Johnson, who was staying with Catharine Burnham, went shopping the next day. Late in the afternoon she returned to Miss Burnham's apartment to find the telephone ringing. It was her agent, Elizabeth Otis, who had been having a secretary call the apartment every 20 minutes since noon. Ian Ballantine had stayed up all night reading Miss Johnson's stories and was offering a contract with a $5,000 advance.

"I just couldn't believe it!" Miss Johnson said. "I told my agent I didn't believe it and she said, 'Well, it's true and you better get down here quick.' I went to her office that day and signed the contract. I almost died."

Miss Johnson returned to Whitefish and stayed long enough to repack her suitcases. By mid-April, she was in Missoula to begin work with the press association. Her mother remained in Whitefish to pack their belongings and sell the log house at 836 Columbia Avenue.

Near the Continental Divide, Miss Johnson bestrides the headwaters of the Missouri River.

CHAPTER TEN

Aunt Dorothy

O N C E HE HAD READ AND SELECTED THE STORIES, Ian Ballantine wasted little time in getting Dorothy Johnson's second book in print. *Indian Country*, dedicated to Professor Harold G. Merriam, appeared in July 1953.[1] Included was the following foreword by Jack Schaefer, author of *Shane*:

Dorothy Johnson went home to Whitefish, Montana, in the truest meaning of that old worn phrase. She had been away and she had come back and because she had been away, she came back with a better understanding of the region and the people she had known before. She began writing stories again and they were stories that only Dorothy Johnson could write.

During the last four or five years these later stories have been appearing in national magazines. They are not the usual popular magazine stories, not slickly published and fitted to the usual romantic formulae. They are stories of straight-forward personal distinction. They have the strength and honesty of the high plains and mountains of Montana.

The eleven stories presented here are stories of bitterness and bloodshed, of courage and endurance, of sorrow and triumph—

---

[1]Later published in paperback, *Indian Country*'s 11 stories include "Flame on the Frontier," "The Unbeliever," "Prairie Kid," "Warrior's Exile," "Journey to the Fort," "The Man Who Shot Liberty Valance," "War Shirt," "Beyond the Frontier," "Scars of Honor," "Laugh in the Face of Danger" and "A Man Called Horse." In a note to teachers and parents in a paperback edition for high school students, Richard Tyre, chairman of the English department of Germantown Friends School in Pennsylvania, wrote: "Quite simply, this is *the* best collection of stories about the American frontier available in paperback. By "best" I mean that it combines detailed historical and anthropological accuracy about the Minnesota-Montana frontier settlements and the Cheyenne, Crow and Sioux Indian customs, with a lean, unadorned, understated story-telling style reminiscent of Hemingway at his best . . . . "

and always of people, of individual human beings meeting and matching and sometimes surmounting the hard facts of frontier life in *Indian Country*. They are as varied as the region and the people they depict. Yet they share a gallant kinship. All of them breathe the same spirit, the spirit that grew out of the bigness and the reaches of the American West and gave a new dimension to what we now call the American heritage. They face forward. They affirm life. They assert that man, in defeat as in victory, can be equal to his fate.

And always people . . . . These are stories of white people, men and women and children, and of Indian people, men and women and children, and always, to Dorothy Johnson, they are all people. The integrity of her writing never wavers. Her sympathy encompasses them all. No one has written with more understanding of the mountain men who first penetrated the Indian wilderness and of the white settlers who met hardship in hostile Indian territory. And no one has written with keener perception of the Indians themselves, the displaced persons who saw their lands being taken and their way of life crumbling before the inevitable white advance. Here is no glamorizing, no romantic gilding, of settlers or of Indians. Here is something finer and more gripping, the honest portrayal of good and bad, of strength and frailty, of the admirable and the contemptible, in both white settlements and Indian villages.

And always people . . . . They throng these pages. They leap into life, unforgettable, out of the text, each complete, fully realized, fully known. And their stories are told in a lean, stripped, strong prose, told with a resolute economy of words. Yet the writing has a richness of texture rare in modern fiction. The stories move, flow forward with swift, at times almost racing, vigor and then, like a nugget in the rewarding ore, comes the sudden singing sentence that implies more than it says and gives depth and significance to the whole.

Still the flood of western fiction rolls from the presses. It sweeps over the counters of the bookstores and the racks of the newsstands. It is the paramount escape-writing of our time. Much of it is cheap and simply sensational and most of it offers nothing more than exciting and adventurous entertainment—the glamorized or deliberately dirtied surface trappings of the western frontier. But there are a few writers who do much more, who match and surpass the others in the sheer vigor and excitement of the writing itself and who dig deep into reality and are uncompromising in the authenticity of their material and the integrity of their treatment of it. Slowly they are building a body of true literature about the American West. Dorothy Johnson is one of these. To read her stories is to know: This is the way life was lived in frontier settlement and in Indian village. This is part of the American heritage.

Indian Country was well received. In *Saturday Review,* Seth Agnew commented that Miss Johnson had written western stories at their best.

"There is no romanticizing of the noble savage or of the intrepid pioneer," Agnew wrote. "Here are credible men and women in credible situations. Here are stories told with pace and suspense and skill."

John T. Frederick, reviewing *Indian Country* for *The Rotarian,* said its stories held appeal equally as narratives of exciting action and as fiction of literary excellence.

"These stories are big in theme, wide in range, profound in sympathy. . . ," Frederick wrote. "Few recent books of fiction offer so much lasting pleasure . . . ."

Reviewing *Indian Country* for *Montana-The Magazine of Western History,* John T. Vance III wrote: "It is a book that all students of western history must read. Her stories of warriors and squaws, white men and women, boys and girls are written in some of the best prose it has ever been this reviewer's pleasure to read. Miss Johnson's writing is as lean and spare as the people in her stories."

When *Indian Country* appeared, Miss Johnson had been secretary-manager of the Montana State Press Association for almost four months. In Missoula, she had purchased a house on Benton Avenue using her share of Ballantine's $5,000 advance as partial payment.

"We would have had the money from our house in Whitefish except that something went wrong with the first sale and we didn't get it for quite some time," she said. "My $4,500 advance from *Indian Country* made all the difference in the world between buying a little shack or something livable."

Miss Johnson's first months with the press association were hectic:

"I was trying to catch on to the job. I didn't have very much chance to learn about it because my predecessor was in a terrible hurry to leave. I got to Missoula in the afternoon just as fast as I could after coming back from New York. I went to a motel and had dinner and then I telephoned 'Din' (W.L. Alcorn, the former secretary-manager). He was going to clue me in on how to run the job. He leaped down my throat: 'Why hadn't I phoned him before?' Well, he hadn't told me he was in any tearing hurry, but he was. I met him up at the Journalism Building and we talked for two hours. He had a lot of instructions written out for me. He told me to take them to my motel and read them and ask questions the next day. So I went and then the next morning we talked for two more hours. That's when I met my new secretary.

"Everything that I asked about, Din would say, 'Well, Mary knows about that.' Well, thank God for Mary McCarthy. She stayed for a couple years after that and by the time she left to work for the Forest Service, I knew about 'that' too . . . . Altogether I had four hours briefing on how to run a job that I'd never even heard of before. I knew it was a trade association but I didn't know what a trade association was . . . . In short, I fell into the job very suddenly."

Affiliated with the press association was the Montana Advertising Service, an advertising representative that placed agency ads in the state's weeklies. MAS, alone, required considerable attention, and Miss Johnson discovered that her secretary had to devote more time to it than to the press association. Miss Johnson studied the ad service operation and concluded that it could be streamlined. She learned, for example, that Miss McCarthy had been told to make extra copies of all advertising orders. The copies were being sent to a Seattle man who had left Seattle years earlier.

"Mary was still making the extra copies and piling them carefully in a cupboard," Miss Johnson said. "She didn't know what they were for, but somebody had told her to do it and had never told her to stop."

Miss Johnson also changed the association's record-keeping. Miss McCarthy had been tediously copying records in a book that seemed to Miss Johnson to weigh "about 40 pounds." Miss Johnson reorganized the system so that it not only was easier to handle but provided better permanent records.

The task Miss Johnson was to enjoy most—and the one for which she would be long remembered by the state's publishers—was editing the association's official monthly publication, *Montana Fourth Estate* (formerly *Montana Press Bulletin*).

"I didn't really know what was supposed to go in the magazine," she said. "All I knew was that I had to fill all the space where there weren't any ads."

She confronted the challenge armed with instinct, her New York editing experience and the well-developed sense of humor that had become her trademark. She examined several back issues and concluded they were dull. She began immediately—and worked hard for the next 14 years—to remedy the situation. In

Opposite: Cartoonist Stan Lynde's inimitable Chief Horse's Neck is a discriminating reader. Lynde, an avid reader of western fiction, had admired Miss Johnson's work for years before he met her in 1964. This cartoon, a portion of one of Lynde's syndicated strips, bore the following inscription: "To Dorothy Johnson—friend, mentor and fellow Montanan with admiration and affection from Rick O'Shay." Miss Johnson also is an avid Lynde fan. *(Permission granted for use)*

While secretary-manager of the Montana Press Association, Miss Johnson's headquarters were in the University of Montana School of Journalism. *(Photo by the author)*

editing *Montana Fourth Estate*, Miss Johnson constantly scanned some 90 weeklies and 10 dailies in the state, seeking both humor and news of new techniques, equipment and personnel:

"I found that some of the papers had awfully good columnists, usually the publisher, himself. Also, there often would be news about the paper in the paper—they got a new press or the linotype broke down and they had to go clear over to someplace a hundred miles away to get their type set. Often there were entertaining quotes from the editorials. Scanning the papers took considerable time, of course. There was lots of writing to do and I just loved it because that had been my specialty at Gregg Publishing Company."

In addition to publishing *Montana Fourth Estate*, the press association served unofficially as an employment agency for persons with newspaper skills:

"We often got phone calls or letters from printers or reporters wanting a job. We tried to get them together with our members, who would suddenly telephone that they were losing their best reporter to the nearest daily or that their linotype man had got drunk again and was in jail. Once in awhile we could make a connection. The biggest problem was that the available people often were not available by the time a frantic plea came from a publisher who needed them."

Among the last things "Din" Alcorn had told Miss Johnson was that she would be responsible for the association's annual convention.

"He told me I'd never know anything about running a convention until I'd been through one," she said. "That wasn't very much help, although I'll admit that really is the way to learn to run one."

The 1953 convention had been scheduled for August in Glacier National Park. Although Ken Byerly had the program well outlined, there still was plenty for Miss Johnson to do:

"I was afraid to ask anybody to help me, so I had to try to be at the registration desk and also at the meetings at the same time. At the meetings I was supposed to run a tape recorder to get down what people were saying. Tape recorders scare the wits out of me. That first year I didn't even have a machine. I took almost all of it in shorthand and then had to transcribe it. I'm not a court reporter and I didn't get it verbatim, but . . . I got a lot of it. I had to because that was part of the association's permanent record."

During the 14 years she was to serve the press association, Miss Johnson's ability with mechanical or electrical equipment improved little over her *Whitefish Pilot* days when she struggled with press cameras. Her difficulties at conventions became a legend, as indicated by comments from Helen Peterson of the *Hardin* (Montana) *Tribune-Herald* and Richard Adams of *The Whitefish Pilot*.

Helen Peterson: "I can remember only two things that really got under Dorothy's hide. One was a press association president who wouldn't make plans or stick to a schedule. The other was a recalcitrant tape recorder that refused to perform properly even though it cost a pretty price."

Adams: "We had the 1963 convention on Big Mountain. As host publisher, I worked quite closely with Dorothy in getting the

Miss Johnson, secretary-manager of the Montana Press Association, in her office at the University of Montana School of Journalism.

details set up and holding her hand while she fought with tape recorders. Those famous tape recorders. Dorothy had more trouble with them than anybody else in the world. All through the convention I was being called frantically from some meeting to come and help Dorothy fix the tape recorder.

"Don't get me wrong. She was well organized and she knew exactly what she wanted to have happen at the conventions. With people and other arrangements, there was no problem. But when it came to extension cords, microphones and tape recorders, she had problems."

Miss Johnson devoted considerable time and energy to learning her job—including the convention aspect:

"I soon realized that I couldn't—and didn't have to—do everything at the conventions. I had been *so* afraid to spend any of the press association's money to get something done I thought was my duty. I found I could usually hire a girl or two from whatever hotel the convention was in to run our registration table and take care of the money. Conventions were always terrifically big things with a lot of pressure—everybody wanting something at the same time. If you were at the registration table, you had to keep your cool while a couple of men waved twenty-dollar bills and a couple more signed their names and a couple more shouted, 'Have you seen my wife?' "

In each of her responsibilities—including preparation of a weekly confidential bulletin—Miss Johnson gained a reputation for her conscientious handling of the association's affairs. Their affection for her and their awareness of her constant concern for the organization's welfare soon had the state's publishers calling Miss Johnson "Aunt Dorothy." She liked the nickname and occasionally signed bulletin items with it. As her rapport with the publishers developed, she began referring to them simply as "the boys." The feeling for Miss Johnson is indicated by the comments of Harold G. Stearns, former publisher of *The Harlowton* (Montana) *Times* and the Ryegate (Montana) *Clarion:*

"Dorothy was a great asset in making our advertising agency work. She was a gem as far as correspondence and details were concerned. However, she most endeared herself to us all by her wit, clever little notes regarding all problems and her tremendously jovial reports of her doings.

"These were so replete with her humor and cuteness that they brought the house down invariably. In my estimation she was the greatest public-relations gal for the newspaper fraternity we could possibly have ever obtained . . . . Her bulletins were loaded with wit and wry observations we all miss . . . . Prior to getting 'Din' Alcorn as secretary, the president of the association had had to do most of the work of contacting members and traveling constantly . . . . This work later fell largely to the secretary. We could depend on Dorothy for much detail and she was great to work with."

Publisher K.A. (Doc) Eggensperger of the Thompson Falls *Sanders County Ledger:*

"She was like a mother hen to us. She worried about us constantly. She was very definite in how she managed things and what she wanted she wanted. Nobody was about to shove off any substitutes on her. As far as looking after legislative matters and being concerned with the financial status of the association and handling the magazine and running an efficient office, she did a tremendous job. I think to a lot of us her successor now and those in the future will be measured by her standards to a great extent."

Miss Johnson, indeed, was a noted worrier. An item from the minutes of an August 16, 1957, executive committee meeting in Great Falls reads: "After a discussion of the taxable status of the Montana Press Association, Dorothy Johnson was advised to take no action and stop worrying about it." An item from the minutes of a similar meeting two days later reads: "Dorothy Johnson was assured that she should not worry about whether the Montana State Press Association is subject to payment of income tax. She said she would worry anyway."

Miss Johnson's energy seemed unlimited. In the fall of 1954, the university provided her with the part-time work Byerly had told her she would need to supplement her press association income. There had been talk of her working mornings or afternoons for the University News Service, but she realized that the press association would suffer for it. She described the new job and how she got it:

> "Carl McFarland met me in a corridor one day and asked if I'd like to teach the magazine courses in journalism. I didn't even know they had any. I didn't have any connection with the school. My office was there and I was officially an assistant professor. I had a contract that said so. Without duties and without pay. I always thought that was very funny. But it did give me some faculty privileges and that was very pleasant. When President McFarland asked me to take over the magazine courses, I said, 'Why, yes, I guess so.' McFarland didn't even ask Ole Bue, the acting dean. He just went right over his head."

Thus, with little warning, Miss Johnson was teaching a three-credit magazine course each quarter. The only similar thing she had ever taken had been a magazine-editing course at New York University.

"I knew how useless a course like that could be if not handled properly," she said. "My instructor at NYU had worked for only one magazine and he didn't really know very much about the great outside world."

Just as she had had to learn the press association job on her own, Miss Johnson was faced with the problem of teaching herself how to teach:

"Thank God it was only one course each quarter. I looked through the library to see what textbooks were available, but generally I had to make up my own lectures on awfully short notice. I had been out of school so long. Most people who teach go into it right after they get out of school themselves. They remember how somebody did things well or how somebody did things poorly. I'd been out since 1928 with the exception of my evening courses in New York. Besides, my work with the press association was terribly tight then.

"I was flying around like crazy and staying up late at night trying to figure out what I was going to do in class the next day. It got better after the first year, but I do wish I could have had some help and advice from somebody. I learned a lot from the students. I only had about five in the first class, but later the registration began to build up. At first, I had to write my lectures down verbatim because I simply could not talk off the cuff. Later I got over that."

Miss Johnson continued to find time for her own writing. Another short story, "Too Soon A Woman," had been published in the March 1953 *Cosmopolitan*.

Others that followed included "Journal of Adventure" (*Collier's*, March 19, 1954), "The Last Stand" (*Cosmopolitan*, November, 1954), "I Woke Up Wicked" (*Collier's*, February 18, 1955), "The Man Who Knew the Buckskin Kid" (*Cosmopolitan*, June 1955), "Lost Sister" (*Collier's*, March 30, 1956) and "Young Devil" (*Collier's* paid $2,000 but folded before the story could be published).

Many of Miss Johnson's older stories were reappearing in anthologies and foreign magazines. Among these were "The Unbeliever" (*John Bull*, England, February 7, 1953), "Flame on the Frontier" (*Argosy Book of Adventure Stories*, 1953), "Journey to the Fort" (*John Bull*, 1954), "A Man Called Horse" (*The Spirit of Adventure*) and "Journal of Adventure" (published in Dutch, Swedish and Danish).

In addition to her press association duties, her teaching and her writing (she also was a contributor to *Redbook*, *Charm*, *The Great*

Northern Goat, Montana-The Magazine of Western History, Ford Times, Lifetime Living, Everywoman's and *Montana Library Quarterly*), Miss Johnson had become a popular speaker. In September 1953, for example, she delivered back-to-back addresses—the first in Great Falls at the 40th anniversary convention of the Montana Society of Certified Public Accountants, the second a day later in Billings before the District 12 convention of Zonta International.

In December of the same year, speaking to delegates at the fall meeting of the Montana Interscholastic Editorial Association, she presented an optimistic appraisal of the future of women in journalism. Other groups to hear her included the Missoula Camp Fire Girl Council (1954), the graduating classes of the Plains and White Sulphur Springs high schools (1955) and members of the Spokane chapter of Theta Sigma Phi (1956).

As 1957 approached, Miss Johnson, at 51, showed no signs of slowing the brisk pace she had set for herself as a girl. If anything, she was working harder, although her health had begun to suffer increasingly. Still, the work had its rewards. The greatest were yet to come.

Miss Johnson tries her hand at the Indian stick game on the Flathead Reservation. *(Photo by Carling Malouf)*

CHAPTER ELEVEN

The Hanging Tree

It was a long time ago that I knew the Lucky Lady. There is nothing left now at Skull Creek, they say, but scattered logs where buildings used to be, and windrows of gravel where, in later years, dredges went through the gulch to glean the sparse remaining gold.

They were three arrogant people, Doc Frail and the Lucky Lady and the young fellow who called himself only Rune.

When the news came to Skull Creek about the lost lady, old Doc Frail was trying to pick a squabble with me. I was annoying him by agreeing with everything he said. If we ever got mad at the same time, both of us knew, I would leave or Doc would throw me out. He was smaller, but a man of his reputation might as well be a mile high.

Just before the road dipped down to the gold camp on Skull Creek, it crossed the brow of a barren hill and went under the outthrust bough of a great cottonwood tree.

DURING A PERIOD OF WRITING AND REWRITING spanning 10 years, Dorothy Johnson tried many openings for her second novel.[1] The fourth of those above—telling of the ominous cottonwood tree—was her final choice. Some 65,000 words at its completion in the mid 1950s, the novel had been pared to a 39,000-word novelette by June 1957, when Ballantine Books published it in hard cover

---

[1]The first, written in 1939 in Greenwich Village, was not published.

with nine other Johnson stories.[2] The collection, later published in paperback form, bore the name of the dramatic novelette, *The Hanging Tree*.

The Hanging Tree is the story of grim, gun-toting Dr. Joe Alberts (alias Joe Frail), who drifts into a frontier gold camp in the early 1870s. Doc Frail is embittered, made so by a scandal in Missouri between his wife and his brother. At war with himself, he finds the cynicism born of experience constantly at odds with his compassionate instincts as a doctor.

Frail heals a young sluice robber, Rune, who has been wounded while stealing gold. Later, a road agent holds up a stagecoach 40 miles from Skull Creek, killing a wandering schoolteacher named Armistead and causing the horses to stampede. Armistead's 19-year-old daughter, Elizabeth, is thrown from the wreckage. After wandering for days in the blazing sun, she is temporarily blinded. Eventually, a scheming prospector named Frenchy Plante finds her and brings her to Skull Creek, where she is treated by Frail. In her bewilderment, she is grateful to Plante and mystified by the remote, yet kindly, Frail.

Elizabeth's misfortunes result in a psychotic disorder. Frail helps her recover, after which she is determined to remain in the gold camp. Unable to change her mind, Frail helps her again, providing her with an anonymous grubstake to help her get another start. She uses the gold, which Frail has hidden in her woodpile, to stake other miners. Their claims pan out and Elizabeth becomes the wealthy Lucky Lady.

Only when a mob is about to lynch Frail for shooting a wild-eyed, rabble-rousing, old zealot who calls himself a preacher is Elizabeth able to help him. In effect, she also helps herself. She relinquishes her wealth, which has become foremost in her life; recognizing her love for Frail, she buys him from his would-be executioners.

The hate and fear that have tortured Frail disappear. He knows that in Elizabeth he has found the peace he has been seeking.

---

[2]"Lost Sister," "I Woke Up Wicked," "Journal of Adventure," "A Time of Greatness," "The Man Who Knew the Buckskin Kid," "The Last Boast," "The Story of Charley," "The Gift by the Wagon" and "Blanket Squaw."

Soon after publication of *The Hanging Tree*, Miss Johnson received a note from Betty Ballantine of Ballantine Books:

June 7, 1957

Dear Dorothy:

The first lovely order for *The Hanging Tree* is in from the Army, for 822 copies. We have been told that there will be a review in Tuesday's *New York Herald Tribune*, tho' no amount of gentle probing was productive of what the review says. Will send you a copy as soon as we can lay our hands on one.

Best,
Betty Ballantine

The *Herald Tribune* review, the first of many of *The Hanging Tree*, appeared June 11. The reviewer was John K. Hutchens, a former Montanan who had been a college classmate of Miss Johnson's. Hutchens wrote that while he would not take an oath that Miss Johnson was ready to join the company of H.L. Davis, A.B. Guthrie Jr. and Conrad Richter, she "certainly was on the way . . . . "

Another review appeared in the *Herald Tribune* on June 16, this time by Curtis W. Casewit.

"Women are no longer scarce in the American West, but there is still a scarcity of important Western fiction written by women," Casewit commented. "Dorothy Johnson is one of the few exceptions . . . . "

Casewit discussed "Journal of Adventure" and "The Gift by the Wagon," then turned to Joe Frail and *The Hanging Tree*.

"There is something magnificently touching about this man's arrogance and loneliness and his aloof care for the girl in distress," he observed. "Yet there isn't a shred of sentimentality or melodrama here, and a minimum of dust and gunplay. Miss Johnson is a fine literary writer."

Critic Charles Poore of *The New York Times* also reviewed *The Hanging Tree*, describing it as "Western fiction at its best . . . . " Other newspapers and magazines were enthusiastic about the book. *The Great Falls* (Montana) *Tribune's Montana Parade* stated that Miss Johnson had "won a place in that select company of writers—Jack Schaefer, A.B. Guthrie Jr., and Willa Cather—who have portrayed with honesty and compassion the people of the American West." Lillian Carleton of the Boston (Massachusetts) *Sunday Herald* said *The Hanging Tree* was "beautifully written," calling it "fast, good, reading." The *Hilo* (Hawaii) *Tribune-Herald* said Miss Johnson had written her "spare, clean-cut" stories with a "fierce restraint." Kimmis Hendrick of the *Christian Science Monitor* wrote that "More than anything else, *The Hanging Tree* was a collection of stories about the tenderness in the hearts of people who made the new country." Alphin T. Gould of the *Providence* (R.I.) *Sunday-Journal* said he believed the stories of both *The Hanging Tree* and *Indian Country* would be rated high in literature about the West.

"The author has a superlative ease in dealing with complex characters in situations unique to the American frontier," he wrote.

Critic Victor P. Hass of the *Chicago Tribune* thought *The Hanging Tree* was a collection of short stories worthy of the most discerning of readers.

"Dorothy M. Johnson is a miser with words; she spends them as grudgingly as ever Scrooge spent a shilling," he commented. "It is this admirable penury that gives the . . . stories in this volume their unique distinction. Without an ounce of literary fat, they are taut and springily muscular."

Time magazine, highly complimentary, said that in her tales of Indian, settler, miner and badman, Miss Johnson had "subtly suggested the tragedy of collision between aborigine and invader, and sometimes the more complicated tragedy of their collusion . . . ."

"There is a day in most men's lives when they give up reading cowboy stories because they cannot believe them anymore," *Time* observed. "Dorothy Johnson's tales offer a chance to turn back the calendar with a good conscience."

Possibly the greatest compliment came from the *New York Journal-American* in a book-review section called "The Week's Round-Up":

> Week's best new six-shooter fiction: *The Hanging Tree* by Dorothy Johnson. Novelette and nine short stories by the most brilliant woman Western taleteller since Mary Austin.

In reviewing Alan LeMay's *The Unforgiven* for the *New York*

Herald Tribune, John Hutchens again praised Miss Johnson. Having described LeMay's book as a "tale told with shine, authority and dramatic sense," Hutchens added:

> There are not, when you come to think of it, so very many of them in the Western American field in which LeMay works. At the very head of that field among living practitioners is Conrad Richter—and it is not so much to praise Mr. LeMay as to place him that one thinks of him in the Richter company, and that of A.B. Guthrie Jr., H.L. Davis and two relative newcomers, Dorothy M. Johnson and Charles O. Locke.

To add to the critics' acclaim, the Western Writers of America, meeting in Great Falls in June 1957, presented Miss Johnson with its annual Spur Award for her short story "Lost Sister," which it designated the best western short story of 1956. Other Spur recipients, four men, included author Irving Stone, whose *Men to Match My Mountains* was judged the best in non-fiction. Unlike Stone, who was in Rome working on his Michelangelo biography, *The Agony and the Ecstacy*, Miss Johnson attended the WWA convention and received her award.

Another honor came in October. Miss Johnson and author Erskine Caldwell were invited to Seattle by the Pacific Coast Independent Magazine Wholesalers Association, a group that also distributed paperback books. The purpose of their appearance was to stimulate an interest in reading as a leisure activity. Miss Johnson, who read as voraciously as she had during her school years, might have provided the most stimulation. She told association members she could not get by the book racks in Missoula supermarkets without picking up several paperbacks. Caldwell said he read newspapers and a few magazines, but that his writing allowed him little time for books.

The idea for *The Hanging Tree* came to Miss Johnson as the result of two movies she had seen in New York City in the mid-1940s. One starred Gregory Peck, the other John Wayne, but both dealt with men alone in the desert and dying of thirst. Having some time but no story ideas, Miss Johnson decided to apply the so-called "switch" or twist to the desert situation:[3]

---

[3]In using a switch, the writer takes a hackneyed situation, changes one detail and goes from there.

"The detail I thought of changing, just in playing around with the idea, was this: Instead of having a bunch of men lost and thirsty in the desert, how about making it a woman? This makes for a terrible problem. How in the world did she get out there in the first place? This was the germ idea of the story. The woman became the Lucky Lady."

About the story's setting, Miss Johnson was not specific:

"I never said in that story where it happened. The book's dust jacket and some of the publicity said it was about Montana. I never did. It could have been anywhere as long as there was a gold camp not very far from a desert. I didn't happen to know of any deserts that had a gold camp right next door so I never dared say where it was. It never mattered."

During the 10 years she worked on the story, she rewrote it numerous times.

"I did it over and over and I got so tired of it," she said. "But it seemed like such a good idea that I just couldn't drop it. I am definitely not a novelist—I have proved it again and again."

Among the approximately 26,000 words cut from *The Hanging Tree* prior to publication were about 5,000 dealing with Doc Frail and his personality:

"That chapter I remember the best because cutting it out hurt the worst. I had to know how Frail got to be the kind of man he was and that chapter was a terrific piece. Ballantine Books contradicted their own firm beliefs about collections of short stories not selling and insisted *The Hanging Tree* be cut to include several short stories. I write tightly anyway. When you do that and then have to cut out a whole lot just because of somebody's arbitrary order it makes the story jumpy."

Miss Johnson was, perhaps, somewhat at Ballantine's mercy. Her agent, McIntosh & Otis, had sent the novel to several other publishers. After struggling so long with the story, Miss Johnson's disappointment mounted at each rejection.

"It always breaks my heart when somebody turns something down," she said. "It doesn't get any easier to take. You should be able to get calluses on your soul."

Considerable research was required for *The Hanging Tree*. For example, Miss Johnson knew little about gold:

"By the time I had finished, I had been to Virginia City two or three times for information. I held a great big gold nugget in my hand and that was when I really understood what happened during the gold rush. It's *beautiful* stuff. Even if it wasn't valuable, it's *beautiful*. And it feels so good in your hand. I had to find out a lot about gold. I happened to be in Helena where there is a big collection of gold specimens in one of the banks and I bought a booklet for about a quarter concerning gold in Montana. I depended on that booklet a lot for *The Hanging Tree*. By the time I finished the novel I could understand why people did what they did."

About other technical aspects, she wrote:

"Some of my research involved firearms, prices of commodities on the frontier, the nature and cost of a physician's education almost 100 years ago, the discomforts of stagecoach travel, the technique of placer mining, the slang of the gold gulches, the kind of shelters that prospectors built and lived in, the nature of poverty and luxury in a gold camp, and exactly how to go about hanging a man from a handy tree . . . .

"Writers of 'westerns' do more serious research than their detractors give them credit for or their admiring readers suspect. This research may not be used, but it is never wasted. It helps the writer build a world he never knew, in which he must live when he writes about it. Skull Creek never existed anywhere, but it is as real to me, and 1873 is as contemporary, as the campus of the University of Montana right now . . . . "

Miss Johnson dedicated *The Hanging Tree* to "Dr. Catharine A. Burnham, Clinical Psychologist, who understands the Lucky Lady better than Doc Frail did." Dr. Burnham, Miss Johnson's friend from Greenwich Village days, did, indeed, know the Lucky Lady.

Elizabeth Armistead, as conceived by Miss Johnson, was terror-stricken at her father's murder, her own sufferings in the desert and her blindness. Because of those horrors, she suffered from agoraphobia—a fear of open places. She fainted whenever she tried to leave her cabin at Skull Creek.

Miss Johnson did not mention this diagnosis in the story because the word did not exist in 1873. Nevertheless, she had the professional assurance of Catharine Burnham that the phenomenon existed before it was named.

Working at a New York clinic, Dr. Burnham was participating in a weekly psychology seminar in which the members presented case histories of their current patients. As Dr. Burnham's turn approached, she suggested that the group had discussed enough male patients and should look at the distaff side. She obtained several advance copies of *The Hanging Tree* and distributed them to the seminar before presenting her study of Elizabeth Armistead, the Lucky Lady. The elderly Czech psychiatrist who presided over the group was delighted with the idea. Dr. Burnham described what happened:

"The psychology staff was composed of about a dozen hardboiled eggheads who had graduated from reading Westerns after quitting Zane Grey in their pre-teens. We had foreseen a session in which we all made a lot of half wisecracks in deep psychoanalytic terms, the sort of thing most psychologists try to avoid if they

Catharine Burnham, a close friend and
technical adviser on *The Hanging Tree.*

want anyone to pay any attention. The interesting thing is that nothing of the sort happened. Everyone had enjoyed the story and the characters had rung true completely.

"The bantering interactions in which we usually got involved when we presented real cases just didn't 'happen. Our diagnosis, with all concurring, was 'anxiety neurosis precipitated by trauma.'

"Dorothy has an instinctive insight into character that is clinically accurate. My role as adviser in the Lucky Lady's development was mostly as sounding board: 'If she did this, would it make sense in terms of such-and-such a background?' In general, however, Dorothy experiences everything she puts down, and vividly."

In discussing the great cottonwood tree from which the novel took its name, Miss Johnson emphasized no symbolism was intended:

"If it is a symbol, it symbolizes only coming trouble. I wanted the tree to appear near the beginning because it was going to be important in the story. Personally, I don't go for symbolism. Symbolism is something English teachers have taken up since I was graduated. It's all right if writers want to use it but what I don't go for is attributing symbolism to an author who can't defend himself and who didn't intend it. And that's being done. Good Lord is that being done, even with the Iliad and the Odyssey. I know darn well Homer didn't intend any symbolism. He's just telling a cracking good story. It's all right if you, the author, want to use it, but when somebody else decides what your symbolism is, that's dead wrong."

In August 1957, producers Martin Jurow and Richard Shepherd completed negotiations with Miss Johnson's movie agent, Lucile Sullivan, for film rights to *The Hanging Tree*.[4] Con-

---

[4]*The Hanging Tree* was not the first of Miss Johnson's stories to interest Hollywood. Although little came of it, the first talk about a possible movie had been in 1952. The story was "Laugh in the Face of Danger"—the one her former agent had sold without telling her. A Hollywood free-lance writer liked it and Miss Johnson signed a contract giving him an option on it. The writer prepared a good script and tried to sell it. It didn't sell. Years later, he found out why. During the scandal period in Hollywood when many persons were being secretly blacklisted for alleged Communist activities, he was a victim. His career was ruined, even though it turned out that a mistake in identification had been made. Later, the writer got started again with the story idea. Miss Johnson signed another contract with him, this time supervised by her movie agent. Again, nothing came of the script. Before this revival of interest, however, the story had become Miss Johnson's first on television.

siderable correspondence preceded the agreement and for several weeks Miss Johnson was unsure whether one would be reached. She explained how she learned the story had been sold:

> "I was in the *Missoulian* office talking to Dick Morrison, the publisher, when the phone call caught up with me. I had left word at my office on the campus where I would be. Lucile Sullivan said Jurow and Shepherd were going to pay $7,500 for *The Hanging Tree*, plus 3 per cent of the net profits. Sad to say, a rumor got around that the amount to be paid had another zero on it. Would that it had been so!"

At the time her book *Beulah Bunny Tells All* was published, Miss Johnson experienced a marked increase in prestige. When it became known *The Hanging Tree* was to become a movie, she noticed a similar effect. In addition to some further comment on the economics of selling stories to the movies, she later wrote about her new stature:

> When a book becomes a movie, even strangers (even teen-agers!) begin to act respectful. A book is permanent, but a movie is glamorous, and everybody knows that the author of a story bought for the movies automatically becomes rich. This is not true, but just try convincing anybody except another writer who has found out for himself.
>
> When the title story of my third book, *The Hanging Tree*, became a motion picture, I learned some interesting facts about the difference between printed and visual media as well as the changing status of writers and how little money the average non-best-seller brings out of the famed golden coffers of Hollywood. I'm not complaining bitterly about the money. It's a little more than I had, and it came with no effort on my part. All I did was sign a contract of some 45 typewritten pages, of which the only detail I remember is a stern warning that if I should become an object of public obloquy and disgrace I wouldn't get any screen credit.

Jurow and Shepherd became the owners of Miss Johnson's original 65,000-word *Hanging Tree* manuscript. They had requested it so that screen and script writers could learn more about the principal characters. The producers offered Miss Johnson a handsome salary to assist in the preliminary work, but she declined.

"I was reluctant to let university officials and the state press

In 1957, Dorothy Johnson and Gary Cooper talked books and movies in the University of Montana Lodge. Cooper was in Missoula with producers Martin Jurow and Richard Shepherd to discuss *The Hanging Tree*. *(Photo by Dick Harris)*

Actor Gary Cooper and Miss Johnson quickly formed a mutual-admiration society.

association find out they could get along without my services," she said.

The evening of October 30, 1957, Jurow and Shepherd arrived in Missoula to confer with Miss Johnson and to begin seeking possible filming sites. Favorably impressed by the two young producers, Miss Johnson later referred to them as "alert, earnest, highly literate young businessmen, hard-working and thorough."

"All I ever knew about movie producers is what I had seen in cartoons," she continued. "They were always shown as stupid oafs who wore gaudy sport shirts, berets and dark glasses, and who said idiotic things to their subordinates."

Jurow and Shepherd were accompanied by a widely known traveling companion, himself a former Montanan. His name was Gary Cooper, and he had just been named the star of *The Hanging Tree.*

On October 31, Miss Johnson, Cooper, Jurow and Shepherd met in the University Lodge for a news conference. Shepherd told reporters that he and Jurow planned to visit Helena, Virginia City and Three Forks in search of a site. Jurow said Montana's scenery was unequaled and that he hoped the movie would prove it to people throughout the country. Cooper discussed Miss Johnson and *The Hanging Tree.*

"When you read stacks of stuff that aren't any good, you really grab at something as interesting and beautifully written as Miss Johnson's book," he said. "You have a great talent in Miss Johnson."

Cooper and Miss Johnson posed together for numerous pictures. Among the photographers was Cyrile Van Duser of the University News Service, who had been a campus classmate of Miss Johnson's some 30 years earlier.

Miss Johnson and Cooper got along famously. During one of their conversations, Cooper asked the author if she would like a pheasant. He had shot several while hunting with Ernest Hemingway near Sun Valley, Idaho, and had given them to the chef at the Florence Hotel. Miss Johnson, though not a cook, accepted the pheasant anyway, thinking she could have it prepared somewhere and use the feathers for a hat. When Cooper handed Miss Johnson the bird, wrapped in heavy paper, neither he nor she realized that the chef had removed the plumage and prepared it for the oven. Determined to have a memento of Cooper's visit, Miss Johnson, after enjoying her pheasant with Cyrile Van Duser, saved the wishbone. She had it copper-plated and still considers it one of her most prized possessions.

Cooper's contract with Jurow and Shepherd became final early in November. Among the first to find out was Columnist Louella

Parsons. After informing her readers why Cooper would not be taking a planned vacation to Paris, she wrote:

> While I was talking to Gary I got another story. His picture after the Mirisch western is *The Hanging Tree.* Martin Jurow and Richard Shepherd bought this from a collection of short stories by Dorothy M. Johnson . . . . Dick Shepherd told me "The Hanging Tree" was originally written as a novelette and he added, "Two young producers like us are very lucky to get such a story, plus Gary Cooper."

Production of *The Hanging Tree* began in June 1958, but not in Montana. Instead, Jurow-Shepherd moved their cameras to Washington's Yakima Valley. Many Montanans later joked that Hollywood apparently had found scenery that looked "more like Montana than Montana."[5] Amid tall evergreens and rock out-croppings at the confluence of the Rattlesnake and Little Rattlesnake rivers, 35 miles northwest of Yakima, the frontier mining town of Skull Creek began to take shape.

Throughout the creation of the set and the subsequent shoot-ing, the activities of the movie makers were well covered by the Washington press. Many Yakima residents got their first crack at being actors when Director Delmer Daves called for extras for his mob scenes. The prime attractions, however, were Cooper, Swiss actress Maria Schell (Elizabeth) and veteran actor Karl Malden (Frenchy). Miss Johnson never visited the set; indeed, there were several things she did not do during the latter part of 1958.

In late February, she had accepted an invitation from the Whitefish school board to deliver the May commencement address at the city's high school. On March 7, the Whitefish Jaycees had designated her guest of honor for their 10th annual Gala Days celebration August 2 and 3. She had accepted the invitation of Fred Stacey, a Gala Days committeeman, to ride in the parade, but emphasized that because of other commitments she

---

[5]Miss Johnson explained in *Montana Journalism Review* the cause for the shift. "They wanted to make the movie in Montana but were concerned about the probability of rain at the time and in the place selected. They knew more about Montana weather than Montanans do. They had checked the probabilities of rain at Bannack on the basis of weather reports for the preceding ten years. They . . . chose the Yakima Valley . . . because they had almost a guarantee of sunshine in May and June."

could attend only one day of the celebration.

Miss Johnson spoke at the graduation exercises but did not attend the Gala Days. As August approached, she considered herself fortunate to be alive. It was July 19, and she had been to a Stevensville nursing home to visit her mother. Driving back, she was feeling pleased because her mother liked the home and seemed content. Then, about 3 miles south of Missoula, although she was not tired, her eyes kept shutting. Later, in a grim article warning others of what had happened, she wrote:

> Need more air, I thought, and opened the little butterfly window on the left side. The big window there was already wide open.
>
> That extra window didn't help, so I decided to pull over to the side of the road. But there wasn't any place to pull over. No shoulder on the road, no scenery, nothing. Not even fog. Just nothing. Take ten deep breaths of fresh air, I advised myself, and stop the car. But what I breathed was not fresh air. It was a lethal gas.
>
> The next thing I knew, somebody was pulling me out of the wreckage of the car, waking me from the deepest, blackest sleep I have ever experienced. I couldn't see my rescuer because my face was covered with blood and my glasses were smashed. But I heard someone say that my car had collided with another one. An ambulance was coming.
>
> In the nearest hospital, a surgeon stitched me up for several hours, then had me x-rayed and put to bed. Meanwhile, a woman passenger from the other car was in the operating room. She had a fractured hip and back, they told me.
>
> My doctor asked me a great many questions, and then said, "You were overcome by carbon monoxide."
>
> The world that simply hadn't been there at the side of the road when I wanted to stop—that void was due to a phenomenon called narrowing of the field of vision, caused by carbon-monoxide asphyxiation. The deadly gas had also affected my judgment—though I had wanted to stop the car, I couldn't. The overpowering drowsiness and the deep blackout were typical. Carbon monoxide . . . affects the brain—sometimes terribly and permanently—even when it doesn't kill.
>
> A week later, leaning on a cane, still shaken, I limped into my study at home, saw the unfinished work on my desk, and realized I almost hadn't gotten back to this.

Knowing that news of her accident would upset her mother, Miss Johnson had called the nursing home and asked the management not to let Mrs. Alger see any newspaper stories. A nurse had obligingly clipped the story and picture from the next day's *Missoulian*, a deed that brought a sharp reprimand from the indignant Mrs. Alger. The censorship worked, however, and not until three weeks later, when Mrs. Vedder Gilbert drove Miss Johnson to Stevensville, did Mrs. Alger hear of the accident.

Miss Johnson sustained several broken ribs, a badly lacerated forehead, a knee injury that plagued her for eight years and severe facial bruises.

"My face was so black and blue that visitors coming into the hospital room to sympathize with me burst out into hearty laughter instead," she said. "I was a sight to behold, but the woman in the other car was a lot worse."

The accident resulted in a $50,000 damage suit against Miss Johnson. Only three weeks after moving into a new home on Duncan Drive in the Rattlesnake Valley, she was faced with losing it and considerably more. The suit continued well into 1959, and not until October of that year was it finally settled out of court by the insurance companies.

"For 15 months I have been bumbling along with the equivalent of a long, dreadful illness, and I can't quite realize yet that it is now over," she wrote her friend Mel Ruder of the *Hungry Horse News*.

There was more encouraging news from Hollywood as the end of 1958 approached. A press release from the Warner Brothers studio in Burbank told the story:

> Skull Creek had a short life, but a wild one.
>
> One day it was a roaring boom town, its streets jammed with covered wagons and mule trains, and gun fights and drunken brawls raging on every other corner as miners celebrated a new gold claim.
>
> Five weeks later the town was dead, completely erased from the earth. Only Hollywood could build and destroy a town with such a mixture of ease and violence, and only Gary Cooper could survive the short but perilous life of a town like Skull Creek . . . .
>
> The mining town . . . had a genuine air of permanence about it. It had a frame hotel, two stories high; a general store, an assayer's office and a huge saloon. There was Mame's Eatery, a barber shop, a blacksmith shop and a dozen other stores, as well as more than 50 miners' tents and shacks—and high on a precipice the cabin of Gary Cooper, a gunslinger doctor.

For the five weeks of its existence, Cooper, the other stars and 250 bit and extra players went in and out of the stores and up and down the streets as love and violence played out the story of "The Hanging Tree."

Before construction was started, Warner Brothers and producers Martin Jurow and Richard Shepherd had to have dozens of huge Ponderosa pine trees felled and a road bulldozed in from a nearby logging highway. Then a crew of 100 technicians, carpenters and laborers went to work to build the town as it might have looked in 1870. They even built a waterwheel, 15 feet high, to provide water for the miners' sluice boxes. The course of one of the streams was temporarily diverted to operate the contraption.

On the last day Director Delmer Daves filmed the burning of the town by a horde of drunken miners celebrating a new strike.

There could be no retakes on this sequence, for once the fire took hold, the frame dwellings would go up fast. Daves used four cameras shooting at once, each placed at a strategic spot to get the best and most dramatic angles. More than 250 actors took part in the flaming scene.

Before sundown, Skull Creek was a smouldering ruins. The next day a cleanup crew went to work. By nightfall, they had erased every trace of the town, leaving only the new dirt road to remind residents that *The Hanging Tree* had been filmed there.

The filming was over and editing was well under way. Next would come plans for the world premiere.

A world premiere showing of *The Hanging Tree* was a gala event at the Fox Theater in Missoula, Montana, the night of February 18, 1959. The official world premiere had been in Yakima, Washington, three days earlier. *(Photo by Cyrile Van Duser)*

CHAPTER TWELVE

1959: "Quite a Year"

"I came to town to search for gold
And brought with me a memory . . . . "

THE VOICE—POWERFUL, YET MELLOW—WAS
that of singer Marty Robbins. The song—done in
semi-folk style on the Columbia label—was "The
Hanging Tree."[1] Within 10 days of its release it was
in second place among the nation's most popular tunes. Within
two weeks it was at the top of the charts, where it stayed for almost
a month and a half.

By March 1959, theaters throughout the country were filled with
the melody. People were whistling it on the streets. The movie *The
Hanging Tree* had opened in New York City's Roxy Theater on
February 6. A day earlier, at the Montana Theater Association's
biennial legislature theater party in Helena, Montana lawmakers
had a private screening. On February 15 the official world premiere
was in Yakima, Washington, and three days later, the movie
opened at Missoula's Fox Theater.

For Miss Johnson, the Helena and Missoula premieres proved
the most action-packed. She attended the former on the invitation of Clarence Golder, then president of the Montana Theater
Association. The theater owners made her their guest of honor,
stating, "This is the first time in the history of motion pictures that
we have had a Montana story with a Montana star and written by
a Montana author." Miss Johnson later described her visit to
Helena:

---

[1]Written by Mack David and Jerry Livingston.

"I took a day off from the press association duties and went, not knowing what I was getting into. Nobody had warned me what was involved. First, they took me in to see the governor. I kept running into people I knew in the corridor. It was a great turmoil. Then the man in charge of me dragged me over to some radio station where he thought I was going to be interviewed. The people at the station didn't know anything about it and were quite cool.

"Next, we landed in the House of Representatives. I believe I was the attraction just after the high school band from Lewistown. One of our representatives from Missoula County introduced me with a beaming smile. I waved at a couple of people I knew and then we went into the Senate chamber. This was much worse because there I was escorted with great dignity up to the platform where Lieutenant Governor Cannon was holding forth. I saw a couple of senators I knew and I waved at them. They didn't wave back. I thought, 'Oh dear, there's something wrong.' Both of them did wave after a minute and I realized they hadn't known I was waving at them.

"And then Mr. Cannon introduced me and kind of bowed as if I was supposed to say something. I said 'Thank you' and sat down. Afterwards, somebody said that was the best speech they had ever heard in the Senate chamber because it was the shortest. Nobody had told me I was supposed to make a speech. I had never been in a situation like that before.

"That evening the theater owners had a marvelous buffet supper in the lobby of the Marlow Theater and then showed *The Hanging Tree*. Then they asked me to get up on the platform. For this I was prepared—I had a few notes on a card. At the very moment I began to speak, somebody thrust a beautiful bouquet of roses into my arms. I couldn't get at my note card. Anyway, the footlights were shining in my face so it was a more impromptu speech than I had intended to make.

"Afterward, they had dancing. Somebody wanted me to dance. Well, of course, I can't because I never learned. And so I handed him over to the governor's wife and they went dancing off. You don't tell the governor's wife who she should dance with, but she was having a good time . . . . The legislators all said they liked the movie. What *could* they say? They were getting all of this free."

In Missoula, prior to the opening of *The Hanging Tree* at the Fox Theater, Miss Johnson was guest of honor at a dinner sponsored by the Missoula Community Theater in cooperation with the Fox and the Hotel Florence. During the dinner—in the hotel's Bitterroot Room—Alan Bradley, then mayor of Missoula, proclaimed

February 19 as "Dorothy Johnson Day" in tribute to her talent and contribution to the community. Miss Johnson was introduced by Harold Merriam, her former English professor, who told the audience, "She became a successful writer the only way it can be done—by writing, writing and writing."

During the presentations, Miss Johnson received a leather-bound copy of *The Hanging Tree* with the inscription, "For our friend and associate, Dorothy Johnson, on the occasion of the Missoula premiere." The book bore the signature of Dr. Gordon B. Castle, acting president of the university, on behalf of the faculty and staff.

Some 250 persons listened and laughed while Miss Johnson described Gary Cooper as "my hero" during the dinner. She quoted a New York newspaper as saying that Cooper thought so highly of her story that he had agreed to go into the production on a percentage basis.

"My hero," she said, "is a man of literary judgment."

In a brief speech several hours later at the theater, Miss Johnson still was in high spirits.

"There was one thing that bothered me," she said about a *Hanging Tree* review she had read in an entertainment magazine. "It said the movie promised 'strong b.o.' Turned out b.o. means box office, people buying tickets. It means you. I'm perfectly willing to buy a ticket myself, and I've already seen it twice."

Generally, Miss Johnson liked Hollywood's treatment of her story. She was to see the picture seven times, vowing after the seventh never to see it again unless somebody handcuffed her to a theater chair:

"The story was greatly changed in the transfer to another medium. Such changes are supposed to infuriate authors, but in *The Hanging Tree* they made sense, and I will even admit that they improved it. I wish I had thought of some of them myself. . .

"I visualized Doc Frail, the hero, as of medium height and 33 years old. When the news came that Gary Cooper would play this role, I hastened to read my story again—and lo, Doc Frail had grown taller and older. When I began to adore Gary Cooper from afar, both of us were considerably younger than we are now.

"When Elizabeth, the heroine, left my typewriter, she was a dark-haired girl from Philadelphia and afraid of her own shadow. As played by Maria Schell, she is an admirably determined blonde from Switzerland (to allow for Miss Schell's German accent), with great strength of character.

"The movie Elizabeth can afford strength of character, because her problems have changed in the transfer from one medium to another. The problems and the plot changed because in a motion picture the audience has to *see* the conflicts.

"In a written story, readers contribute more than they realize. They fill in for themselves the backgrounds that the author only sketches; they visualize faces and costumes, understand mental turbulence that the author suggests. The author can tell what's going on in people's minds, and if he uses this privilege frugally, readers accept it. A motion picture or a stage play must *show* all this, and that takes longer. A writer can say in ten words enough to require ten minutes of visible action and dialogue . . . .

"Miss Schell's Elizabeth suffered, but she recovered from her mental troubles in a hurry, thanks to some harsh treatment by Gary Cooper as Doc Frail. *Time* called him a 'frontier Freud,' thus infuriating the clinical psychologist who was my technical adviser when I was writing the story. Miss Schell's Elizabeth fared forth to mine gold in partnership with the juvenile lead, Rune (Ben Piazza), and the jovial villain, Frenchy (Karl Malden).

"My Elizabeth did her gold mining by grubstaking miners; the gold came to her, and she stayed in her cramped, dismal cabin. How dark and gloomy that would have been in a motion picture! Without the agoraphobia—the major theme in the written story—the action could move out into the sunshine.

"The cabin changed, too. Miss Schell's Elizabeth lived in one that would have been a palace on the frontier. This bothers nobody but me, and it doesn't bother me much.

"Several characters who were dear to me, because they were my children and I knew them well, did not get into the motion picture at all. In fact, there are enough good ones left over for another movie. Some new ones appeared—total strangers to me. I was glad to make their acquaintance, but I grieve a little for those who were abolished: Tall John, the scholarly miner who had studied in Rome; Wonder Russell, whose name was given to a man the screenplay writer invented; an old dragon known as Ma Harris; a dance-hall girl named Julie, who cut her own throat after Wonder Russell was buried.

"Doc Frail's past changed. He is still racked by conscience, but for a different reason. My Doc Frail had killed a man, but his anguish arose from the fact that he had not killed another one who shot his friend Wonder Russell. Building up the past I saw for Doc Frail would have taken up another couple of hours of screen time . . . .

"Messrs. Jurow and Shepherd had certainly read the story. They knew more about it than I did. I wrote it for ten years, reduced its length by almost half at the publisher's demand, and then cut the silver cord. When a story is in print, the author shouldn't go on brooding over it. The producers did not yet have a screenplay when we met in Missoula. They were intensely concerned with a story that, for them, was not finished. They talked earnestly about the people—not characters but people. They wanted to know what happened to the people after the story ended . . . .

"One thing neither the publisher nor the producers changed: The title. The publishers almost called the book "Red Men and White," which wasn't an attractive title even when Owen Wister used it. The producers worried because "The Hanging Tree" sounded violent and might scare off women. Martin Jurow telephoned to ask whether I had ever used any other working title for the story. Yes, I had—The Prisoner at Skull Creek. I could hear him shudder all the way from Hollywood.

"My title stayed, and they even had a song written to match it. I liked the song so well that I bought two records of it (in case one wears out) and a phonograph."

Gary Cooper and Maria Schell in a scene from *The Hanging Tree*. (*Warner Brothers photo*)

Gary Cooper as "Doc" Frail in *The Hanging Tree*.

Maria Schell as Elizabeth in *The Hanging Tree*.

Karl Malden, who played "Frenchy" in *The Hanging Tree*.

Not all the critics were as enthusiastic about the movie as they had been about the original story. *The Commonweal* commented that the plot tried to crowd too much into its 106-minute running time.

"Director Delmer Daves, who knows how to make outdoor movies that have some depth in characterization, is so busy packing his picture with incident after incident that he has little time to develop his trouble-laden characters," the magazine contended. "Even those that get started never seem to arrive."

Time called *The Hanging Tree* a "psychological western based on the rather odd premise that the American West was won on the consulting couches of Vienna." Later referring to the production as "slick and artificial," *Time* granted that the moviemakers, in places, had been successful.

"Actress Schell, holding a hard rein on her sentimental excesses, gives a gracious, intelligent performance," *Time* observed. "And though actor Cooper, when required to produce the piercingly analytic stare, can do no more than push out his chin and look as though he is about to whinny, he demonstrates in a hundred subtle little platitudes of the prairie that he sure does know his oats."

Newsweek, describing *The Hanging Tree* as "fine fantasy from a frontier folk tale," stated that although the film offered ample gunplay, fist fights, gambling scenes and a lynching party, the underlying mood was more suggestive of Malory's *Morte d'Arthur* than Bret Harte's *Poker Flat*.

"Like all legends of chivalry, this one shuffles action, poetry, humor and a sense of morality together in an atmosphere that is not quite real and not quite meant to be," the magazine commented.

Hollis Alpert of *Saturday Review*, offended by the movie's theme song, nevertheless saw good points.

"*The Hanging Tree* manages to avoid several of the more flagrant Western cliches," he noted. "Not once, for instance, is anyone offered a horse that merely requires extensive breaking in; the hero and villain do not shoot it out on a lonely, empty street in the last reel; and no one is challenged to drink more whiskey than is good for him . . . . "

In the *New Republic*, critic Stanley Kauffmann used *The Hanging*

Tree and the film version of A.B. Guthrie Jr.'s *These Thousand Hills* to illustrate some general observations on Westerns. Both authors, Kauffmann wrote, had taken considerable pains to reproduce an era with some care, and to avoid the character and story cliches of the inferior straight Western.

"In both cases," he added, "the movie-makers have taken just so much of the historical milieu and the originality as would fit within the conventional framework. They have shown a nose for whatever of the tried-and-true lurks in these stories and have used just enough of the books' individuality to distinguish them from the last Western we saw."

Alton Cook of the *New York World-Telegram* had more favorable reactions. He disagreed with *The Commonweal*, stating that the movie showed "unusual concern for the inner workings of its characters." He added that *The Hanging Tree* had "enough sheer action to qualify for television" and a "mature attitude" that made it "outstanding in its field."

Archer Winsten of the *New York Post* also approved, claiming that *The Hanging Tree* contained some of the best pioneer Western material ever offered by the movies.

Variety praised Director Delmer Daves' camera work, pointing out that Daves and his crew did not lose a chance to show the "rugged and beautiful" location backgrounds.

"The natural splendor of the Washington mountains and forests is thoroughly exploited in Technicolor, but Daves doesn't allow his scenes to become such that one can't see the plot for the trees," *Variety* commented.

Harrison Carroll wrote in the *Los Angeles Herald & Express* that while it took "a lot of picture" to top Gary Cooper's classic *High Noon, The Hanging Tree* "definitely did it." Carroll said the film was "bound to be a box office block-buster." Bosley Crowther disagreed, commenting in *The New York Times* that the picture was neither "sharp" nor "searching."

"There is no particular theme or moral to it, except that bread cast on the waters will be returned," Crowther wrote. "The haunting symbol of that tree, which is presented at the outset, is even neglected until the very end."

"Doc" Frail (Gary Cooper) and Elizabeth (Maria Schell) in a scene from *The Hanging Tree*.

Paul V. Beckley of the *New York Herald-Tribune* agreed with Crowther.

"Despite the fluent direction by Delmer Daves, who showed in '3:10 to Yuma' . . . how tight a grip he can get on a tense situation, *The Hanging Tree* lacks conviction," Beckley wrote. ". . . Daves has given the picture an undercurrent of excitement, but the facts don't bear close examination."

John Beaufort of *The Christian Science Monitor* also saw flaws. Among minor ones were narrative gaps—"beyond the film editor's power to conceal"—and side action that repeatedly got "side-tracked." Beaufort believed that although greater attention to details would have made the picture more "tightly knit," it rated as a "better-than-average" Western to which its stars gave "solid frontier performances . . . . "

Larry Tajiri noted in *The Denver Post* that while old-style westerns had been "pretty elemental, with sharp divisions between white hats and black hats, good guys and bad," the newer ones had been "influenced by Dr. Freud." The movie, Tajiri claimed, was an example of "psychology on the lone-prairie . . . . "

The Hanging Tree had been in theaters for fewer than three weeks when another of Miss Johnson's short stories, "The Lady and the Killer," appeared in *The Saturday Evening Post* (February 21, 1959). In addition, book sales of *The Hanging Tree* were climbing steadily. The hard-cover edition had entered a fourth printing and paperbacks in book stores were moving rapidly.[2]

If Hollywood's movie had added little to Miss Johnson's reputation, her original story had. In a March 30, 1959, cover story on westerns and the West, *Time* commented that "only since World War II had the cliches been rescued by a serious set of younger writers—A.B. Guthrie Jr. (*The Way West*), Tom Lea (*The Wonderful Country*), Dorothy Johnson (*The Hanging Tree*)." Miss Johnson responded to the compliment in a letter to *Time*'s editor:

Sir:
Thanks, pardner, for including me as one of the "younger

---

[2]Miss Johnson also was selling to *Seventeen* and *True Western Adventures*. In addition, many of her stories continued to be purchased for foreign reprint and various anthologies.

writers" of westerns. You make me feel coltish, gray-haired as I am.

Another "younger" writer, whose book *Shane* you mentioned with approbation, wasn't named at all. No story exists without an author, so let the name Jack Schaefer be blazoned on your pages. He wrote *Shane.*

Occasional setbacks occurred. In the spring of 1958, Miss Johnson had written the script for a musical, "Jack o' Diamonds," at the suggestion of Michael Martin Brown, a New York composer. A western, "Jack o' Diamonds" was set in the non-existent Prickly Pear Mountains of Montana. On April 4, 1959, Brown arrived in Missoula to discuss several script revisions with Miss Johnson. The two worked diligently, but on April 7, in a letter to Mel Ruder concerning press association business, Miss Johnson indicated that the play still needed changes:

> "The past three days my collaborator . . . has been here so we could work on our musical show. I took most of yesterday off. Will take a few days after school is out in June, hole up somewhere and revise like mad. That's no way to spend a vacation but I've done it before . . . . "

Later, Brown finished the lyrics and tried to sell the play. When, after many months of trying, he found no backers, "Jack o' Diamonds" joined Miss Johnson's 1939 Greenwich Village novel in her "lost cause" file.

A later lost cause was a collection of short, pithy, non-fiction pieces Miss Johnson called *Over the Coocoo's Nest.* The circumstances surrounding the book would be a sore spot with her for years after the project had been scrapped:

> "The idea for the book was suggested by Ian Ballantine, president of Ballantine Books . . . . What he had in mind was the sort of thing done by Harry Golden of the *Carolina Israelite.* He wanted kind of a Harry Golden of Montana approach. The idea tickled me because I had many short pieces that had been in the *Great Falls Tribune.* I enjoyed doing them. I sent Ballantine an outline of what I proposed to write about and that was fine. We had a contract that paid $500 down . . . .
>
> "I spent a year working on that book, revising some old stuff and writing some new ones. Every once in awhile I would write to Ballantine's editor and send him one or two of these to see if I was on the right track. I asked him to return them with his comments. He never returned a single one and never made a single comment.

Naturally I assumed everything was all right. I gave him every chance to say this wasn't what he had in mind.

"I got the manuscript typed and sent it away to my agent, who sent it on to Ballantine. Then, after a long delay, his editor wrote back and said, very blithely, 'This isn't exactly what they had had in mind.' There wasn't a thing I could do about it . . . . One time after that, Ballantine phoned from New York to ask if I wanted to do something for him. I told him no and I told him why. I told him what his editor had done and that I thought it was outrageous. Even then—although he said he was sorry things had turned out that way—he defended his editor, who was his great white hope. Later the fellow quit him and went to work for another publishing company . . . . "

Although *The Hanging Tree* had brought Miss Johnson many tributes, none, perhaps, pleased her as much as that paid her by the people of Whitefish, the city she considered her home town. The Whitefish Chamber of Commerce began planning for a celebration soon after the movie's release in February. On April 24, the eve of the event, *The Whitefish Pilot* told of the plans in its

The Hanging Tree Restaurant and Lounge in Whitefish was named in honor of Miss Johnson's book. *(Photo by the author)*

lead story:

> Whitefish will honor its hometown girl who made good on Saturday afternoon when Dorothy M. Johnson returns here after winning national acclaim as an author of western stories of high quality . . . .
> Hailed as one of the finest writers about the American frontier, Miss Johnson will be presented with the key to the city by Mayor Roy Duff in public ceremonies Saturday at 1 p.m.

Also on the front page, next to a two-column picture of Miss Johnson, was the following:

PROCLAMATION!

WHEREAS, one of Whitefish's own, Miss Dorothy M. Johnson, who was raised and educated in our community, has achieved recognition on an international scale and received nation-wide honor and distinction for her authorship of the book *The Hanging Tree*; and,

WHEREAS, she has brought honor and glory to Montana and our community through her fine stories, articles and book; and,

WHEREAS, she has achieved the distinction of, "The most brilliant woman western taleteller since Mary Austin"; and,

WHEREAS, many of us, who know her personally, are proud and happy of the success she has achieved and know that she is worthy and deserving of the same; and,

WHEREAS, it seems only fitting and proper that we take notice of such success and achievements and acknowledge our appreciation of the momentous events that have occurred as a result of her great talents:

NOW, THEREFORE, I, ROY M. DUFF, as Mayor of the City of Whitefish, do hereby proclaim and designate Saturday, April 25, 1959, as and to be "DOROTHY JOHNSON DAY" in the City of Whitefish in tribute to her talent and contribution to our community, and I urge the people of the City of Whitefish to observe "DOROTHY JOHNSON DAY" with appropriate public ceremony in recognition of her achievements.

IN WITNESS WHEREOF, I have hereunto set my hand and caused the Seal of the City of Whitefish, Montana, to be affixed.

Done at the City of Whitefish this 20th of April, 1959.

Roy M. Duff, *Mayor*
I.O. Graff, *City Clerk*[3]

---

[3]To add to her honors, Miss Johnson, on April 5, was named one of four "Women Trail Blazers" during the 28th annual Matrix Table award dinner sponsored by the University of Montana's Kappa Chapter of Theta Sigma Phi.

Publisher Gurney Moss of *The Whitefish Pilot* introduces Miss Johnson in front of the Orpheum Theater. At left is Sterling Rygg, president of the chamber of commerce. *(Photo by Lacy Studio, Whitefish)*

The Whitefish Chamber of Commerce sponsored "Dorothy Johnson Day" on April 25, 1959. A mounted escort met Miss Johnson at the outskirts of town and took her to the main ceremoney by buggy. In the background, from left, are David Morris, Elmer Smith, Park Ellis and Dr. John Whalen. In the rig with the guest of honor is Art Harlow.

From left, John Tatsey, nationally known Blackfeet newspaper correspondent; Milo Fields, publisher of Browning's Glacier Reporter; and Miss Johnson. *(Hungry Horse News photo)*

Made an honorary member of the Blackfeet Tribe in 1959, Miss Johnson was given the name Kills-Both-Places.

"Dorothy Johnson Day" was an immense success. Hundreds of Whitefish residents—who had bedecked the town in a "Hanging Tree" motif—greeted Miss Johnson as she rode in a buggy to a platform near the Orpheum Theater on Central Avenue. The buggy belonged to Whitefish resident Art Harlow, who met Miss Johnson at the outskirts of town to bring her to the celebration in true western fashion. Accompanying Harlow as a mounted escort were riders David Morris, Dr. John Whalen, Park Ellis and Elmer Smith, all members of a local saddle club.

Holding a bouquet of red roses and the large ceramic key to the city, Miss Johnson was introduced by her former boss, Gurnie Moss of the *Pilot*. Numerous speakers paid tributes, as did the 82-piece Whitefish High School band and the VFW Drum and Bugle Corps. Several coffee hours ensued, followed by a Founder's Day banquet at Big Mountain chalet and a visit to the Orpheum to see *The Hanging Tree* in its last Whitefish screening.

In July 1959, Miss Johnson was honored again, this time by the Blackfeet Indians. On July 4, during North American Indian Days in Browning, Montana, she and Publisher Milo Fields of Browning's *Glacier Reporter* were inducted into the Blackfeet Tribe. Among the Blackfeet, a name is a thing of value and can be given only by someone who has a right to it. Miss Johnson's sponsor, Charles Crow Chief Reevis, gave her his grandmother's name, Nah-chee-kah-poo-neh-kee (Princess Kills-Both-Places). Fields' sponsor, Daniel Bull Plume Sr., gave Fields the name Chief Running Rabbit.

"I was so pleased with my name, but Milo—thinking his sounded cowardly—wasn't a bit pleased," Miss Johnson said. "I looked his up in a book about the Blackfeet, though, and found out they once had an important chief by that name. Milo felt better then."

The Winter 1959 *School of Journalism Communique* had reported that "unless someone heads her off at the pass, this is going to be quite a year for Dorothy Johnson." Indeed, as 1959 ended, the statement had been proved true.

CHAPTER THIRTEEN

The Pace Quickens

F A M O U S *LAWMEN OF THE OLD WEST*, WRITTEN by Dorothy Johnson and published by Dodd, Mead and Company in August 1963, contains brief biographies of 11 frontier peace officers. Aimed at a juvenile audience, the 151-page volume marks a major turning point in Miss Johnson's writing career.

A few minutes spent studying a list of Miss Johnson's publications clearly indicates that as early as 1958 something was happening to the American short-story market. Miss Johnson still was writing and selling fiction, but for previously unpublished sales no year in the late 1950s had produced the kind of results she had enjoyed throughout the 1940s and into 1950. There were abundant sales in the late 50s, but they were previously published stories that were enjoying immense popularity both in European and American anthologies and in European magazines. This trend culminated in 1960, when every story Miss Johnson sold went for reprint rights.[1] Miss Johnson had been slow in recognizing the situation:

"I must have been asleep for a couple of years there. There finally was a realization that I just wasn't selling short stories any more and that maybe I better find something else to do. After all, if you're going to be a writer you have to be published somewhere.

"The realization should have come before it did. A friend who lived in Missoula at that time had published a lot of books for children, but the juvenile field had *such* a cloud over it. It was something people apologized for because a lot of people write

---

[1]Examples: *Indian Country* published in England by Andre Deutsch; *The Hanging Tree* published in England (second time) by Corgi Books; "Scars of Honor" in *Out West*, anthology published in England, and "A Man Called Horse," *Hilton Bedside Book*.

children's books who can't write anything else. As a result, many children's books are bad. It was something I really didn't want to get into, but I went to the children's room at the public library and looked things over and discovered that some very well-known writers were writing children's books.

"I decided it probably wasn't going to ruin any reputation I had acquired if I tried it. I began trying to find out what there might be a market for. I discovered that my agent, with whom I'd been dealing for years, had a special department with a woman who handled only children's books."

That she had not immediately noticed the deteriorating short-story market probably is more attributable to Miss Johnson's schedule than to lack of awareness. Aside from considerable night-time article writing, her duties with the press association and those as an assistant professor of journalism, she had undertaken a vigorous crusade against carbon-monoxide poisoning. Armed with voluminous information she had gathered from highway patrols, the National Safety Council and other agencies, she spoke and wrote frequently on the subject. Among her earliest talks was one on February 22, 1960, to the Missoula Lions Club. She told the group her close call in July 1958 had aroused her anger and that if something that could not be seen or smelled had caused her to crash, it could do the same to other drivers.

"I'm tired of news stories in which a deputy sheriff is quoted as saying the driver must have gone to sleep," she said. "Maybe he did. But if carbon monoxide got him, he went into an abnormal, deadly sleep—total black unconsciousness. And he needn't have died."

Sadness, too, was a part of Miss Johnson's life in 1960. On December 28, two days before her 81st birthday anniversary, Mary Louisa Alger died at Daly Memorial Hospital in Hamilton. From the early 1940s, except for the two and one-half years she had lived in the Stevensville nursing home, she had been a companion and confidante—and the most loyal of fans—to her daughter. For her part, Miss Johnson had sacrificed often to accommodate her mother. Through the years, both had adjusted to the physical and social disadvantages of living together.

For several reasons—namely the need to earn a living and what she considered her responsibilities to her mother—Miss Johnson never had done the traveling she had wanted to do since her girlhood. Thus, in the summer of 1961, she flew to the British Isles and Greece. The latter was the trip's high point:

"I had a wonderful teacher in college named W.P. Clark. He taught Latin and Greek, neither of which I wanted to take because of the horrible time I'd had with Latin in high school.

"I wished later I had taken them. He taught another course called Influence of the Classics on English Literature. I don't remember a thing about it except that he was in love with ancient Greece and he made all of us love it, too. The first time I could afford to go to Europe, Greece was where I wanted to go."

While in Greece, Miss Johnson enlarged by one her fine collection of pistols. She visited the flea market in Athens with a friend, Doreen Magazian, spotted an antique pistol and bought it. Immediately she was confronted with the problem of getting it out of the country:

"When I got back to the hotel I gave the pistol to the desk clerk and asked him to mail it to me in Missoula. He sent it over to the post office with a bell boy, who came back with the news that the post office wouldn't accept it for mailing because it was an archeological treasure. That upset me terribly because I didn't want to lose the money. I wanted to take the gun, but on the other hand I didn't know what they did to people who tried to smuggle something like that out. If it was an archeological treasure they shouldn't have been selling it in the flea market anyhow.

"I hit the roof and phoned everybody I knew who spoke English. They all thought it was terribly funny and they laughed merrily. I remember pacing back and forth in the lobby of the Athenia Palace Hotel with a bell boy by my side patting me and saying, 'There, there, madame, not worry, not worry.' The concierge, kind of a sour fellow, said, 'Madame, why not put it in your suitcase?' I told him the authorities might open it and that I might go to jail. He shrugged his shoulders.

"I paced some more with the help of the bell boy and finally thought, 'Well, a Greek jail is not a place where I want to spend very much time, but maybe nobody will even notice.' This was my first trip and I didn't know how customs operated. Scared to death, I wrapped the pistol in my spare girdle and put it in my suitcase with everything else. Nobody opened the suitcase and nobody cared in Greek Customs. As my Athenian friend said, 'Anything is all right as long as you don't try to steal the Parthenon.'

A tourist with sore feet, Miss Johnson takes five near the Bay of St. Paul and the village of Lindos on the island of Rhodes while on a European trip in the early 1970s.

"When I got to London nobody there opened my suitcase, either. But when I got to the United States, *there*, of course, they made me open them. The customs man started looking through the one and he saw the pistol and his eyes got bigger and bigger. I had it listed with my purchases, so I wasn't trying to sneak anything in. I had unwrapped it from the girdle. Then he said, 'Hey, Joe!' I was frantic. All he wanted from Joe was to know whether this was legally an antique. Joe said it was. I not only got to bring it in but it was not even dutiable."

Miss Johnson flew to Missoula and was back at her press association job the following Monday morning. At about 10 a.m., she looked up from her work and was startled to see a Missoula police officer in her doorway:

"He asked if I was Dorothy Johnson. I said, 'Yes, and whatever it is I didn't do it because I've been out of the country for three weeks.' I saw what he had in his hand and it said 'warrant for arrest' in big, black type. Then I did get scared.

"It turned out he was looking for another Dorothy Johnson, who had 14 unpaid parking tickets. He had stopped in at the print shop on the main floor and the boys there had been very helpful in telling him exactly how to get to my office. When I found out about the parking tickets I was very helpful in telling him where the other Dorothy Johnson lived . . . .

"Having that policeman waltz in there right after I got home had made me think that Interpol had been right on the job."

Early in 1953, Richard Tyre, chairman of the English department of the Germantown, Pennsylvania, Friends School, wrote in a note to teachers and parents at the front of Miss Johnson's *Indian Country*: " 'The Man Who Shot Liberty Valance' is perfect for a Hollywood western and it would make a fine class exercise to turn it into one." Whether Tyre's pupils undertook such a production is not known. However, John Ford did. Ford was a director for Hollywood's Paramount Studio, which had bought "Liberty Valance" from Miss Johnson early in 1961.[2] By October of that year, he and a half dozen stars—John Wayne, James Stewart, Vera

---

[2]Ford won an Oscar in 1935 for "The Informer" and also considerable acclaim for "Stagecoach" and "She Wore a Yellow Ribbon." Before its publication in *Indian Country*, "The Man Who Shot Liberty Valance" had appeared in June 1949 *Cosmopolitan*.

Miles, Lee Marvin, Edmond O'Brien and Lee Van Cleef—were well into the production.[3]

---

[3]Wayne played Tom Doniphon, who Miss Johnson had called Bert Barricune. Stewart played Ranse Stoddard, who Miss Johnson had called Ransome Foster. Marvin played Liberty Valance, a hired gunslinger who is the terror of a western community. The movie was released in April 1962.

John Wayne as Tom Doniphon in *The Man Who Shot Liberty Valance.* The inscription reads, "Dear Dorothy Johnson: Have you any one else you want shot?"

James Stewart, who appeared as Ranse Stoddard in *The Man Who Shot Liberty Valance.*

Lee Marvin as Liberty Valance in *The Man Who Shot Liberty Valance*.

In September 1961, Miss Johnson—with President J.E. Corrette of the Montana Power Company and Frederick Greenwood, a retired banker—received the University of Montana Alumni Distinguished Service Award, given annually during the school's Homecoming activities. The award recognized graduates or former students who, by distinguished service to the university, the state or the nation, had brought honor to the school and to themselves.

Miss Johnson's 10 days in Greece in 1961 convinced her of one thing: She had to return. This she did in the summer of 1962, a trip that resulted in her fifth book, *Greece: Wonderland of the Past and Present.* About the book, an illustrated description of Greece for younger readers, Miss Johnson commented:

> "When I left on the trip I had the book in mind. Although I didn't have a contract, Dodd, Mead was interested. I knew that if I was going to buy pictures for it . . . I'd have to get them in Greece.
>
> "I hunted photographers with the help of a young, English-speaking friend who lives in Athens. I looked through the pictures taken by the man we chose and ordered what I thought would be needed for the book, which wasn't even written. When I told him what I needed, he said he was sorry but he couldn't possibly get all those prints made in the time I had left in Greece. Then, when he started adding up how much he was going to get, he decided he could."

Flying home aboard a Pan American jet, Miss Johnson did a full day's work, using her shorthand notes to write captions for the thick portfolio of photographs she had purchased.

Miss Johnson was not especially pleased with *Greece: Wonderland of the Past and Present* when it was published in 1964. She had not agreed with Dodd, Mead's editor on how it should be written and had felt unduly restricted in its preparation.

Miss Johnson's sixth book, published by Houghton Mifflin in 1964 as a result of her travels to Greece, was a children's novel, *Farewell to Troy.* Using the Trojan War for background and characters, she told of a young grandson of King Priam who, on an odyssey that leads him through ancient Greece, sets out to seek a new Troy. *The Commonweal* called the novel "ringing drama," while the *Chicago Tribune* referred to it as "an excellent book, shot through with humor and so readable that it will delight even those who think they don't like historical fiction." The best "review," perhaps, came from a Springfield, Massachusetts, school boy. His letter, addressed to "Dear Miss Dorothy Johnson," appears exactly as it was written:

> I enjoyed your book thoroughly and I consider it one of the best book I ever read. The detail was excellent and the way the book was set up was good and the plot was exciting. I have read many book of Troy but yours was the best. The duel between Hector and Achilles was discribed beautifully. I am looking for more of your books and hope they are as good as the book I just read, *Farewell to Troy.*
>
> Your fan,
Paul Sandberg

Miss Johnson's enthusiasm for books and libraries had never lagged. If anything, because of the extensive research she did, her reading had increased through the years. This dedication to books started her, in the mid 1960s, on what would become an extended series of talks in behalf of libraries and their resources. She presented one of the first of these in 1964, speaking on April 16 to the Friends of the Great Falls Public Library.[4] The emphasis of her talk was on her belief in the importance of reading—"whether trash or Toynbee."

"I'm here, " she said, "because I'm a friend of the library—just about any library that will let me get at its books."

In June 1964, one of the worst floods in Montana history occurred in the northwestern and north-central portions of the state. The result of unusually heavy snowfall in early May and from two to five inches of rain early in June, the flood claimed 33 lives and caused an estimated $62 million in damage in northwestern Montana alone.

---

[4] Miss Johnson had become an increasingly popular after-dinner speaker. In addition to Friends of the Library talks throughout the state, she was to address groups ranging from the Montana Home Economics Association to a Jaycee chapter at the Montana State Prison. She entitled each of her talks, "How to Get on a Horse." She explained that the title gave her plenty of latitude in preparing her remarks and saved her the trouble of thinking of new titles.

On Monday evening, June 8, Publisher Mel Ruder of *The Hungry Horse News* learned that the flood situation had created a crisis. He telephoned the owner of Station KGEZ in Kalispell so listeners could be alerted, then set out to cover the story. A year later—because of the energy and talent he displayed and because of a nominating letter from Dorothy Johnson—he would win the Pulitzer Prize for local reporting. Some excerpts .from Miss Johnson's letter described both Ruder's coverage and Ruder himself:

> Mel stayed up all night to give bulletins to the radio station, which competes with him for advertising.
>
> He flew over flooded areas in Glacier National Park in a rented plane. When he couldn't rent a plane, he begged a ride in one. He took pictures, developed and printed them in his own darkroom, and had his engravings made in Kalispell, 16 miles away.
>
> Late on press day, he learned that an accident had occurred. He went after the story and had it in print three hours later . . . . His press normally turns out 3,900 copies. This time he ordered 5,800.
>
> The disaster grew. He found a boat and took pictures *in* the flood. He brought out a Saturday paper, too. This time he threw out the advertising. He dedicated himself to covering the news for his readers.
>
> On some of his news-and-picture expeditions he drove his car on the railroad track because the road was washed out.
>
> Mel covered the story for Associated Press and telephoned late news to some of the dailies.
>
> On Monday, *The Hungry Horse News* came out for the third time in one week with more news. After his two printers had run a total of 12,550 copies for that week, Mel started working on the *next* Friday's paper . . . .
>
> Mel's pictures make other photographers envious. For him, the shadows, the mountain goats and even the mountains somehow move around into the right place! Of course to achieve this, he ventures into some untenable positions with his heavy press camera . . . .
>
> When Mel started his own newspaper, he had never worked on one. He had $4,000 saved from his Navy pay and employment with Westinghouse, but that wasn't enough to buy a paper in a thriving town. He saw an opportunity in Columbia Falls, where four previous newspapers had failed; he took a chance that the construction of Hungry Horse Dam would bring at least temporary prosperity. Later, when the dam was finished, he could have been finished, too, but he had worked hard and long to bring an

aluminum plant—permanent industry—to Columbia Falls. He deserves credit not only for a good newspaper but for reviving a community that for decades had been half dead.

Ruder never learned who placed second in the 1965 Pulitzer competition for local reporting. He still believes, however, that the judging was so close that Miss Johnson's letter made the difference.

"It was a fine, fine letter," he said. "She had a sense of the dramatic and nobody else could have written that letter."

In the summer of 1965 Miss Johnson went to Europe for the third time. On a jet somewhere between Lisbon and London—and then at the latter's Strand Palace Hotel—she recorded some impressions of her travels. Her comments appeared in *Montana Fourth Estate* under the headline "Notes on the Fourth of July":

The Portuguese captain of this plane just said the temperature in London is 50 degrees. That'll be a nice change. Last week in Seville it was 122. I considered trying to sneak back into the cathedral after dark to sleep on the floor near the metal casket that holds the bones of the late Christopher Columbus. It was probably only 110 degrees there.

I've eaten cous-cous in Morocco, barnacles in Lisbon, ripe figs in Algeciras (they taste like sunshine), kangaroo-tail soup in Amsterdam and so much chicken that I'm haunted by indignant clucking. It will be good to get home to my own haphazard cooking and enough green salad.

Too bad barnacles are so scarce in Montana. They're served in a great clump, boiled in sea water. You twist off the top of each one and reveal an object like a stout rubber band. It tastes a lot better than it looks.

The stewardess just said we're over the Bay of Biscay.

Spain has seen the last of me, but Portugal is a dream. An old lady helped me across a busy street in Lisbon, lecturing volubly about (I suppose) the hazards of traffic.

Next time I feel sorry for myself because there are so many Dorothy Johnsons, I'll remember that Maria Duarte has worse problems. I counted 84 of her in the Lisbon telephone directory!

Thirty-five minutes to London. Land—the British Isles?—has appeared dimly down below, along with a rainbow.

Just read an international edition of the *New York Times*. Good to know what the problems are back home in America. Got a London paper last week, but can't tell which side to be on in their public fights.

Two more days and I can find out what's going on in Montana.

Reading matter got so scarce that I was reduced to trying to translate travel folders in Portuguese.

Four objects below are certainly ships, so we aren't over land. Presumably the plane captain knows where he's going.

Wish I'd studied geography harder back in the Whitefish Public Schools. But the boundaries have changed anyway, principal products always bored me and we even seem to have more continents than I recall memorizing.

Land ahead, and we're slanting down. But in England I'll still be a foreigner.

London Airport: In Madrid the other day there was sudden flurry at the airport and squeals of "Beatles! Beatles!" Debarking from a flight coming in from Paris were a dozen businessmen trying to look unassociated with the entourage surrounding some hairy apparitions that were, I suppose, Beatles.

Here, the observation roof is jammed with waiting watchers, and a big sign says, "I say, it's absolutely spiffing to have you home again, chaps."

Strand Palace Hotel: Four years ago I decided that Brown's Hotel was too grand for me. Now I think that nothing is, really. This one is just as expensive, but the service is poor and the hall porter is surly.

A head waiter seated a bunch of us colonials together—two women from Pennsylvania heading for Russia, three from Austreyelia escaping their winter by heading for North America, and me. The Australians' travel agent has them booked into Buffalo for three days, poor things. It takes half a day at most to look at Niagara Falls.

Maybe I'm tipping too low or too high, but I cannot figure any percentage of shillings and pence or even identify the coins here. The Australians said they're changing to the decimal system next year. South Africa has already done it very successfully.

Trafalgar Square: Fountains, pigeons and Lord Nelson in well-earned bronze majesty on an immensely high column. At the column's base is a swarm of teenagers who resemble maggots more than any other human beings I've ever seen.

They all wear pants, shoulder-length hair and no makeup. You can't tell the gruesome boys from the ghastly girls. Was it to produce horrors like these that their parents suffered through six years of war?

A public meeting is in progress, quietly guarded by dozens of competent-looking bobbies. There are lots of banners. Several identify chapters of the Young Communist League. One says "Anarchists Against Tyranny." A neglected elderly fellow in a business suit has a sign advising "Get ready—Jesus is coming."

A man with an American accent is making a rabble-rousing

speech over a p.a. system. He says his name is Cipriano and he's from San Francisco. He's talking about "President Johnson's barbarous war in Vietnam" and saying that the press of the United States is distorting the facts.

Listen . . . . Why, that scoundrel is attacking my country—and his—on its birthday! Here's what I wish for him: That he should spend the rest of his life wanting to go home and never getting there.

Last Independence Day, at the Indian Pow-Wow at Arlee, I heard Chief Walking Mouse make a good patriotic speech.

Strand Palace Hotel: Down, blood pressure. Let's think of pleasanter things. Not of the Emperatriz Hotel in Madrid, where I waited six hours in the lobby to get into the room they had reserved, but of the funny Barbary apes on Gibraltar and how every guide on a 12-day bus tour appeared right on schedule.

Of the Arabs at Xauen in Morocco, straight out of National Geographic, and the tourist who muttered, "I've seen at least half the Forty Thieves already." Of the chanting that woke me there around three in the morning so I thought a bunch of the boys had decided to charm a cobra, but it was only the muezzin at the mosque, calling the Moslem faithful to prayer.

Of the man in jellabah and fez who said in Tangiers, "Come wiz me to ze Casbah," so I went, with six other ladies, and it turned out to be the king's palace but he wasn't home.

Of flying from Vancouver to Amsterdam in nine hours and looking down on Iceland. Probably the Icelanders love it. Of two busy, happy days in Amsterdam collecting material for a magazine article with the help of competent hostesses from the local tourist bureau.

Not of the horrors of bull fights but of the reflection that this is some improvement over the Inquisition, during which thousands of people were burned to death in the name of God in the public square of Madrid. Of the charm of Portugal and a fairy-tale castle at Pena that should be used for a movie set.

Of the occasions when my scraps of Spanish actually worked, but not of those when somebody responded with a volley of which I couldn't understand one word. Of the time when, wanting my two red suitcases (maletas), I bewildered a porter by demanding two red lards (matecas).

Nine o'clock, and it's not dark yet here in England. Fourth of July, and of course the heating system doesn't work, so I'll go to bed wearing the sweater I bought four years ago today in Edinburgh. Tomorrow I'll go home. What a lovely place that is!

Miss Johnson's seventh book, a series of short biographies about frontier women entitled *Some Went West*, was in stores by the fall of

1965. Published by Dodd, Mead and written for girls, *Some Went West* was well received by critics and customers alike. Kenneth Hufford commented in the *Christian Science Monitor*:

> In this book . . . Miss Johnson vividly tells the stories of a number of courageous women who made the arduous trip west . . . . She gives an excellent description of wagon train travel and the grueling daily chores which these women took for granted . . . .

Montana, The Magazine of Western History published a review by Therese Westermeier, a former instructor at the University of Colorado and author of several articles concerning the social history of the West. Describing the book as "delightful and highly narrative," she commented:

> Miss Johnson has a distinctive feminine flair for portraying the woman's angle, which makes for a very sympathetic understanding of the countless "little things" so dear to a woman's heart, whether she lives in luxury or in a log cabin.

With a note telling her to "pray that the newspaper strike doesn't spoil things," Rosemary Casey of Dodd, Mead sent Miss Johnson a copy of a review scheduled for *The New York Times*:

> *Some Went West*, built on solid research and not fictionalized at all, treats of a variety of female pioneers . . . . By including a wealth of significant detail and drawing heavily on her heroine's own stories, the author admirably recreates the early West from a feminine viewpoint . . . .

Although the review did not make the *Times*, sales of *Some Went West* continued to run high enough to elicit another memo from Rosemary Casey:

> SING OUT FOR BOOKS! For *Some Went West* in particular. Enclosed find the fourth and fifth major reviews on this book, and all favorable. Think we could do a *Some More Went West*, or *Some Went Wester*? I'm just as pleased as I can be, and so happy for you.[5]

---

[5]She gave the manuscript of *Some Went West* to the University of Montana Friends of the Library for the Northwest history collection. Her eighth book, *Flame on the Frontier*, was published in July 1967. It contained short stories of pioneer women. All but one—"Virginia City Winter"—had been published before ("Flame on the Frontier," "Journey to the Fort," "Beyond the Frontier," "Lost Sister," "A Wonderful Woman" and "A Woman of the West").

Just as she had been doing since the early 1930s, Miss Johnson continued to do her own writing at night. By 1966 she had turned almost exclusively to articles and books owing to the decline in the short-story market:

> "*Collier's* and *The Saturday Evening Post* had competed vigorously for short fiction. They competed by paying substantial sums of money to writers. But *Collier's* died, and the *Post* almost did. In its convulsive effort to maintain life, the *Post* changed its editorial policy violently and often.
> "It went in for stories I didn't want to read, let alone write. And there was *Cosmopolitan*, never a top market, but it did buy a story of mine occasionally. . . . The magazine's whole function now is to advise its female readers how to trap the wily male, and since a lot of women want to know, *Cosmopolitan* is prospering without me."

Among Miss Johnson's last short stories to appear in a major American magazine was "The Ten-Pound Box of Candy," published in the April 1966 issue of *McCall's*.[6]

Miss Johnson had written "The Ten-Pound Box of Candy" several years earlier but had added it to her "lost cause" file in the belief that it was too long. She had to rewrite it, but the effort brought a $2,000 check.

Had it not been for physical ailments, Miss Johnson might have continued for several more years the pace she had set in 1953. Although the thought had occurred to her, it was her doctor who finally told her she would have to reduce her activity with the press association, the School of Journalism (where she continued to teach the magazine sequence), or in her writing. To Miss Johnson, one thing was indispensable:

> "I couldn't quit writing; that was what I was working for. I just couldn't give that up . . . . I decided to quit the press association but to continue teaching. I didn't see how I could afford to drop my entire assured income. Those paychecks coming in regularly were awfully nice."

Making it clear she would remain until the executive committee found a replacement, Miss Johnson resigned as secretary-manager

---

[6]Her previously published stories continued to enjoy great popularity in foreign magazines and numerous anthologies. In addition, *Indian County* was in its third printing in England.

of the press association in December 1966.

On March 22, 1967, Helen M. Peterson of Hardin, then president of the association, announced that Robert E. Miller of Helena would take over the post. Miller, who retired April 1 as editor of the *Helena Independent Record*, began his duties April 15 and the association's offfice was moved to Helena.

In March, Miss Johnson had assembled the material for her final issue of *Montana Fourth Estate*. The issue appeared in April and contained an editorial in which "Aunt Dorothy" said goodby:

> This is my last issue of *Montana Fourth Estate*. My first one was April 1953 and I forgot to put my name on the masthead.
>
> Now, in my 169th issue, I don't mind admitting that I write poor heads (this is not just my own prejudiced opinion) and have no talent for pasting up a dummy.
>
> But I'm going to miss a privilege that I've enjoyed for fourteen years—that of sounding off in print with nobody to warn, "You shouldn't say that!"
>
> I'll miss more about this job than editing the magazine, but let's be brief about that lest I drip a tear and you-all catch on that Aunt Dorothy loves you.
>
> Robert E. Miller, MPA's new secretary-manager, called his final editorial in the *Helena Independent Record* "We Lay Down Our Pen."
>
> George Remington, his successor there, called his first editorial "We Take Up Our Pen."
>
> Bob Miller will pick up his pen again with the May issue of *Fourth Estate*.
>
> Don't let any of us kid you. Messrs. Miller and Remington actually use typewriters, like anybody else. And although I'm calling this a swan song, I sing like an English sparrow.
>
> *Dorothy Johnson*

Because her health had continued to deteriorate, Miss Johnson also resigned from the University faculty in June 1967. There was no particular income problem since, to supplement her numerous royalties, Miss Johnson had purchased stocks and various rental properties in Missoula.

The sentiments of John F. Kavanagh and Richard A. Mauritson of *The Shelby* (Montana) *Promoter* were typical of publishers throughout the state as Miss Johnson stepped down:

This week is indeed a regrettable one for members of the Montana Press Association. The association's secretary-manager, Dorothy M. Johnson, well-known Montana author, journalism teacher and a good friend to all newspapermen, will drop the reins of her dedicated work on behalf of the *Fourth Estate* and devote full time to writing more great books.

"Aunt Dorothy" . . . has delighted press association members with her wit, gaiety and fervor at meetings, in weekly bulletins and in the association's monthly magazine . . . .

She will be greatly missed, but we look forward to her future published works, which are sure to be among the greatest.

In her 14 years with the press association and 13 with the University of Montana, Miss Johnson earned the esteem of friends and colleagues. Billings cartoonist Stan Lynde, creator of Rick O'Shay, thought highly of her work long before he met her in a Billings hotel during one of her 1964 speaking engagements:

"Dorothy has a remarkable mind, great talent and a really amazing understanding of people. Her writing seems to me not so much the telling of stories, but the sharing of personal experience. Her male characters ring as true to me as do her females, a rare gift in women writers.

"I think Dorothy is one of the finest writers of western fiction I've ever read. She writes the kind of fiction that is told so truly that it often becomes more 'true'—or better reflects how it really was—than actual historical fact . . . . "

Commented Helen Peterson of the Hardin (Montana) *Tribune-Herald:*

"I knew Dorothy Johnson only by correspondence before the Montana Press Association convention of 1959, held in Yellowstone Park just after Montana's most recent and destructive earthquake.

"I had just come back to the newspaper business after a ten-year 'vacation. . . .' I felt a little strange in the business and just a little green—and I was in awe of Dorothy.

"The awe vanished long before the convention was over. But the admiration I have for her has been growing ever since. Nothing daunted her—not the earthquake (which was still shaking us up a little), not even the fact that a fire started in the Lake Hotel right in the middle of a business meeting. Her hands might tremble a little, but her voice was steady as a rock. No matter what happened, Dorothy managed to say something that made it awfully funny . . . . Certainly a bat that invaded her room one year at East

Glacier . . . didn't ruffle her composure. She'd gotten a choice room at the hotel and was soon commenting that she supposed the bat was just another special feature . . . .

"Aunt Dorothy scolded her editors (as circumstances warranted), stiffened their spines and often encouraged them to do just a little better than they had been doing before. No matter what you did, Dorothy was there with a pat on the back.

"She is one of the best one-woman audiences I've ever encountered, and she could be depended on to say the one thing that would bolster your ego the most . . . .

"Dorothy has met illness with great courage and she's overcome some tremendous obstacles. Through it all she's kept the most delightful sense of humor to be found anywhere in the continental limits of the United States—or in Alaska or Hawaii for that matter . . . .

"Though I lost my awed feeling in Dorothy's presence, I certainly didn't lose my respect for her. . . ."

Virginia Gehrett, wife of Publisher J.O. Gehrett of *The Silver State Post* in Deer Lodge, commented:

"Dorothy Johnson was our house guest on the occasion of her talk to prisoners at our state institution . . . . She had a full-time audience in our three children. She didn't let them down. The dinner hour was consumed with stories of Liver Eating Johnson and other non-gastronomical characters . . . . It seems rare to find a person with her story-telling ability who also could handle as 'rare' and diversified group as Montana's newspapermen with tact and patience. . . ."

Professor Warren J. Brier, named dean of the Montana School of Journalism in 1968, met Miss Johnson when he joined the school's staff in 1962:

"She did not match the image of the woman I had conjured up in my mind, the writer of western stories. I think it was because she was smaller and a little older. Somehow she didn't look like the kind of person who would be writing about gun fights and so on . . . . The first thing I ever read that she wrote . . . was an article in the first *Montana Journalism Review*, a history of Montana's first newspaper, *The Montana Post*. It was a fascinating article and she had dispelled several myths about the paper . . . . As to historical accuracy, her research is magnificent and greatly detailed. I have an idea that for any book she has written she probably found enough material for three books. She simply refines it and takes the best of it."

Brier said Miss Johnson usually was the final authority when differences of opinion arose in the journalism school over points of writing, grammar and editing:

"Dorothy always had the definitive answer, in my opinion. When these controversies would come up, I would immediately go down to her office for her viewpoint. That was good enough for me because she knew her writing . . . . There was no question about it."

In Brier's opinion, Miss Johnson's greatest contribution to the School of Journalism was her experience:

"She was teaching magazine article writing, and while she was teaching it she was practicing it. She was selling articles, books and short stories. . . . Her eminence as an authority on the subject was such that you couldn't question it. You couldn't even begin to question it because she could wave a $2,500 check at you . . . . Other than her experience, just having her around was delightful. She always seemed to be in good humor and always had a funny story to tell. It was fun being around her . . . . She was always busy, too. In the entire time I knew her around the school, I don't believe I ever saw her when she wasn't occupied . . . . "

Nathaniel B. Blumberg, former dean of the school, commented on Miss Johnson's writing:

"Her greatest virtue is simplicity—very simple sentences and direct, marvelous control of mood, environment and characterization . . . . She eliminates unnecessary words and has a crisp, clear style."

He said of her years in the journalism school and the press association:

"She made it possible for the school to offer a highly qualified instructor in the magazine sequence without having to take on someone else to handle other areas. We needed versatility on the staff and she took the magazine sequence requirements off our hands . . . .

"As secretary-manager of the press association, she often smoothed over ruffled feelings and eliminated misunderstandings that would crop up between members of the state's press and the School of Journalism . . . .

"Dorothy has very strong feelings about Montana. She was

gone for years, but she wasn't one of those hypocrites who talk about what a marvelous place Montana is but somehow manage to live elsewhere. Dorothy came back. She's a real Montanan who feels very much at home here. I think everybody feels very much at home with her, too."

During her years on the campus, Miss Johnson frequently hiked and played hearts with a group of faculty members that included Professor Robert M. Burgess. Burgess commented:

"Dorothy was a regular hearts player for a long time. We played during the noon hour. You could always hear Dorothy laughing. . . . How she loves to laugh! Some people laugh but it is not out of mirth. When Dorothy laughs she is really amused. She had a wonderful laugh and always was fun to be around."

If Miss Johnson was slowing her pace, it was not noticeable. On May 5, 1967, she was in Jackson, Wyoming, to address a tri-state library conference. Two weeks later she was in Banff, Alberta, Canada, to speak to delegates to the Centennial Conference on the History of the Canadian West. Within two months of that speech, her next book, *Witch Princess*, was receiving favorable reviews. Published by Houghton-Mifflin, it was followed the same year by *Flame on the Frontier*, published by Dodd, Mead.

Miss Johnson in the early 1960s.

Miss Johnson was proud of her pistol collection.

CHAPTER FOURTEEN

The Gentle Critic

AGAZINE EDITORS WERE NOT THE ONLY persons with whom Dorothy Johnson conferred before returning to Montana in the fall of 1950. She also wrote to several New York newspaper book-review editors offering her services as a reviewer of books about the West. Despite *Beulah Bunny Tells All*, some 35 short stories and dozens of articles to her credit, she was not considered widely enough known and was ignored. Only after the publication of - *Indian Country* three years later did the situation change. Requests for her opinions began mounting.

Among the first books Miss Johnson reviewed were Howard Pecklam's *Captured by Indians* and Daniel W. Whetstone's *Frontier Editor*. She reviewed both for *Montana, The Magazine of Western History*, the former in July 1955, the latter in the Winter 1957 edition. Excerpts from her commentary on *Frontier Editor* illustrate the tone of her subsequent reviews:

> This is not just another book of personal reminiscences by another country editor—it is a history of economic change written by a man who was and is keenly aware of the meaning of events. The Cutbank *Pioneer Press* has recorded up-and-down history, near ruin, and present prosperity . . . .
>
> Seldom does a book of facts contain so many good stories of oddballs and their antics as does this one. The stories about real people (who presumably won't sue the author because they are either illiterate or dead) make *Frontier Editor* brisk reading even for those who don't care much about history. This is a hell-for-leather, ripsnortin', really readable book about the dramatic interim years between open range rascality and "civilized" respectability which allegedly followed. It's as fresh and warm as next spring's chinook!

When Miss Johnson reviewed fiction, she studied the characters to see if they seemed real. She had to determine if the story sounded plausible. It was the exception, not the rule, for her to severely criticize an author's efforts. In most of her reviews, she seems to have remembered the adage, "If you can't say something nice about someone, don't say anything at all." Miss Johnson said:

> "There was one book I didn't like one bit but I never did say the nasty things I was thinking. The book reviewer has such tremendous power and can ruin a writer. I don't want to ruin any writer. If the tone of my reviews usually indicates that the books are well done, it fortunately is because that is the kind I usually get.
>
> "Once, though, I refused to do a review because the book was so bad. I just didn't want to have anything to do with it. I'd rather refuse a review than write a scathing one about a bad book. Writing a review is particularly hard if the author happens to be someone I know. This has happened once in awhile. In that case, when I write or wire the editors, I warn them that this is a friend of mine. I let them decide, although usually they say to go ahead anyway.
>
> "In one sense, I have to review books. I feel an obligation not to crush the author, especially if he is a new one. But I also feel an obligation to tell the reader what I really think about a book. Presumably my opinion counts or the editor wouldn't ask me. It's a delicate situation and I don't like it."

One of the few books Miss Johnson disliked was John Williams' novel *Butcher's Crossing.* She thought it was "detestable" and commented:

> "The jacket blurb said it was about a young man who went out to shoot buffalo to find himself. Well, he didn't find himself; he started out an absolute neurotic and he was still one when the book ended.
>
> "He hadn't found anything except a few buffalo. I was disgusted with it because I think people like that are the product of contemporary civilization. I don't think an author should put a 20th century man back into the 19th century."

In her review, she made her point but also managed to compliment Williams: "The author has a truly creative imagination. His descriptions are spectacular."

Miss Johnson also was unsympathetic toward August Derleth's novel *The Hills Stand Watch.* For the *New York Herald Tribune Book*

Review, she wrote, in part:

There is plenty of plot and action, but none of it is very convincing because the people are not. Because they lack reality, adultery does not seem reprehensible (or inevitable, except that the plot requires it), death by fire does not seem terrible, and passion is just something to read about.

She then wrote to the *Herald Tribune*'s book review editor, Irita Van Doren:

April 29, 1960

Dear Miss Van Doren:

I don't want this review of August Derleth's book to sound snippy, but it is not a good book. He has gone through the motions conscientiously, but his characters are cardboard.

Years ago I used to dote on his fantastic stories about werewolves and monsters from the deep. It's too bad he went legitimate. Don't quote me!

In reviewing Professor K. Ross Toole's *Montana, An Uncommon Land,* Miss Johnson demonstrated she could be funny as well as firm:

The most uncommon thing about Montana, you will learn from this book, is its politics. Compared with Montana's political fights, the Custer Massacre (to which the author gives a dutiful paragraph) was as momentous as a free-for-all on a grade school playground . . . .

When Toole gets to the copper kings—William A. Clark, Marcus Daly and F. Augustus Heinze—and politics, he really chews the scenery. This is obviously what he was leading up to. He doesn't much like the Anaconda Company or its predecessors.

"The Company" has been criticized and "exposed" many times in print and, as far as I know, defended only once, in *Anaconda,* by Isaac F. Marcosson (Dodd, Mead, 1957). Mr. Marcosson wrote the company's corporate biography with admiration akin to awe, like a Renaissance public-relations man doing a Sunday feature on the current Borgia. There must be a tale to tell that would come somewhere between crusading attack and reverent defense.

The author stretches the facts when he says, "Today Montana's daily press is still owned and controlled by the. Anaconda Company." When he wrote, six dailies were, of the nine dailies, including the very influential *Great Falls Tribune.*

Miss Johnson was sharply criticized for one review. After some persuasion from Dr. Robert G. Athearn, book review editor of *Montana, The Magazine of Western History*, she agreed to critique Richard Lancaster's *Piegan*, a book dealing with Chief White Calf of the Piegan Blackfeet.

"Yes, indeed, I'll be delighted to review *Piegan*," she told Athearn in a letter dated September 15, 1966. "I've been away from it long enough now so that I'm no longer mad at the author."

Miss Johnson, who was Rocky Mountain regional editor for *Montana*, wrote in her review:

> The author adores James White Calf, age 109, the man the book is about, but has a tendency to sneer at most other Indians, including some outstanding men on the Blackfeet Reservation. This makes me mad, and I trust that the men he undercuts will read this book and get equally mad.
>
> Putting aside my personal animosity toward Mr. Lancaster for taking cracks at some of my Blackfeet friends, I must say that this is a very lively, informative and sometimes hilariously funny book. I'll even try to ignore his use of Blackfoots as a plural.
>
> Mr. Lancaster lived in James White Calf's home, recorded his stories, asked the right questions to get illuminating answers, and kept a perceptive journal. His book is about the good old days recalled by his aged informant and about the bad new days as observed by the author himself. It is a rich mixture (and by mixture I don't imply that it's disorderly) of history, anthropology, folklore and current social and economic problems.
>
> The author's specialty is linguistics. He went to the Blackfeet (Blackfoots?) to study the language. He's way beyond most of us in his use of esoteric English, too. What is a "fulgent, smaragdine smile"? What is "sequacious"? What is a "thick, sciuroid tail of dust"? No, no, don't tell me. I'd rather just worry about it.
>
> This is a man with firm opinions and strong feeling about everything he thinks about. So this *is* a good book.

The spring, 1968 edition of *Montana* contained a letter from Nancy McLaughlin, a reader from Sequim, Washington, and the illustrator of Lancaster's book:

> Re: Dorothy Johnson's review of *Piegan* by Richard Lancaster in your Autumn issue, 1967: I was both surprised and disgusted that Miss Johnson had obviously not read the book thoroughly before reviewing it. I can find no other excuse for her statement that Mr. Lancaster "has a tendency to sneer at most other Indians." Certainly the book's introduction explained the author's use of

the term "Blackfoots" which perturbed Miss J. Perhaps the explanation lies in her apparent inability to use the dictionary: e.g., "what is 'sequacious'?"

I find it gratifying, however, that she at last conceded *Piegan* was "a good book," since among its many other awards, it was selected to grace the American Library Association's list of 60 notable books published internationally in 1966 and goes into a French language edition this year.

Having had the honor to illustrate this fine book and having therefore worked closely with Mr. Lancaster and his many Blackfoot friends, I find he has more empathy, truth and sincerity with Indians than ANY white person I have known. Consequently, I am looking forward to his future publications as he continues to work among the Bloods, Piegans, and "Blackfoots."

Miss McLaughlin was only guessing, of course, that Miss Johnson had "not read the book thoroughly before reviewing it." Her guess was wrong. Miss Johnson explained her technique in reviewing books:

> "I read every book at least twice and maybe more than that. I read it the first time and make notes as I go. Then I look back to see what those notes mean. In writing the review, which I do four or five times, I go back again. It's an awful job for such a small piece of writing and such low pay.
>
> "Of course, for *Montana* magazine I do reviews for love. They don't pay at all. The others pay me $25 to $50, which is not very much money if you have to spend four or five days on the review. Maybe I'm not very competent; maybe I shouldn't spend that much time, but I do."

Miss Johnson began reviewing books for *Saturday Review* in 1958. In discussing *Crow Killer*, the gory history of a legendary Montana character named Liver-Eating Johnson, she wrote:

> Jim Bridger, John Colter, Kit Carson—these and a few other trappers are known to everyone who cares enough about the great days of the frontier to read about them. These men had biographers. Until now Liver-Eating Johnson has had none. He has been a shadow, mentioned casually in obscure reminiscences, with most of the details wrong.
>
> However, thanks to the patient scholarship (and admirably dramatic writing) of Raymond W. Thorp and Robert Bunker, he emerges as flesh and blood, with the emphasis on blood. Liver-Eating Johnson was not the kind of frontiersman whose adventures can be prettied up for children's stories or television shows.

His story is the material from which grand opera might be made, except that Richard Wagner died too soon.

The mountain men were the violent, heroic, doomed gods of the American frontier, and their Valhalla was the Rocky Mountains.

About Don Berry's novel *Trask,* Miss Johnson wrote what perhaps was her most complimentary review:

> The most exciting book I have read in years. Very few writers can evoke truly a time and a way of life that they have experienced only in imagination. Once in a long while this controlled dreaming, which makes real what never happened, creates a novel that can be called great. This is the kind of imagination that Don Berry has.
>
> At the age of 27, he has produced a book which I must call great . . . . The narrative begins quietly, gently, and increases in suspense until it has the power of an avalanche . . . . Here is all manner of conflict, and triumph of the most admirable kind.

Miss Johnson's humor often was present in her reviews, as shown by a comment in her critique of *The Book of the American West* for the *New York Herald Tribune* and its syndicate: "This volume is impressive for bulk, beauty and scope, but it will never be popular for reading in bed. A reclining reader risks internal injuries."

Miss Johnson sometime found reviewing books difficult because of the rush involved:

> "The editors wire you and give you just a few days. They ask you if you will review such and such, which you've never heard of, of course. Maybe you've never even heard of the author. And they have to have the review by a certain date.
>
> "Some of them don't realize that Missoula, Montana, is not right across the river from New York City. It takes awhile for the book to get out here.
>
> "Then you search your soul to see if you can drop everything else for a few days in order to read the book and write the review. With *Saturday Review* they don't even send the book. They send the galley proofs, great long things tied up with string. This is not the easiest way to read a book. Usually they are not corrected and you keep running across errors that worry you. Sometimes the preface, which may be very important to you, is not with it."

By the end of 1968, Miss Johnson had reviewed more than 40

books of the West for the *New York Herald Tribune Book Review* and *Book Week, Saturday Review, Oregon Historical Quarterly* and *Montana, The Magazine of Western History*.

"Usually there isn't time to do much outside research for reviews," she said. "Editors assume when they choose a reviewer that he already has some background. Occasionally, I find myself very much handicapped by not knowing what an author has done before. When that happens, I just have to struggle along."

Miss Johnson

CHAPTER FIFTEEN

Dorothy Johnson on Writing

Youth passes, and youth was short for Marjory.
One day last summer I saw her,
And her face was old in the sunlight—
Marjory, old at nineteen!
In two long years we had never spoken,
And she had been married.
She lost her beauty in those two gray years
Cooking over a rusty kitchen range,
Slaving her life away for a fool,
The slack-mouthed idler she married—
All because her dying mother had made her promise.
Oh, the dead have no right to bind us,
Us, who have our young lives to live!

THUS BEGINS "MARJORY" IN THE MARCH 1924 issue of *The Frontier*. Some observers consider the poem—based on an emotional experience while she was in high school—the best product of Dorothy Johnson's brief career as a poet. The deep emotion underlying "Marjory" is important in understanding Miss Johnson's philosophy of writing. To her, good writing is born of emotion. In an interview granted Kathryn Wright of *The Billings* (Montana) *Gazette*, she discussed the subject:

> "The important thing is that the short story starts with an emotion in the writer. At least mine do. And other writers I've talked with say the same. A writer should feel strongly about something. Strongly enough . . . to want to communicate that feeling to others. I start with an emotion. Then I try to think of people—characters—who might fit that emotion. People who

would have logical connection with it. Then these people make the plot. I don't think about the plot first. I find an emotion. Probably through seeing something—people, maybe—or hearing something, or learning something. It's harder that way. Maybe. But that's the way I do it. Inefficient, perhaps. It's hard work. You get calluses off a typewriter just like off a shovel."

In an article, "Emotion and the Fiction Writer," Miss Johnson wrote that while she never had tried classifying her emotions, those most useful to her in fiction writing were pity and admiration:

"We pity someone because of the situation he's in, and we admire him because of the action he takes. It might be wise for every fiction writer to decide what kind of people he admires, and why. Some fiction I have tried to read lately indicates that the authors thereof don't admire or pity anybody. I don't see how their characters can stand them or one another.

"A fiction writer must be willing to feel. He must accept his own emotions, not trying to evade them. Then he must learn to extend them to purely imaginary people, the people he invents."

There are other emotions, however: "Once in awhile, it's whatever emotion it is that makes you giggle. Then I write a really funny story, one like 'I Woke Up Wicked.' I don't know what emotion that one would be but it's a kind of feeling in the pit of your stomach that makes you want to laugh out loud."

That compassion figured in Miss Johnson's short stories is indicated by a comment from the late Dr. Harold G. Merriam, her English professor at the University of Montana: "The tendency . . . was for her to reveal conditions of working people. I remember one story . . . called 'The Fruit Tramps' in which she shows great sympathy for the working class. That probably has been characteristic of her throughout her life."

Apparently Professor Merriam's evaluation is correct, judging from Miss Johnson's comments about Washington's Okanogan Valley migrant workers who inspired the story: "I felt sorry for them because people were always talking about them in Okanogan during the fruit season. Everybody was suspicious of them because they were a footloose lot . . . . People at that time who stayed in one place were suspicious of wanderers."

In a series of lectures delivered in 1959 at Concordia College in

Moorhead, Minnesota, Miss Johnson described whom she admired and therefore chose to bring to life in her stories: "I like to write about Indians and the rugged characters of frontier days. I admire physical courage. Perhaps one reason is that I am not endowed with courage myself."

She stressed the importance of research—asking questions and reading: "You must be willing to bother. You must be explicit in what you write. The writer owes the reader answers to all questions, but the writer must first think of the questions."

Human actions or deeds Miss Johnson could not comprehend or identify with—actions for which she felt genuine disgust—affected her sympathy, altering it to the pity of contempt or transforming it to an emotion that precluded creation of a story. Once, while in the Missoula County sheriff's office to get fingerprinted for a pistol permit, her sympathy was aroused by an impoverished young man and woman being released after a night in jail. Miss Johnson became concerned about the couple's apparently limited resources—48 cents, a wallet, a comb and a marriage license—and the next day phoned a deputy to see if a modest fund could be established to help others leaving jail needing a stake. When the deputy told her why the two had been detained (they had damaged the home of an old woman who was in the hospital), the emotion that might have given birth to a story was transformed. Miss Johnson wrote:

> I cannot understand the young couple who did that. Therefore, I cannot write a story about them or anyone like them. I pity them, against my better judgment, and wonder what made them into monsters. The strange thing is that I can understand armed robbery and even murder without having tried either one. I can write about outlaws and killers, identifying myself with them. But young, attractive people who commit wanton vandalism I cannot understand or write about. From this experience. . . there remains my unwilling pity, but I cannot translate it from life to a story.

Miss Johnson once said that "fiction writers tend to reach out for new experiences and variations on emotions, because these are the seeds of stories. We need a store of these for future use, a private little granary. If we ever use them all up, how can we write anything more?" She used an anecdote to illustrate her point, then explained its significance:

When I was about eleven, I went with a small group of people to a town 15 miles from home. That was quite an excursion. We traveled by bus . . . and took a basket lunch for economy's sake. Then we had to find a place to eat, and the place we found was somebody's front yard.

I have never forgotten the people who invited us to have our lunch in their yard. They were a very old couple, cordial and eager. They shared with us what they had, rhubarb sauce. It was very sour. After we left them, I mentioned this, wondering why they hadn't put sugar in it, and someone explained quietly, "They're so poor they can't afford sugar."

Then, as even now, that understanding had a strong emotional impact. Not even sugar to sweeten the sauce made from rhubarb they raised—but they gave strangers some of what they had . . . .

These were old people, with a bleak present and very little future. They were wonderful people. I could write a story about people like them. They seem real . . . whereas the young vandals do not.

What I have told about these old people . . . is the kind of thing from which a story might develop when the emotion is translated from fact to fiction. There is no real beginning—we just happened to ask permission to eat in their yard. There is no end—we never heard another thing about them.

If a writer used that emotional experience as a seed for a story, he might change every single thing in the actual event. He need not be bound by facts at all. He might not even use the emotional realization he started with. He would start with that bit of heartbreak and go anywhere his thoughts took him. But if he made a story from it, it would have some meaning that it doesn't have now.

A fiction writer translates his emotions and creates people. This is why he writes. He *becomes* these people, and this is sometimes a tormenting experience. I have been Indian warriors and cowboys and homesteaders' wives and gold miners and captives of Indians. I have been bloody-handed outlaws and the grim men who strung them up, the victim and the victor, and pursued and the pursuer. I have been defeated and triumphant—but never "beat." Twice I have been killed.

A writer who creates characters is every one of them. This is probably why writers write. They get away from their own little world with its known dangers into a boundless great world where anything can happen. They live vicariously a thousand lives.

This is the finest kind of adventuring. There is no escape from reality so splendid as the escape of a writer dreaming over a sheet of paper.

In an article for a handbook on writing, Miss Johnson remembered the time she was lost in a swamp. Having read that three gunshots were an SOS, she drew the .38 revolver she was carrying, fired three rounds and "stood around waiting expectantly for somebody to come plunging through the woods" to lead her out. Nobody came. After a reasonable wait, Miss Johnson, "avoiding the sinkholes," retraced her route, located the right trail and found her own way out. She wrote:

> This is exactly what a fiction writer always has to do—find his own way out. Firing three shots is the equivalent of waiting for somebody to show him exactly and infallibly how to write. Finding his own way out is the equivalent of actually writing stories—blundering around, rewriting, discarding, changing, trying over and over.
>
> The analogy has a weakness, because there is one big difference between writing stories and getting out of a swamp. If a story gets too troublesome, you can tear it up and forget it. But if you are physically lost, you'll keep struggling for a long time before you quit, because giving up can be fatal.
>
> Planning a story is a matter of exploring in order to get out of a swamp—not by just any route but by the best one.
>
> Absolutely everything in a story not yet written—or written but not competely satisfying—is subject to change. No words of a fiction writer are sacred. A writer should keep his mind open so that he is able to change, able to give up a good dramatic scene or sacrifice some wonderful dialogue because it doesn't fit.
>
> And still, I'll admit that if he keeps too open-minded and doesn't hang on to some landmark idea, he can dream off in too many directions and never get a coherent story at all.

Miss Johnson described a short-story course she took at New York University in which the instructor cautioned against forgetting the value of "if":

> Your characters are in a certain situation that seems good. You know how you plan to get them out of it. But there may be better ways. What happens if Joe loses his temper? What happens if a planned meeting doesn't take place? What happens if . . . practically anything.
>
> In brief, it's wise not to start with an ironbound, unchangeable idea of what the story is going to be, because there may be better ways to tell it than the first one you thought of, or there may be better stories to be found in the same material.

But you do have to start with something, some landmark-idea. From that, you explore outward. You may find such a promising trail to travel on that you'll get clear away from the beginning idea and never go back to it.

Important to Miss Johnson was the concept of searching or exploring for a story. She believed that many writers simply made up some characters and some action, then "brutally moved the characters around to take care of the action," inventing something for them to say.

"The writer, himself, doesn't really believe it but he hopes he's writing a story," she said. "I found out when I was quite young that this is not the way I can do it. I have to search and find out what the story is supposed to be."

An example of finding a story—not making it, but searching and exploring for it—is provided by the following commentary:

I spent my first vacation after the war in southeastern Montana. I got there, on purpose, in time for the spring calf roundup. I followed cowboys around, asking questions of anybody who would talk, and looked constantly for story ideas. (A writer who is serious about his business doesn't sit back and wait for ideas to strike; he looks for them all the time.)

Nothing remarkable happened during the roundup—no romances, no injuries. But it was all new and wonderful to me, and I got lots of authentic background material, all of which went into a notebook for future study. I spent most of the time around camp or at the branding corral.

There was nobody around camp when the cowboys were out on circle except a couple of lady dudes and the cook and his wrangler. The wrangler carried water, cut firewood and rounded up the cavvy (cowboy slang from the Spanish "caballard"—herd of horses) when the riders wanted fresh horses. Wrangling was, I felt, beneath him; he was as competent a cowhand as any of the others, but he had been drafted to do the chores because somebody had to do them.

He didn't complain, but I began to feel sorry for him.

Now the valuable If went to work. What if the wrangler were a teen-age boy, eager to prove his skill in a man's job, but sentenced by his youth and bad luck to slave for the cook?

What if the roundup cook were a bad-tempered, autocratic, sharp-tongued old man? (Oscar of the Roundup wasn't. But good roundup cooks are rare, and they can be cantankerous if they want to.)

There were two pretty good characters, with continuing conflict between them. Fine and dandy. Now for romance—and puppy-love romance can be very touching.

The girl would have to be very young and pathetic, out of place. Then she couldn't be a ranch girl; she'd have to be a dude.

How did she get out there in a roundup camp eighty miles from the nearest town? A female relative brought her, because the family said she had to. The girl was ignored while the female relative courted a cowboy. (And don't think dude girls wait for cowboys to court *them*!) Our little heroine had to hang around camp with the cranky cook and the troubled young wrangler.

The payoff, as I saw it, was that the girl hurt her ankle badly and the boy wrangler sneaked out of his bed-roll to sit outside her tent and talk to her all night, just to comfort her. The other men found out about it and he became the laughing-stock of the county.

The girl never forgot his kindness, and from that childhood romance grew a later, adult one.

It was all very touching, but it wasn't quite believable. I wasted a lot of time and effort on that story—and then started over.

This time the roundup background, which had started the whole thing, was omitted entirely. (I'll use it sometime, though. Nothing a writer learns is ever really wasted.)

Everything was changed in the new story. The hero was a cowboy, but a rich one, part owner of a family cattle empire. The girl was still an Easterner, but she worked for a living. They weren't teen-agers, but in their romantic twenties. And they didn't meet in Montana, but on a dude ranch fifty miles from New York City. There was no cantankerous old roundup cook; instead, there was the hero's bossy, magnificent old grandmother.

The second time, the story was light and funny rather than pathetic. *Argosy* published it as "Hold That Bull!"—not Miss Johnson's title and not under her name, either. Instead, the by-line read, "By L.R. Gustafson."

Still another story generated by the "if" factor and published by *Argosy* was "Warrior's Exile," originally called "The Man Who Could Not Dream."

The facts on which the story was based were these: The Indians of the plains admired personal courage. They proved their courage, and won honor, by performing dangerous deeds. Their courage was bolstered by their faith in personal magic protection called "medicine." Young boys and men starved alone on hilltops until, exhausted and terrified, they went into a dream state. From what they experienced in the medicine dream they learned what their own protective magic was.

Now none of that is fiction. Generations of Indians lived by those beliefs.

The If was this: What if an Indian, completely normal in all other respects, always failed to get a medicine dream? He would be a failure in his own environment. He might be a hoodoo for his tribe, scorned and feared.

The story of "Warrior's Exile" concerned a Crow Indian's final desperate attempt to dream a magic dream or die of cold and starvation and weakness.

That's out of the ordinary; not every writer wants to write about Indians. But pick some other man, not an Indian, put him in an environment that he doesn't fit but cannot leave, give him enough strength of character to keep trying to adjust to it—and almost always, I think, you will have the kind of conflict that makes a story.

Miss Johnson believed that fiction writers profited little by being stubborn about story ideas. She contended that from the same material that produced an unsatisfying or unconvincing story, a writer might find a good story that was entirely different. The evolution of her short story "The Man Who Shot Liberty Valance" is a good example. It also illustrates one of her favorite devices—the switch:

Story ideas can come from anywhere. Some of mine come from western movies.

One came from a trite old gimmick that used to be popular in bang-bang horse operas, the old faithful situation in which the hero walks with measured tread down a dusty street to shoot it out with a villain.

There's a hackneyed situation, good for cat-calls from the gallery in your neighborhood theater. It was new, I suppose, when Owen Wister used it in "The Virginian." It was good; it had wonderful suspense. But it's worn out now—and the reason it got worn out is that it was good.

In "iffing" around with that tense but trite situation, I tried an experiment in technique. Could that old impending-duel scene possibly be used again?

Writers are always looking for rules to go by. Here's one, to be used cautiously: When puzzled, try the switch. That is, turn a situation around and see how it looks from another angle.

In these street duels, the western hero is always bold and brave. He straps on his Colt and off he goes while you hold your breath. You're not worried about his control of his iron nerves—only about the state of his health.

The switch I tried was this: What if the hero wasn't bold and brave? To add to his tribulations, what if he wasn't even a good shot?

Still "iffing" around, unsure of everything in this still-nebulous story idea, I had this problem: How would a scared man who wasn't a good shot ever get into a street duel anyway? He didn't fit the situation. He had no personality, no motivation. He was nothing but a wild idea, and so far from normal that no reader could accept him without a thorough explanation.

How did he get into this duel? For revenge, maybe. Why? What was he mad about? By "iffing," by eliminating a lot of possibilities, I got a picture like this:

A man is beaten and robbed on the prairie and vows vengeance. To seek it is suicidal, but he has nothing to live for anyway. (Therefore he is a cynic, a drifter.) If he is not a good shot, he is not a typical frontiersman; therefore he has recently come from the East. He has been exiled by his well-to-do family, whom he had disgraced. He was by no means an admirable hero, but he improved in the course of the story.

What kind of man would have attacked and robbed him and set him afoot on the prairie, perhaps to die? A hard-case bully, of course, and there were such men among the gun-toters of the frontier. (I have a hard time believing in villains, but recollecting the infamous and historic Boone Helm of Montana gold-rush days restores my confidence. Boone Helm ate two men. But it was for other activities that the Vigilantes hanged him.)

A name for the villain came out of the air: Liberty Valance.

Still fumbling, I came up with another If: What if the hero only thought he killed the villain, but somebody else's shot really did it? There was a fresh angle!

So a third man got into the act—one who really could shoot. He was not admirable, either. But he was convincing. His name was Bert Barricune.

Bert was originally a brother of the girl who was in love with the hero. But what if, I thought, he's not her brother but a man who loves her in vain, has no hope of getting her but is so stubbornly faithful that he will save the life of the man she loves? Right there Bert stopped being her brother.

Another If came in: What if the hero didn't get a mere bullet nick, as they usually do in the movies? What if he had a crippled arm for the rest of his life? So he did. As a result, he had to change his temporary occupation—which was swamping out the Prairie Belle saloon—and study law. He became governor and then senator, and his political enemies didn't overlook his lurid past.

There was much more to the story. Actually, the duel scene didn't take up very much of it. But the idea of the duel was the original spark.

I didn't *make* that plot. Neither did it just grow. I *found* it, piece by piece, fitting together and discarding, moving and changing.

Although "fitting together and discarding, moving and changing" worked well, it resulted in an embarrassing oversight in "Liberty Valance" as first published by *Cosmopolitan* in 1949. The period is established at the outset: "Bert Barricune died in 1910." The hero, Ransome Foster, by this time a senator, returns to town for the funeral. From that starting point, most of the story is told in a flashback to the late 1800s. But as the story ends, the year still 1910, the senator and his wife are being driven to an airport following Barricune's funeral.

"I did some rewriting and changed the time of it and didn't get that airport out," Miss Johnson said. "I remember announcing to the editor by letter or on the phone or something that he should have caught that."

The airport error also appeared in the first edition of Miss Johnson's book *Indian Country*, the 1953 short-story collection that included "Liberty Valance." She warned the book's editor of the mistake, but that warning also went unheeded.

Miss Johnson had definite views on how to begin a story:

If the writer starts too far before the climax, the story can be slow. If he starts too near it, he can get tangled up with awkward flashbacks.

Finding the approach that has the greatest impact is a big problem for me. Of all the possible ways to begin any narrative, which one will hit the hardest? This problem arises, unfortunately, after all the "iffing" seems to be done for the story skeleton, and just when I yearn to go ahead before the bright light of inspiration fades.

Besides sorting out all the Ifs involved in finding out what the story is about, I have to grope around finding the best way to start it. I can't find out until I try it—sometimes fifteen or twenty times.

Anybody can plot a story mechanically and follow the plot without deviating and come out with some kind of narrative. I've tried it—often!—but it has never worked out. Finding a story is harder than plotting one, but for me it works better. In fact, it's the only way that does work.

Story ideas, Miss Johnson believed, could come from anywhere. How to develop the story—how to find it and help it grow from the idea—depended, she thought, on how the writer was feeling at the time:

> Too much introspection can lead to madness, but a writer must look inside himself, because that's where his stories come from. How do you feel right this minute? Why you feel that way doesn't matter; the story doesn't have to be about your own troubles or triumphs. But they influence your current, fleeting emotional state, and that state will influence whatever story you are working on . . . .

Miss Johnson believed that a writer should "listen to dialogue"—that he should be so familiar with dialogue that when it was written, it was not wordy, dull or hard to read. Dialogue, to her, was simply conversation that was clean, sharp and lean . . . .

"Listen to people talk," she said. "Listen and let it soak in. Then write it so that it's easy to read, understandable and gives an understanding of the person who's talking it. It takes a lot of writing."

Significantly, Miss Johnson's characters did not curse or utter obscenities. It is not unreasonable to expect that in attempting to portray the speech of cowboys, outlaws, trappers, lawmen and scouts, she might have required an occasional obscenity. Not so, said Miss Johnson: "My theory is that if you give the tone, the reader will supply the word. Some of my characters are rough, tough and nasty, but the reader knows they are and he can supply the language."

Miss Johnson remembered that at one time *The Saturday Evening Post* would not permit words such as "damn" in fiction:

> "One time I used the word 'fanny' and the *Post* took it out. I didn't think that was bad. It was when Beulah Bunny was learning to fence. This happened to me in a fencing lesson: The fencing master kept saying, 'Straighten your back, straighten your back!' Well, I straightened it until it was practically broken. Finally, one of the other pupils next to me said, 'He means pull in your fanny.' Well, I had that happen to Beulah Bunny in the story and the *Post* took out the 'fanny.' "

In her article "Emotion and the Fiction Writer," Miss Johnson began a brief discussion of conflict by remembering a boy named Edward, the mainstay of one of her earliest literary efforts. Thanks to his 12-year-old creator, Edward was lost in the woods: "I never got him out. I never explained how he got in, either. I skipped all that, because figuring it out would have been hard work. Edward's story started in the middle and never got very far past the middle . . . But at least it wasn't static, as beginners' stories often are. Edward kept trying to get out of the woods . . ."

About conflict, Miss Johnson wrote:

> In any satisfying story, somebody wants something. Usually he makes an effort to get it. He may not succeed, but he does try. If he doesn't try, there may be a story in that: he is the kind of person who just lets things happen to him and then probably complains about it. In that case, the story is depressing and either very dull or very literary, perhaps both. My Edward kept trying. Anybody I write about tries. Let somebody else write about people who give up without an effort. There has to be a very intimate association between a writer and a person he invented. I do not care to associate with people I can't respect—although some of mine are pretty bad.
>
> And some of them are defeated, but they are never "beat." They go down shooting. Most of my stories are about people on the American frontier in the violent years when considerable effort was required just to stay alive. I respect those people, good or bad.
>
> The Tarzan books were popular—and to me forbidden—literature when I was writing about Edward. I borrowed them from a neighbor, hid them under the front steps, and read them privately . . . . Years later, I reread a couple of them and was sadly bored. But they illustrate the point about somebody wanting something and trying to get it. Tarzan was always trying to get from one place to another through the jungle. He was always being hindered by something—usually a hungry lion, as I remember the plots. He always killed the lion and then went on until he met another one.
>
> That is about as simple as narrative can be—somebody wants something but is prevented from getting it and has to struggle. That is conflict.
>
> The forever unfinished story of Edward, an American boy lost in an American forest, had enough conflict and suspense to make me remember it, although the manuscript has been lost for forty years. While I was writing it, I *was* Edward, lost and scared. I admired him. It was an honest story; there was emotion behind it, in the writer. It was my fault, not Edward's, that he never got home.

Miss Johnson always believed in the importance of rewriting:

> "It takes longer and longer to get the story down to where I'm

satisfied with it. 'Bonnie George Campbell,' the first one I sold to the *Post*, I worked on for two days at white heat. Then I was satisfied. I was so excited I just couldn't wait to get it typed and mailed to somebody. But the longer I write the more particular I get . . . . Some of them take years and years before I am happy."

Miss Johnson believed that in the rewriting process, characterization was the least of her worries: "I think the characters are all real to begin with. It's not the characters that have to be polished. It's the wording and clarifying of the story; maybe finding a new scene."

Miss Johnson once told a group of historians in Missoula: "If you write fiction about the Lewis and Clark expedition, you'd better not have Sacajawea be an Irish girl lost from a wagon train." Throughout her career, she tried to remember the difference between writing history and writing fiction. She discussed the difference in an article for *The Roundup*, official publication of the Western Writers of America:

> What right has a writer got to remodel history? It's usually better than fiction to begin with, so why mess up facts and make fiction out of the result?
> It seems to me . . . we owe something to the gullible public. It *is* gullible. Some people will believe anything. I get mail from readers who assume that my short stories are all gospel truth, picked up from pioneer settlers. They give me credit for a good memory, which I haven't got, but no credit for imagination.
> You know how it goes from there: They have some old diaries kept by Grandpa, who once saw Kid Curry get on a horse, and all that's needed is for somebody to "make a story of it" and we'll both get rich . . . . I did write a story that might have been about Kid Curry, after talking to a man who knew him, but by calling him the Buckskin Kid I took off the shackles of history.

In her tips on fiction writing, Miss Johnson said: "Don't use real people. Let them give you ideas or emotions. Then go from there with your knowledge and imagination."

Speaking in 1967 to delegates to the Centennial Conference on the History of the Canadian West, Miss Johnson again discussed history versus fiction while reviewing use of historical material in writing for the mass media. She said:

> "Forgive me if I define fiction and nonfiction. You probably

know the difference, but I have to do this for my students at the University of Montana and for many other audiences.

"Magazine articles are nonfiction. They are usually packed with facts. They may also include some opinion. The facts come from interviewing and research and sometimes from experience.

"*Stories* are fiction. They are inventions. There doesn't have to be one single true thing in them. But a good story *seems* true. The people in a good story seem real, although they are probably entirely the creation of the writer.

"Maybe the reason it's harder to write fiction than articles is that you don't have to stay inside any fences. Facts are fences, and very handy. Outside those fenced boundaries a writer can get lost. The only requirement in fiction is that the people must *seem* real and the sequence of events should *seem* inevitable. This is a pretty big order.

"It is not so easy to base fiction on historical fact as it might seem. Starting with facts, you have some foundation to work on; you have less imagining to do. This should make historical fiction easy to write. But it's not easy to write. Because the facts get in the way of the imagination.

"How much does a writer dare change? How much will his conscience let him change? How much dialogue may he attibute to his characters when he can't prove that these real people really said any such thing? He has a battle with his conscience—or he should have one."

Miss Johnson posed a hypothetical situation in which a writer was producing fiction about the Sioux chief, Sitting Bull. Soon after leading his people into Canada following the Battle of the Little Big Horn, Sitting bull confronts a Mountie (whom the Sioux trusted). The writer wants to relate the conversation, but is unable to find a record of it. Miss Johnson answered her rhetorical question, "What are you going to do?" as follows:

"Maybe you'll figure out what they *should* have said and put the words into their mouths. Maybe you can't bring yourself to do that. If you were a hack writer, you wouldn't hesitate to invent conversation or even events. A hack writer might make the Shoshone girl, Sacajawea, the mother of Sitting Bull, who was a Sioux.

"If you're an honest writer, you have to face this problem or else not write about Sitting Bull. There is some wonderful historical fiction in which great writers face the problem and solve it to the satisfaction of everybody. It can be done.

"But I don't do it. I get around the problem instead of crashing through it. I take off from a real event but change the people's names. So I'm not pretending to write historical fiction. It is just fiction for which history was the springboard."

The importance of emotion to Miss Johnson's writing helps, perhaps, to explain why she chose not to "crash through" the problems presented by straight history or straight historical fiction:

"A writer who uses history as a source looks for the emotion in it. You may think of me, therefore, as sentimental, and I can't argue. But if I don't feel strongly about something, I don't write about it.

"History is full of tremendous emotion, but if you're writing straight history so many facts have to be crowded into so few words that the emotion sometimes gets squeezed out.

"Historians have to boil down a dramatic event, stressing what led up to it and what the result was. In some survey courses, a student who stays home with a bad cold may miss a couple of major wars."

Miss Johnson stressed that as a writer she wanted to be read by "lots of people, who want to be entertained." Of those people, she said:

"The layman wants to see something happening to people. If they don't seem alive when he's reading, he'll leave you. The little things are important to him. He's reading for pleasure, not for college credit.

"I'm not a historian. I'm a layman. The layman wants detail. He doesn't want to read *about* something. He wants to see it happen in his mind. He wants to feel it."

In this connection, it's appropriate to mention that action was among the most important elements of Dorothy Johnson's fiction:

"One big trouble I had for several years was that my people never did anything. They just sat around and thought at each other and didn't say very much and didn't move very much and didn't do very much. This went on up until the early 1940s, when I finally began to publish in the *Post*. Some people still write that way and get published but I don't read very far in that sort of thing."

Miss Johnson regarded herself as a storyteller who wanted to tell a good story because she owed it to her readers:

"Something I didn't realize for a good many years is that my readers don't owe me anything. They are doing me the courtesy of reading what I wrote, so I owe them a good story. This is why I can't read many of the stories that are being published, especially in *The New Yorker*. Those stories bore me to death. Those authors owe me something and they aren't coming across with it.

"The people, the action—if any—plows along. There seems to be no movement. If you tried to graph one of those stories, it would just go right across the graph paper. It wouldn't go up or down. They do a lot of talking but it's pretty tiresome conversation to me."

Many of Dorothy Johnson's most successful stories came from historical accounts. If the number of reprintings is any indication, "Lost Sister," reprinted 24 times in several languages, is among the best stories. Miss Johnson traced the development of the story for the Canadian historians:

"Down in Texas, in 1836, a group of settlers was attacked by Comanche Indians. Several of them were killed, and three or four were captured. One of the captives was a little girl named Cynthia Ann Parker. She was nine years old.

"She grew up as an Indian, married an Indian, had two sons and a daughter—and was captured by white soldiers when she was 33. As a true story, this is tremendously moving. She had become an Indian, and now her white family expected her to become white again. She never did adjust. She grieved. She suffered. And she died at 37.

"Just one photograph was ever taken of her—after the whites took her back to civilization. That's the saddest face I ever saw. She wasn't a white woman any more. She was a captive Indian. She couldn't speak English. I think she died of heartbreak. One of her sons became the great Chief Quanah Parker. She would have been proud of him.

"I was so moved by her picture that I had to write a story . . . .

"But only a student of western history would guess that it (the story) has any connection with Cynthia Ann Parker. History was my jumping-off place. I could change anything I wanted to and keep anything that seemed good for the story. It doesn't purport to be history. I had no battle with my conscience. The story I wrote didn't mention Cynthia Ann Parker, and what happened to the woman I wrote about was not what happened to Cynthia Ann Parker."

In "Virginia City Winter," a story in her book *Flame on the Frontier*, Miss Johnson used facts from history "without any qualms at all." Incidents used as background include the hangings of Sheriff

Henry Plummer and his road agents, the hanging of Joseph Slade and the wild flight into town of the latter's wife, Molly, when she learned what was happening.

"There was no need to change any of that," Miss Johnson said. "The story I wrote is about a hard-luck family, purely imaginary, that was there at the time and was influenced by these events."

For Miss Johnson, "sometimes a tiny bit of history is enough to start the dreaming process that produces fiction." Once, in the New York City public library, she read in Paul Wellman's *Death on Horseback* a footnote that told of the Eastlicks, a frontier family living in a Minnesota settlement raided by the Sioux.

The father and three of the five boys are killed. Before her capture, the mother hides her infant son, Johnny, and charges her only other surviving son, 11-year-old Merton, with his care. Eventually Mrs. Eastlick escapes. She is found by whites, "crazed with the belief that her whole family is dead." While she is being taken to another settlement, however, Merton and the infant are found.

"The lad had carried the baby every foot of the way, hiding from the Indians and subsisting on berries," Wellman's footnote said. "He was an emaciated skeleton, with the flesh worn off his bare feet and was unable to speak for days afterward. But the baby was safe and sound."

Miss Johnson said:

"I went home and went to bed but I couldn't go to sleep because there was all this massacre going on right there. I tried for an hour or so to sleep but these were real people and there were terrific scenes of violent action and dreadful fear. I didn't know how these scenes hooked up and I didn't know who these people were, but finally I gave up trying to sleep and got up and started writing in shorthand just as fast as I could go . . . . I didn't know if there was a story and I wasn't thinking about that. These things were actually happening in my mind without being invited. Heaven knows I had to go to work the next day. I think I wrote until 2 o'clock or 2:30 and then I went to bed. The next day, after a full day's work (she was managing editor of the *The Woman*), I came home and transcribed all this stuff on the typewriter. It surprised me.

"I had given it a little thought on the subway, but the rest of the day I had been working for Farrell Publishing Corporation and I didn't have time to think about it. I transcribed it and I still couldn't see how it hitched up. I didn't understand who these people were and what was going on. But I . . . found that if I did a little moving, I could find out how the scene connected. Then I had to invent and create some new characters to flesh out . . . . "

"Flame on the Frontier" originally was almost 8,000 words. Miss Johnson thought the story was a sure winner, but the editors of major magazines did not. Her agent turned to *Argosy*, then considered a secondary market, and the story sold for $750. That was about half what it would have brought from *The Saturday Evening Post* or *Collier's*.

"I called it 'Family Album' because it seemed to me that's what it was about and I wanted a very quiet title for a bloody story," Miss Johnson said. "But *Argosy* doesn't like quiet titles and they called it 'Flame on the Frontier.' "

Miss Johnson's late-evening bout with "Flame on the Frontier" indicates the pattern of her writing schedule in subsequent years. Until the spring of 1967, the only time she had for writing was at night or on weekends. Night hours became a habit with her.

A victim of insomnia, which began in the late 1930s as she worked on a novel, she saw a definite link between her mind being productive and her inability to sleep.

Miss Johnson may not have enjoyed her reading of George Gissing's *House of Cobwebs* during her senior year of college, but the experience was valuable. In classifying Gissing's "gruesome, melancholy little essays" as to whether they were short stories or sketches, she provided herself with a quick course in form:

"Form was of greatest importance to me then, and it still is. A story has a beginning, a middle and an end.

"A sketch is not a story, but just a piece of something. This slice-of-life business I never did go for. It starts in the middle of something and ends in the middle of something and nothing has been resolved and nothing really has happened. This doesn't interest me in the least. Something has got to happen and something is either changed or not changed because of it. That's what makes a short story.

"Sometimes I do start in the middle, but something has happened before that is of consequence. Someone has made a decision, one way or another, and because of it his life has been changed. It's usually character that makes for this change or lack of change—maybe the man just hasn't got gumption enough to change. That doesn't happen very often with my people, though, because they are usually strong characters one way or the other, good or bad."

Miss Johnson's friend, Opal Colbert, emphasized that authenticity was of prime importance to Dorothy Johnson even in the early part of her writing career. The concern for detail remained. In a 1943 article, "Research for Writing," Miss Johnson provided some guidelines for authenticity that are as applicable now as they were then:

> If you must place a scene in a period you don't remember, read the popular fiction of that period. Let your mind lie open, though you may have to hold your nose. Visualize the ideal of the period (realizing that it was probably never attained), and you will have better background for characterization than you would get from remembering . . . .
> The fashion drawings are useful for descriptions of clothes. Sometimes I make rough (very rough) sketches for my notebook; sometimes I jot down brief descriptions.
> I should mention that doing research is not writing, and that you can get so fascinated by it that you will never get any work done. If you have run out of excuses, you may welcome this as a new reason for avoiding the typewriter.
> Even if you do not have to start a character way back in the early 1900s but are willing to stay in the present, there are countless details to be checked. Details give plausibility to a story, but they must be accurate. If you have somebody picking cherries and apples at the same time, a wide-awake editor will probably save you from public embarrassment—and, of course, from publication. Editors are paid for being suspicious.
> When you need specialized information, consult a specialist. For one story, I had to confront my physician with this problem: What lingering ailment, painful but not incapacitating, could take the patient off suddenly and expensively? He found one. It was not at all what I had chosen before I had sense enough to ask him.
> For the same story, I had to ask an automobile mechanic which tire should blow out in order to send a car over a cliff at the left-hand side of the road. We drew a little map, and he figured it all out. His professional interest was aroused, and he wanted to know what model the car was. I told him, and said it landed upside down in the river, but they got the body out. He said, "But that model had a wooden top and would have smashed on the way down." So I changed the car.
> For some reason, most people really like to help a writer out of a puzzling situation. Even ethical people will connive with you in

crimes. An honest and respectable attorney once helped me to fix a coroner's jury so as to keep my hero out of jail . . . .

Writing letters is not . . . the best way to find out things as a rule. Only writers really like to write letters, and most of the people who have the answers simply never get around to taking pen in hand.

It's important to keep listening. You may not find out what you started after, but you are likely to get something else that's better. I used to set out with a notebook and ask baldly, "Do you know any good stuff for stories?" That approach was flattering, but it wasn't productive. It scared people out of talking. When you lead up gradually, you get better results. Precise questions get useful answers.

Miss Johnson believed that almost every poet, fiction writer, artist and creative scientist has a helper to whom he never can give credit in public because of the helper's name, Genius. In a 1961 article, "The Years and the Wind and the Rain," she discussed the concept of genius as defined by the ancients. She also described how she believed it influenced her writing:

Sometimes the writer writes more profoundly than he really can, and he knows it. But he can't admit it. He can't give proper credit to his genius, because that would be boasting, which in our culture is not permitted. Therefore he must pretend that he did this fine thing all by himself—and that is not only boasting but a big lie besides.

The trouble is the word "genius." We think of it as "extraordinary power of invention, native intellectual power of an exalted type." We equate genius with a high IQ . . . .

Centuries before I progressed through the public schools of Whitefish, Montana, . . . genius had another meaning. The religion of the ancient Romans held that every person had his own genius. It was an attendant guardian spirit allotted to him at birth to govern his fortunes and determine his character and finally to conduct him out of the world.

This makes sense. What everybody has, nobody can boast about. To an ancient Roman, it was no more remarkable to possess a genius than it was to have ten toes. They were all part of the package. I suppose a successful man could assume that he had an especially good genius, and a failure could find comfort in the thought that he wasn't entirely to blame.

We have lost, except in dictionaries, this meaning of "genius." Maybe everybody doesn't have a tutelary spirit now. Maybe it's still there but dormant, silent and powerless because we don't know about it or don't believe in it.

A creative artist is likely to know he has a genius, although he may prefer to let the world think that he wrote his book or composed his music or painted his picture all by himself. Of course, the genius isn't always on the job. Many a book is written entirely solo and it would be an insult to one's genius to give it a by-line.

Now that I've gone into the antique meaning of "genius," I can admit modestly that I have one, in the sense that everybody is entitled to one, and mine is free to help me because I recognize its existence and am grateful to it . . . .

My genius is a flibbertigibbet, here today and gone tomorrow, or more likely here yesterday when I was too busy to listen and unaccountably missing today when I have a couple of free hours and a fresh ribbon in the typewriter.

Miss Johnson remembered her poem "Old Mine," first published in *The Frontier* and later in *Northwest Verse*. The poem's last two lines are:

And the years and the wind and the rain
Heal everything.

She subsequently wrote:

That was written by an 18-year-old girl, a student . . . who was describing something she saw from a train window. Nobody ever said it was great poetry. But I insist that no girl of 18 could possibly be wise enough to write those last two lines. They did not come from experience, from inside; they came from an attendant genius who was wiser than the girl who wrote them down.

The girl was, in fact, doubtful about that statement. *Did* the years and the wind and the rain really heal everything, or was she just guessing? I remember the circumstances vividly because I was the doubtful girl.

I am a girl no longer, though often still doubtful. More than 50 years of living have proved to me that those lines were truly written. I wish I could have been sure long ago. Certain subsequent events would have been easier to endure if I had believed my attendant genius.

For a long time after seeing the old mine I had the idea that there was something especially inspirational about riding on a train and always took along a notebook. But the skittish spirit doesn't always take the same train I do. Once, however, she shared my seat on a plane eastbound from Billings, and we wrote an awfully good story as soon as we got to a typewriter.

Long ago she lost interest in writing poetry, finding the short story more comfortable. There is no depending on her. She comes and goes and cannot be enticed. In fact, she is away so much that I sometimes wonder whether I am sharing her with somebody else.

One of the most important lessons Miss Johnson learned about writing is that attempting to follow a success formula—trying to imitate others—is useless. In college, after reading Ernest Hemingway's early short stories, she was impressed enough with his lean, objective style to try to emulate it. She liked Kipling's stories and subsequently went through a Kipling period:

"I think every beginning writer tries to adopt the style of somebody he admires. It took a long time before I found out how I was supposed to write.

"Hemingway's objective approach—where he told what people said and the reader understood—appealed to me. But I used to do things the hard way. I was always looking for limitations; I think most fiction writers do: If you could only find out what the rules are that a successful author follows, then you could be successful, too. But after you have been writing for a long time, you find there are very few rules and that you might as well forget about formulas and stop buying books that tell you how to write stories.

"Nobody can tell you how. Everybody has to find out for himself."

A statement she made in a 1958 speech before the Polson Chamber of Commerce summarized best, perhaps, Dorothy Johnson's view of her craft: "Some people think writing is like building a house; you draw your plans and work from them. But writing is more like drilling for oil—you don't know for sure where the oil is, but you must find it, pump it out and refine it."

CHAPTER SIXTEEN

Courage

O
N THE MORNING OF JANUARY 28, 1969, Dorothy Johnson left Missoula on the Northern Pacific's North Coast Limited for a 34-hour train ride to Minneapolis. From there she traveled to Rochester, home of the Mayo Clinic. Twice before leaving the clinic more than three weeks later, she underwent minor surgery for the removal of a skin cancer from her nose (for the fifth time) and in preparation for later skin-grafting. She also arranged to return later for additional steps in the plastic-surgery procedure.

Miss Johnson went to Rochester on the advice of her physician. Since November 1968, he had been trying to learn what, aside from her ulcers, was causing a lingering and sometimes severe abdominal pain. Whatever the difficulty, it prevented Miss Johnson from taking a long-awaited trip to Australia, New Zealand and the South Pacific in December. Having to cancel the South Seas trip was not the first disappointment of this nature. An intestinal affliction, diverticulitis, put Miss Johnson in St. Patrick Hospital's intensive-care unit for eight days in the spring of 1968, causing her to forgo a trip to Turkey with her friend Catharine Burnham. Recuperating through the summer and fall, she postponed several shorter trips, one of which would have taken her along the historic Bozeman Trail. She did get to Great Falls for the 1968 Montana Press Association convention, where she received a standing ovation.

Though illness deprived her of much of the time and energy she gained by resigning her jobs, Miss Johnson continued to write. Her tenth book, a biography of Sitting Bull entitled *Warrior for a Lost Nation*, was in book stores by late March 1969. Published by

Westminster Press, it was dedicated to Mel Ruder. Her eleventh book, *Western Badmen*, a volume for juveniles dealing with famous outlaws of the Old West, was due at the publishers in June. *Montana*, a book describing the Treasure State and written for a "States of the Nation" series, also was scheduled to be published.

Miss Johnson's most ambitious project, a book about the Bozeman Trail, was scheduled for completion in June 1970. McGraw-Hill was to publish the book, part of the American Trail series that was being edited by Pulitzer Prize-winning novelist A.B. Guthrie, Jr. Its title was to be *The Bloody Bozeman*.

Periodically, Miss Johnson was asked to take other writing assignments. Stewart Richardson of New York's Doubleday & Company Inc., requested her to consider a novel about a circuit rider. Thanking Richardson for considering her, Miss Johnson declined. She explained that she had to "be" the people she wrote about and that she could not "see herself in a circuit rider's shoes." Miss Johnson also was asked to serve in an advisory capacity in the preparation of a television documentary about artist Charles M. Russell. The film, to be narrated by NBC's Chet Huntley, interested Miss Johnson. She worried, however, about her lack of experience in the television medium.

Another highlight of Miss Johnson's career was a July 1968 telephone call from Sandy Howard, a Cinema Center producer, informing her that filming of her short story "A Man Called Horse" was to begin in October. Howard had held an option on the story for several months and only recently had taken his second option. The stars of what *Life's* Shana Alexander called "the most authentic Indian movie ever made" were to be Irish actor Richard Harris and Australia's Dame Judith Anderson. In her column "The Feminine Eye," Miss Alexander wrote:

> Harris plays the horse and Judith Anderson is his Indian owner, but the 300 other members of the cast are all authentic Sioux, scooped up *en masse* from the Rosebud Sioux Reservation in South Dakota and imported to some remote mountains in Mexico which the movie's scholars say most resemble Sioux lands in 1830. It may be the largest Indian mass migration since Wounded Knee. To accomplish it, the moviemen spent months on the reservation learning the ancient ways, brewing the old dyes, and winning the hearts

Richard Harris in *A Man Called Horse*.

and minds of the tribal elders. Their passion for authenticity grew so strong that they even decided to do the entire movie in the authentic Sioux language without subtitles . . . .

Frequently ranked among the premier writers of the American West and the author of a dozen books, scores of short stories and numerous articles, Dorothy Johnson still considered herself obscure in the late 1960s. At 63, though, she thought she finally was learning to relax. She said she was happy to be doing so, but her friends wondered whether she meant it. They hoped so. Although most had their own ways of wording it, they agreed that her illnesses were rooted in the relentless way in which she had driven herself.

Once while lecturing at Minnesota's Concordia College, Miss Johnson told an audience that she wrote about Indians, pioneers, outlaws and other rugged characters of frontier days because she admired courage. She suggested that perhaps she admired that virtue because she was not endowed with it. Miss Johnson no doubt believed that, for she was not a woman prone to false modesty. Her friends, however, would have argued that she was among the most courageous persons they knew.

CHAPTER SEVENTEEN

The Bloody Bozeman

N JULY 28, 1862, GOLD WAS DISCOVERED IN eastern Montana. By the time winter weather curtailed operations, the amount mined was valued in excess of $700,000.

Prospectors made even richer discoveries the next year. Hoping to become guides for the resulting flood of eastern immigrants and commercial travel, John M. Bozeman and John M. Jacobs, both long-time wanderers in the Rockies, in the spring of 1863 blazed a new road by way of the eastern base of the Big Horn Mountains and the upper Powder River to Deer Creek Crossing on the North Platte.

Their route was 400 miles and six weeks shorter than the connection with the Oregon Trail west of the mountains. At Powder River, the returning pathfinders and a wagon train consisting of more than 100 persons were informed by a party of Sioux that "You can't go in the direction you are going . . . . We will keep this land. Go back or we will kill you."

The train, except for Bozeman and nine men, turned back and took the long route over the mountains. During the next five years, however, other immigrants by the thousands gambled their lives trying to reach the Montana gold fields by the shorter route. For their protection, the military established three forts: The fortification was self-defeating since the retaliating Sioux under Chief Red Cloud not only killed many travelers and soldiers along the route, but also forced the government, in 1868, to abandon the forts and to close the road.

Indeed, the road became the bloody Bozeman, but Dorothy Johnson's extensive book about the subject encompasses more. A sizable portion is about eastern Montana, since the trail led only to that one place and the history of the two are inseparable.

Miss Johnson's research for *The Bloody Bozeman* was thorough, as always. Montana State University made available to her extensive primary materials in the form of manuscripts, journals, diaries, references and recollections. Some of the research that she had done for juvenile works such as *Western Badmen* also proved useful. In addition, she used much of the knowledge about the gold rush of the 1860s that she had acquired in researching *The Hanging Tree*.

The Bozeman was a short-lived trail, and Miss Johnson's book covers the years between 1864 and 1868. As she had done before, Miss Johnson brought history alive in terms of people—both those recorded by history and those who are "unsung." One of her devices for doing so was to follow an individual's life throughout the four years covered by the book. Frank Kirkaldie, a prospector who writes homesick letters to his family in the Midwest, appears and reappears. For Kirkaldie, wealth and a reunion with his family are always just around the corner. However, they never materialize in the narrative.

Much of the book consists of a series of profiles, and familiar names such as Thomas Meagher become real through Miss Johnson's detailed treatment. She portrays Meagher, Montana's acting governor in 1864, as a flamboyant, egotistical and unstable person. She offers no solution to the mystery of his drowning off a riverboat.

With a narrator's skill for rounding out a story, she closed the book with an epilogue that finishes the stories of some of the reappearing figures. She also commented that "most of the descendants of the Indians who fought so hard for the Powder River country now live on reservations and not so well as other Americans."

"Overall, the fascinating accounts of personal experiences, the novel and interesting style, and the admirable format will captivate the attention of both laymen and historians interested in the American West," Professor Ernest Wallace of Texas Tech University commented in a book review for the *Journal of American History*.

Indeed, *The Bloody Bozeman* was well-received, and eventually would be reprinted in a soft-cover version.

CHAPTER EIGHTEEN

The Bedside
Book of Bastards

F OR HER NEXT EFFORT, MISS JOHNSON collaborated with the late Robert T. Turner, a University of Montana history professor, to write a book about evil people.

Published in 1973, the book described the escapades of cannibals, torturers and mass murderers.

The authors called their work *Great Villains of History*, but couldn't interest a publisher in printing it. When they changed the title to *The Bedside Book of Bastards*, it was promptly accepted by McGraw-Hill.

Miss Johnson and Professor Turner figured that at some time or another everybody had had a bad day because of a bastard. A bastard, as defined by the authors, was an "obnoxious or nasty" person. The frustrations of such bad days inspired the book, which describes bastards of history from the fourth century B.C. to the 19th century.

Turner, who taught at UM for 28 years and once served as dean of the College of Arts and Sciences, died two weeks after he and Miss Johnson completed the manuscript for the book.

"He would have enjoyed so much seeing the book come out," Miss Johnson said later. "He was looking forward to it."

Following publication of *The Bedside Book of Bastards*, Miss Johnson described for an interviewer the days when she and Turner had been professors at UM. She said he often would say after a bad day that he was going to write a book about bastards. One day she asked him, "Well, why don't you?" They discussed it, and soon launched their joint venture.

"We decided the book would have to stop with the year 1900 because we wanted it to be light and funny, if possible, and you cannot be funny about anything that happened in this century," Miss Johnson said. "The people who lived at the time these dreadful people were living didn't see anything funny about it, either."

In a review, the late K. Ross Toole, UM professor of history, called the book "irreverently hilarious." He added, "It's just plain fruitless to try to review a book like this because the joy and hilarity of it lie in the way it is written. Every fourth line is a punch line and yet, *mirabila dictu*, there is not a single monotonous page."

Not all the chapters in the book are funny. One is about Captain Henry Wirz, who was in charge of the prison camp at Andersonville, Georgia, during the Civil War and was court-martialed and executed in 1865.

"I don't know when I have been so mad," Miss Johnson said. "I read the court-martial proceedings and there is no humor whatever in it. I don't think the book is going to sell very well in the South—not after somebody notices that chapter. The execution of Henry Wirz is still a very bitter subject in the former Confederate states. They haven't forgiven the Yankees for it yet."

The dedication of the book is a full-page list of first names. The list is a combination of the names of friends in the authors' address books, none of whom, they explained, is a bastard. The first three names are of Turner's cats and the last name is of a cat that belonged to one of Miss Johnson's neighbors.

On reading *The Bedside Book of Bastards*, many people wondered whether Turner had done the research and Miss Johnson the writing.

"This was not true," she said. "Each of us did his own research and writing, and each of us did about half the people in the book."

At the end of their book, Miss Johnson and Turner left a space for the reader to list his or her own eligible nominees for infamy.

The year 1973 was noteworthy in another way for Miss Johnson. During the University of Montana's graduation ceremony in June, she was awarded an honorary doctor of letters degree in recognition of her growing list of books and achievements.

Miss Johnson receives a ceremonial cross-section from a tree. The gift bore the names of those present at a luncheon in her honor at Whitefish's Hanging Tree restaurant. Seated with her is the late J. Hugo Aronson, former Republican governor of Montana. Behind her is the late Col. Joe Montgomery of Lewistown, who had fought in the Spanish-American War, and Ken Byerly, publisher of the *Lewistown Daily News* and the Cut Bank Pioneer Press. *(Mel Ruder photo)*

Dorothy Johnson and the late Sen. Lee Metcalf of Montana soon after they received honorary doctor of letters degrees from the University of Montana.

CHAPTER NINETEEN

The Golden Saddleman Award

UNDAUNTED BY CONTINUING HEALTH problems, Miss Johnson kept busy writing a new novel, magazine articles and, as always, letters to the editor of the daily *Missoulian* newspaper.

Travel also occupied some of her time, and on June 24, 1976, she went to Billings, Montana, to receive the prestigious Levi Strauss Golden Saddleman Award from the Western Writers of America. Presented annually, the award was to honor a writer for bringing "dignity and honor to the history and legends of the West."

At the Western Writers convention, Miss Johnson received a borrowed trophy. The real one—a bronze figure of a cowboy with a saddle on his shoulder—hadn't been ordered on time.

Other winners of the award included actor John Wayne and director John Ford.

Miss Johnson, left, receives the National Cowboy Hall of Fame's Western Heritage Outstanding Novel Award during a 1978 ceremony in Oklahoma City. The award was for her novel *Buffalo Woman*.

CHAPTER TWENTY

Buffalo Woman

ISS JOHNSON'S NEW NOVEL, PUBLISHED IN
1977 by Dodd, Mead, was titled *Buffalo Woman*. The
book traces the life of an Oglala Sioux woman from
childhood to her death from old age and starvation
while on a long foot journey north to a Canadian haven.

Called Whirlwind as a child, she later is known as Buffalo
Woman because her family was sufficiently well-to-do to provide
the honorary Buffalo Maiden ceremony for her.

Buffalo Woman is an ideal Indian woman—strong and
courageous, skilled at the tasks performed by women, proud of her
culture and community. As an old woman, she saves her infant
grandson from a grizzly, though she, herself, is badly mauled.
Later, she who had prided herself on having the bravery of a warrior gives up mentally after her tribe's camp is attacked and her
daughter-in-law and nephew are killed.

Still, Buffalo Woman recovers her strength when she sees that
the spirit of the others is broken. She becomes the inspiration that
pulls the camp together. Her final act also is one of courage and
strength: She starves herself to death, giving her food and life and
strength to her hungry people.

Throughout the story, Miss Johnson saw events through Indian
eyes. In doing so, she conveyed the message that the Indian world
was a civilization with a distinct order and pattern. The novel,
historical fiction at its best, chronicles the real people and battles
of the Lakotas. Inevitably, it is the story of the disintegration of a
culture. As a child, Whirlwind belongs to a prosperous family and
lives a comfortable life; in her final days, she is part of a ragged
band trying to reach Canada ahead of pursuing soldiers after the

Battle of the Little Big Horn.

But even as her culture disintegrates around her, Buffalo Woman retains her strong beliefs. She remains proud of the way she has lived, and she waits for her chance to go to the Land of Many Lodges where she will, she knows, be reunited with her loved ones.

Buffalo Woman was a triumph.

The book, in April 1978, won for Miss Johnson the National Cowboy Hall of Fame's Western Heritage Outstanding Novel Award. Presented at an Oklahoma City banquet by the board of trustees of the Cowboy Hall of Fame and Western Heritage Center, the trophy was a replica of Charles M. Russell's bronze sculpture, "The Night Herder." It was given in recognition of Miss Johnson's "outstanding writing of the great stories of the West."

Buffalo Woman was chosen over 50 other books nominated for the annual award.

On hand for the presentation were Gene Autry, outgoing president of the Cowboy Hall of Fame, and fellow members Roy Rogers, Dale Evans and Glenn Ford.

"There were a lot of rich Texans and Oklahomans dressed up in tuxedos, but they still had cowboy boots on underneath," Miss Johnson later told a reporter.

CHAPTER TWENTY-ONE

All the Buffalo Returning

T
HE DODD, MEAD COMPANY PUBLISHED MISS Johnson's 16th book, *All the Buffalo Returning*, in the spring of 1979

The novel picks up where *Buffalo Woman* ended, with the Lakotas settling in Canada. There is further dissolution of their culture.

Warfare isn't allowed, so the young braves have no way to prove their courage and are discontented. Eventually, a lack of buffalo and the frustration of the young men force the Lakotas to return to their homeland. The misery of life on reservations—with white people's blind attempts to inflict their culture on Indians—is graphically portrayed.

Focus of *All the Buffalo Returning* is Stormy, Buffalo Woman's grandson, who was only eight when she died. Stormy is sent to an Indian school in Pennsylvania, where he surreptitiously clings to the old ways in the midst of a white world. After school, Stormy tries living like a white man, but always with the goal of gaining as much experience as possible to make him useful to his people.

He returns to the reservation but finds only misery—tough bread and fry bread to eat, sickly children and old people who can't survive any illness. He feels unneeded, as though his years at the white school were of no use. He has lost his faith in the old gods and now can believe in neither the white god nor the Indian one. Unhappy, he works for a white trader who cheats him.

Stormy regains his faith when he travels, illegally, with his family to Pine Ridge, South Dakota, to see the Ghost Dance. Made dangerous by the possibility of soldiers chasing them, the journey of Stormy and his family fulfills the Indian way by calling for the courage that gives meaning to life.

All the Buffalo Returning, originally titled *The Dance of Spirits Returning*, ends with the tragic massacre at Wounded Knee. Stormy and his family are killed. Dying, Stormy realizes that he will be with Buffalo Woman and the others in the Land of Many Lodges.

All the Buffalo Returning and *Buffalo Woman* end with physical defeat and death. Death, however, means spiritual renewal for the characters. Both novels are strongly affirmative and, like Miss Johnson's short stories, tell of strong people who gracefully deal with whatever life sends them.

Autographing books at a Missoula store.

When You and I
Were Young, Whitefish

T AGE 76, MISS JOHNSON'S EXTRAORDINARY life had taken her to many places in the United States and many countries around the world. Still, she loved Whitefish, Montana, and considered the little railroad and tourist community her home town.

She said so in the second paragraph of her 17th book, *When You and I Were Young, Whitefish*, which was published in October 1982 by Mountain Press Publishing Co. The book is a charming collection of reminiscences about growing up in Whitefish in the early part of the century.

"We were kids together," Miss Johnson wrote on the first page. "I was a nice little girl. The town was a sturdy, brawling, mannerless brat that took years to civilize."

In *When You and I Were Young, Whitefish*, Miss Johnson wrote about people and events with the same insight and flair for humor that had brought her fame decades earlier. There was Dad Lewis, a packer who knew how to make a good bed out of boughs and who was noted for his bannocks—baking-powder biscuits fried in bacon grease over a campfire.

There was her childhood hero, police officer George Tayler.

There was the hated A.P. Tills, local manager of Mountain States Power Co., which operated the fledgling telephone system in town. Tills wanted everything done the way it had been done in Chicago, where he once worked.

"The telephoning public had a dark suspicion that we spent our time listening in, and very often the public was right," wrote Miss

Johnson of her days as a relief switchboard operator. "Mr. Tills felt that listening in was a crime just short of manslaughter. They didn't do it in Chicago. Of course not. Nobody in Chicago knew anybody."

And there was Shorty Gammel, the town's only electric and telephone serviceman. A bachelor from Virginia, he belonged to just about every organization in town. He died in 1940 and a funeral procession was held on Whitefish's Central Avenue.

In the last chapter of *When You and I Were Young, Whitefish*, Miss Johnson described the many ways in which Whitefish had changed since she had lived there as a child.

"Whitefish," she wrote, "has become a year-round playground for visitors from far and near. A lot of them liked it so well that they bought land and moved in. Condominiums and luxury apartments have grown where porcupines and grouse once lurked . . . . "

Noting that visitors today call Whitefish a "pretty little town," and that a chamber of commerce brochure calls it "quaint," Miss Johnson wrote: "They should have seen it when it was too raw to be pretty and too new to be quaint, when it was boisterous and howling and always outgrowing its britches."

Miss Johnson and her home town truly had grown up together.

"Now we go our separate ways," she wrote in closing. "Sing a song of laughter, a pocketful of wry."

E P I L O G U E

CRITICALLY ILL IN LATE 1982, MISS JOHNSON HAD HER ATTORNEY burn the unfinished manuscript for her 18th book. The manuscript, which she had been working on for more than two years, was for a World War II-era novel tentatively titled *The Unbombed*.

Later, Miss Johnson rallied and returned to her typewriter. She rewrote the manuscript, and in January 1984 submitted it to her New York City agent under the title *No Bombs Fell*.

Today, at age 78, she continues to live in Missoula's West Rattlesnake Valley.

Miss Johnson was grand marshall of the 1977
Montana Days—University of Montana
Homecoming parade on Missoula's Higgins
Avenue. Parade theme was "Western Books."

APPENDIX

DOROTHY JOHNSON IS AN ENTHUSIASTIC WRITER OF LETTERS TO newspaper editors. Below are some samples:

Quite a lot of people seem to be mad because it's too much trouble for the Missoula County treasurer's office to issue license plates by mail.

You know what? If enough of them stay mad until the next election of county officials, I'll bet we could remedy that situation.

All of a sudden a lot of people, including me, are living on West Greenough Drive. We haven't moved, but new signs appeared on what was Duncan Drive. Nobody asked us, nobody told us—the county commissioners just did it. Pretty high-handed, eh?

I've just had new stationery printed with 2309 Duncan Drive on it and haven't paid the *Missoulian* for the printing job. If I send the bill to the county commissioners, do you suppose they'll pay it? Will our mailman continue to be amiable while mail for families along here comes addressed to a non-existent street for the next several years? Will bills for property taxes still reach us?

Advertising copy writers seem not to be aware that the word "gift" is a noun, not a verb.

"Gift your man with a bathrobe," indeed!

"Perfect for Christmas gifting," bah!

If I should have the misfortune to meet somebody who writes like this, I will gift him a poke in the eye.

Yes, we need an improved airport as recommended by the chamber of commerce. But we can't afford the bond issue or any other bond issue.

Property owners are hurting badly. Owners of rental property have got to raise rents because of the shocking tax increase we already have, so everybody is going to hurt even without any bond issue. Any more increases will make Missoula too expensive to live in, whether you own your home or rent it.

Maybe the members of the chamber of commerce can afford higher taxes, but I know a lot of people who can't. And let's not hear about how Uncle Sugar will pay for part of it. He gets his money out of the same pockets that the state, county and city do.

The *Missoulian*'s new look is fine, especially the color photograph.

But the tiny type in the classified ads and the legals just won't do at all. People pay for these ads because they want other people to read them.

Your Sunday, February 4, editorial, blaming Missoula dentists because our water isn't fluoridated, is unjust—as whoever wrote it must have realized.

Dentists alone can't get the voters to approve fluoridation. There has to be organized support from a lot of other people.

The opposition is well organized. It has defeated the proposition in many communities. Some years ago I wrote a magazine article about the value of fluoridation in preventing tooth decay in children. I got a lot of mail from anonymous crackpots who sent me printed attacks on fluoridation and tried to illuminate my ignorance by warning that fluoridation is a dirty communist plot!

Some opponents are selfish. They claim a constitutional right to drink water without any chemicals added (that kind is hard to get even without fluoridation unless you have your own well), ignoring the right of kids to grow up with sound teeth.

Dentists and the American Dental Association do care. A lot of other people don't.

The way I heard it, the airport wouldn't need a lot of money for enlargement if it hadn't been mismanaged for years, with the planes that use it paying far too little.

Anyhow, property owners simply can't afford that tax increase—which, incidentally, will also burden people who rent. They'll have to pay higher rent.

Although I use plane transportation more than most of the people who would have to pay for the proposed bond issue, I'll vote against it. As for the argument that fresh produce won't reach us unless we enlarge the airport, I'll bet the people who sell the stuff will get it to us.

B I B L I O G R A P H Y

Newspapers

"An Air Warden is Hopeful," *The New York Times*, April 16, 1943, p. 20.

Andrews, Mary Evans. "Farewell to Troy," *Chicago Tribune Book Week*, November 1, 1964, p. 35-A.

"An Eye Out," *The Shelby Promoter*, April 13, 1967, p. 1.

"Author Gives Some Tips on Story Writing," *The FARGO* (North Dakota) *FORUM* and *Moorhead* (Minnesota) *News*, October 13, 1959, p. 11.

Beaufort, John. "Hanging Tree," *The Christian Science Monitor*, February 17, 1959, p. 4P.

Beckley, Paul V. " 'The Hanging Tree,' " *The New York Herald Tribune*, February 12, 1959, p. 13.

Berry, Harland. "Frontier Village Takes Shape in Hills Near Yakima," *Yakima* (Washington) *Herald*, June 1, 1958, p. 7-B.

Butler, Betty. "Montana Author Praised for Book," *Spokesman Review*, February 20, 1959, p. 6.

Carleton, Lillian. "Authentic Settings," *Boston* (Massachusetts) *Sunday Herald*, June 2, 1957, sec. IV, p. 15.

Carroll, Harrison. "Cooper's Film Tops 'High Noon,' " *Los Angeles Herald & Express*, February19, 1959, p. B-4.

Casewit, Curtis W. "Fine Tales of the Old West," *The New York Herald Tribune*, June 16, 1957, p. 4.

Cohen, Lucille. "Caldwell Has Little Time for Books," *Seattle Post-Intelligencer*, October 17, 1957, p. 18.

Cook, Alton. " 'Hanging Tree' Rated as Superior Western," *The New York World Telegram*, February 12, 1959, p. 14.

Cooper, Page. "New Fiction: America," *The New York Herald Tribune Book Review*, September 27, 1942, p. 17.

"An Air Warden is Hopeful," *The New York Times*, April 16, 1943, p. 20.

"CPA Speaker Tosses Problems of Women to Accountants Here," *Great Falls Leader*, September 25, 1953, p. 2.

Crowther, Bosley. "Screen: A Gold Camp in the Montana Country," *The New York Times*, February 12, 1959, p. 23.

"Dorothy Johnson's Book Tells Montana Stories," *Great Falls Tribune Montana Parade*, June 2, 1957, p. 2.

"Dorothy Johnson, Composer Revise Comedy," *The Daily Missoulian*, April 5, 1959, p. 18.

"Dorothy M. Johnson to be Honored in Gala Days Parade August 2," *The Whitefish Pilot*, March 7, 1958, p. 1.

"Dorothy Johnson Undertakes Crusade Against Carbon Monoxide Poisonings," *The Daily Missoulian*, February 23, 1960, p. 2.

"Editing 'Nooz' Her Favorite Task," *The Villager*, August 12, 1943, p. 3.

"Everyone Needs Books, Dorothy Johnson Says," *Great Falls Tribune*, April 17, 1964, p. 9.

"Gary Cooper Here to Visit MSU Author," *Montana Kaimin*, October 31, 1957, p. 1.

"Gary Cooper, Producers Visit Campus for Talk With MSU's Dorothy Johnson," *Montana Kaimin*, November 1, 1957, p. 1.

Gould, Alphin T. "A Cavy of Western Tales," *Providence* (Rhode Island) *Sunday-Journal*, June 23, 1957, sec. VI, p. 6.

" 'Hanging Tree' Opens February 6," *The Daily Missoulian*, January 18, 1959, p. 26.

Hass, Victor P. "A Miser With Her Words," *Chicago Tribune*, July 14, 1957, part 4, p. 6.

"Hell Gate Said Proposed as Monument," *The Daily Missoulian*, December 16, 1954, p. 2.

Hendrick, Kimmis. "A Woman's Wild West," *The Christian Science Monitor*, June 20, 1957, p. 7.

"Honor Author Dorothy Johnson," *The Missoula Sentinel*, February 19, 1959, p. 2.

Hufford, Kenneth. "Go West, Young Woman, Go West," *The Christian Science Monitor*, November 4, 1965, p. B-10.

"Hundreds Greet Western Writer Dorothy Johnson Here Last Saturday," *The Whitefish Pilot*, May 1, 1959, p. 1.

Hutchens, John K. "Book Review," *The New York Herald Tribune*, June 11, 1957, p. 23.

Hutchens, John K. "Book Review," *The New York Herald Tribune*, December 30, 1957, p. 13.

Johnson, Dorothy M. "A Fruitless Search for the Meaning of Life," *The New York Herald Tribune Book Review*, April 24, 1960, p. 11.

Johnson, Dorothy M. "Beatin' the Drum for Harry," *The Whitefish Pilot*, September 26, 1952, p. 2.

Johnson, Dorothy M. "Christmas Gift for Our Town," *The Whitefish Pilot*, December 19, 1952, p. 2.

Johnson, Dorothy M. "Ex-Street Light Guarder Recalls Hectic Night," *Great Falls Tribune Montana Parade*, December 30, 1951, p. 2.

Johnson, Dorothy M. "High School Graduation Packs One-Time Thrill," *Great Falls Tribune Montana Parade*, May 26, 1952, p. 2.

Johnson, Dorothy M. "Knight in Shining Armor Tames Rebellious Stove," *Great Falls Tribune Montana Parade*, July 20, 1952, p. 2.

Johnson, Dorothy M. "Maybe Harry Isn't Welcome Here," *The Whitefish Pilot*, September 12, 1952, p. 2.

Johnson, Dorothy M. *The Neighborhood News*, November, 1945, p. 1.

Johnson, Dorothy M. "This Is No Lie," *The Whitefish Pilot*, July 20, 1951, p. 1.

Johnson, Dorothy M. "This Is No Lie," *The Whitefish Pilot*, February 1, 1952, p. 1.

Johnson, Dorothy M. "This Is No Lie," *The Whitefish Pilot*, March 27, 1953, p. 1.

Johnson, Dorothy M. "Whitefish Writer Recalls Childhood at Rainbow Dam," *Great Falls Tribune Montana Parade*, March 2, 1952, p. 4.

Johnson, Dorothy M. "Who Can We Blame?" *The Whitefish Pilot*, December 26, 1952, p. 2.

Johnson, Dorothy M. "Wild West on a Wide Screen," *The Washington Post* book section, December 15, 1963.

Johnson, Dorothy M. "Writer Cites 'Ups-Downs' of Riding Experiences," *Great Falls Tribune Montana Parade*, March 23, 1952, p. 2.

Johnson, Dorothy M. "Writer Finds Montana Cattle Roundups Colorful— But Too Hard on Anatomy," *Great Falls Tribune Montana Parade*, June 8, 1952, pp. 8-9.

Johnson, Dorothy M. "Writer Promotes Science By Deserting Field," *Great Falls Tribune Montana Parade*, February 10, 1952, p. 4.

Johnson, Dorothy M. "Writer Says Press Camera Needs Full Flight Crew," *Great Falls Tribune Montana Parade*, February 24, 1952, p. 2.

Johnson, Virginia "Bookmark," *The Missoulian*, July 16, 1967, p. 3.

"Legislative Party Set by Theaters," *The Missoula Sentinel*, February 5, 1959, p. 16.

"Lester Johnson Succumbs," *The Whitefish Pilot*, December 16, 1915, p. 1.

"Miller Will Manage Press Association," *The Missoulian*, March 23, 1967, p. 1.

"Miss Dorothy Johnson, Waukau, Sells Story to Magazine for $400," *The Berlin* (Wisconsin) *Evening Journal*, September 18, 1930, p. 3.

"Montana Woman, 4 Men, Receive Writers' Awards," *Great Falls Tribune*, June 28, 1957, p. 1.

"New Book Tells of Montana's Past," *Hilo* (Hawaii) *Tribune Herald*, June 13, 1957, p. 11.

"Okanogan Girl's Story of Rodeo Published in Post!" *The Wenatchee* (Washington) *World*, October 16, 1930, p. 1.

Parsons, Louella. "Coop's Jammed Schedule Eliminates Paris Jaunt," *Norfolk-Portsmouth* (Virginia) *Ledger-Dispatch and Star*, November 23, 1957, p. 16.

Poore, Charles. "Books of the Times," *The New York Times*, June 13, 1957, p. 29.

"Press Secretary Quits Post," *The Missoulian*, December 25, 1966, p. 7.

"Rampaging Rivers Destroy Homes, Highways, Rails," *The Hungry Horse News*, June 15, 1964, p. 1.

Ruder, Mel. "Just the President Coming," *The Hungry Horse News*, September 19, 1952, p. 2.

Sloan, Agnes Getty. "From Greenwich Village to Montana Cabin," *The Spokesman-Review*, October 21, 1951, p. 5.

Tajiri, Larry. "Cooper, Schell Star in Psychiatric Oater," *The Denver Post*, February 25, 1959, p. 45.

Taylor, Tom. "Beulah Bunny Got Lift Here," *The Spokesman-Review*, April 1, 1945, p. 4.

"The Alumni," *North Iowa Times*, July 2, 1896, p. 1.

" 'The Hanging Tree' Preview Will Be Seen By Legislators," *Montana Kaimin*, January 4, 1959, p. 1.

"The Hanging Tree," *Variety*, January 28, 1959, p. 6.

The Villager, May 15, 1945, p. 2.

"The Week's Round-Up," *New York Journal-American*, May 12, 1957, p. 23.

The Yellowstone News, October 1, 1953, p. 2.

"Three Persons Will Be Honored at Homecoming This Weekend," *The Missoula Sentinel*, September 28, 1961, p. 13.

"Welcome Mr. President!," *The Whitefish Pilot*, September 26, 1952, p. 1.

"Whitefish Will Honor 'Dorothy,' " *The Whitefish Pilot*, April 24, 1959, p. 1.

Winsten, Archer. " 'Hanging Tree' Comes to the Roxy," *The New York Post*, February 12, 1959, p. 20.

" 'Writing Like Drilling for Oil,' Says Polson Banquet Speaker," *The Daily Missoulian*, January 21, 1958, p. 6.

Articles and periodicals

Agnew, Seth. "Romance of the .45," *Saturday Review*, 36, August 8, 1953, p. 16.

Alexander, Shana. "The Sad Lot of the Sioux," *Life*, 66, February 7, 1969, p. 14E.

Alpert, Hollis. "There's Gold in Those Theme Songs," *Saturday Review* XLII, February 7, 1959, p. 31.

"Author Paints Bright Picture of Opportunities for Women," *Montana High School Editor*, December, 1953, p. 1.

"Campfire Girl," *Time* LXX, August 5, 1957, pp. 79-80.

"Dorothy Johnson's First Run-In With Sales Competition," *The Colorado Editor*, June, 1956, p. 8.

"Dorothy Johnson's Honors Multiplied by 'Hanging Tree,' " *School of Journalism Communique*, 16, Winter, 1959, p. 3.

"Dorothy Johnson Slated to Speak at Banff Confab on Northwestern History," *Montana Post*, 5, May, 1967, p. 3.

"Endlessly the Covered Wagon," *The Frontier*, VIII, November, 1927, title page.

Frederick, John T. "Speaking of Books," *The Rotarian*, October, 1953, p. 38.

"Historical Stories," *The Commonweal*, LXXXI, November 6, 1964, p. 206.

"Hoka Hey! Klatowa! (Let's Go!)," *Montana Press Bulletin*, XV, March, 1954, p. 2.

"If You Can't Lick 'Em, Join 'Em," *Montana Fourth Estate*, XX, July, 1959, p. 3.

Johnson, Dorothy M. "A Valiant Search for His Vision," *Saturday Review*, 43, March 5, 1960, p. 17.

Johnson, Dorothy Marie. "Bread and Hyacinths," *The Frontier*, VI, March 1926, p. 15.

Johnson, Dorothy Marie. "Confession," "Shams" and "Question," *The Frontier*, V, March 1925, pp. 11, 13.

Johnson, Dorothy. "Emotion and the Fiction Writer," *Discourse, A Review of the Liberal Arts*, April, 1960, pp. 113-118.

Johnson, Dorothy Marie "Fear," *The Frontier*, X, March, 1930, p. 234.

Johnson, Dorothy M. "First Date," *Collier's*, 124, December 31, 1949, p. 29, 67, 68, 69.

Johnson, Dorothy M. "Greece: The Image and the Fact," *Montana Journalism Review*, Spring, 1962, pp. 21-23.

Johnson, Dorothy Marie. "Highways are Happy Ways," *The Frontier*, XI, March, 1931, pp. 249-256.

Johnson, Dorothy M. "How Well do You Like People?" *The Writer*, December, 1943, pp. 365-366.

Johnson, Dorothy "I Was a Teen-Age Poacher," *Montana Sports Outdoors*, 2, May, 1960, pp. 13-14.

Johnson, Dorothy Marie. "I Was Never a River," *The Frontier*, VII, November, 1926, p. 11.

Johnson, Dorothy Marie. "If You Know War Again," *Frontier and Midland*, XIV, March 1934, p. 202.

Johnson, Dorothy M. "169th Issue Swan Song," *Montana Fourth Estate*, XXVIII, April, 1967, p. 2.

Johnson, Dorothy M. "Killer on Our Highways," *Good Housekeeping*, June, 1961, reprint.

Johnson, Dorothy M. "My Favorite Town—Whitefish, Montana," *Ford Times*, 43, May, 1951, pp. 42-47.

Johnson, Dorothy M. "No Scrapbook Needed: Ruder's Pulitzer Nomination," *Montana Journalism Review*, Spring 1966, pp. 5-7.

Johnson, Dorothy M. "Notes on the Fourth of July," *Montana Fourth Estate*, XXVI, July, 1965, pp. 16-17.

Johnson, Dorothy M. "Now George Washington's Dead," *Montana Fourth Estate*, XVIII, May, 1957, p. 2.

Johnson, Dorothy M. "Now There Is No Daydreaming," *Montana Fourth Estate*, XVIII, April, 1957, p. 2.

Johnson, Dorothy Marie. "Old Mine," "The Breed" and "From A Train Window," *The Frontier*, IV, May, 1924, pp. 1, 10, 18.

Johnson, Dorothy M. "One Man's Vendetta," *Saturday Review*, 41, April 19, 1958, p. 21.

Johnson, Dorothy M. "Poor Reporting Deplored," *Montana Fourth Estate*, XVIII, February 1947, p. 2.

Johnson, Dorothy M. "Research for Writing," *The Writer*, January, 1943, pp. 11-13.

Johnson, Dorothy M. Review of *Frontier Editor*, Montana, *The Magazine of Western History*, VII, Winter, 1957, p. 50.

Johnson, Dorothy M. Review of *Montana, An Uncommon Land*, *Oregon Historical Quarterly*, LX, December, 1959, pp. 496-97.

Johnson, Dorothy M. Review of *Piegan*, Montana, *The Magazine of Western History*, XVII, October, 1967, p. 84.

Johnson, Dorothy M. "So History Ain't Good Enough?," *The Roundup*, VII, May, 1959, pp. 9-10.

Johnson, Dorothy M. "Study Folk-Songs and Like 'em!" *Business Education World*, January, 1947, pp. 284-85.

Johnson, Dorothy M. "The Feud of the Fur-Bearing Fish," *The Woman*, XIV, March, 1945, pp. 48-50.

Johnson, Dorothy M. "The Wonderful If," *The Writer*, 65, June, 1952, pp. 191-95.

Johnson, Dorothy M. "Totally We Want to Know," *Montana Fourth Estate*, XVIII, June, 1957, p. 2.

Johnson, Dorothy Marie. "The Fruit Tramps," *The Frontier*, X, January, 1930, pp. 131-134.

Johnson, Dorothy M. "The Years and the Wind and the Rain," *The Montana Insitute of the Arts Quarterly*, XIII, Winter, 1961, pp. 3-4.

Johnson, Dorothy M. "When a Book Becomes a Movie," *Montana Journalism Review*, Spring, 1960, pp. 11-13.

Johnson, Dorothy M. "When a Promise Is Not a Promise," *Montana Fourth Estate*, XVIII, July, 1957, p. 2.

Kauffmann, Stanley. "A Lovely Uncivilized Feeling," *New Republic*, 140, February 16, 1959, p. 21.

"Knighthood in Flower," *Newsweek*, LIII, February 16, 1959, p. 102.

Murray, Gretchen Y. "Miss Bunny Goes to Jail," *Criticism, Suggestion and Advice*, XII, March 7, 1942, p. 3.

"No Bang, No Whimper," *The Commonweal*, LXIX, February 6, 1959, p. 497.

"The New Pictures," *Time*, LXXIII, February 16, 1959, p. 101.

"The Six-Gun Galahad," *Time*, LXXIII, March 30, 1959, p. 57.

Vance, John T. Review of *Indian Country*, *Montana, The Magazine of Western History*, Spring, 1966, p. 73.

Westermeier, Therese S. "Some Went West," *Montana, The Magazine of Western History*, Spring, 1966, p. 73.

"Whitefish-Great Northern 50th Anniversary, *The Great Northern Goat*, June, 1953, p. 7.

Wright, Kathryn. "Dorothy Johnson's Tips on Fiction Writing," *The Billings Gazette Midland Empire Magazine*, September 2, 1962, p. 1.

"YOU Have Reporting Troubles," *Montana Press Bulletin*, XV, July, 1954, p. 2.

Personal interviews

Adams, Richard, interviewed by the author, Whitefish, Montana, January 14, 1969.

Blumberg, Dr. Nathaniel B., interviewed by the author, Missoula, Montana, February 24, 1969.

Brier, Dr. Warren J., interviewed by the author, Missoula, Montana, February 21, 1969.

Burgess, Dr. Robert M., interviewed by the author, Missoula, Montana, February 21, 1969.

Eggensperger, K.A., interviewed by the author, Missoula, Montana, November 11, 1968.

Engelter, Mrs. A.C., interviewed by the author, Whitefish, Montana, January 14, 1969.

Johnson, Dorothy M., interviewed by the author, Missoula, Montana, June 26, July 3, July 10, July 17, August 5, August 12, August 19, September 12, October 16, November 7 and December 13, 1968; January 2 and January 20, 1969. Numerous interviews throughout 1970s and early 1980s.

Merriam, Dr. Harold G., interviewed by the author, Missoula, Montana, August 9, 1968.

Moss, Gurnie M., interviewed by the author, Kalispell, Montana, January 15, 1969.

Ruder Mel, interviewed by the author, Columbia Falls, Montana, January 14, 1969.

Van Duser, Cyrile, interviewed by the author, Missoula, Montana, September 4, 1968.

Telephone conversations

DeVall, Lawrence, Whitefish restaurateur, telephone conversation with the Author, October 22, 1968.

Johnson, Dorothy M., telephone conversations with the author, July 25, October 8, October 19, November 22 and November 27, 1968.

Millhouse, Glenn, Flathead County clerk and recorder, telephone conversations with the author, October 17, 1968.

Noel, Mrs. L.E., Missoula housewife, telephone conversation with the author, November 18, 1968.

Ohnstad, Leone, Department of Vital Statistics, Montana State Board of Health, telephone conversations with the author, October 17, 1968, and February 17, 1969.

Roy, Russell, superintendent of Conrad Memorial Cemetery, Kalispell, Montana, telephone conversation with the author, October 17, 1968.

Letters

Blanchard, Clyde, former colleague of Dorothy Johnson's, to the author, September 16, 1968.

Burnham, Catharine A., longtime friend of Dorothy Johnson's, to the author, January 3, 1969.

Colbert, Opal, longtime friend of Dorothy Johnson's, to the author, September 21, 1968.

Engelter, Mrs. A.C., librarian emeritus, Whitefish, Montana, Public Library, to the author, January 18, 1969.

Frailey, L.E., expert on business correspondence, to Dorothy M. Johnson, July 22, 1935.

Gehrett, Mrs. J.O., Deer Lodge, Montana, to the author, January 27, 1969.

Golder, Clarence, to Dorothy M. Johnson, January 29, 1959.

Johnson, Dorothy M., to the author, December 26, 1968.

Johnson, Dorothy M., to the editor of *Time*, LXXIII, April 27, 1959, p. 4.

Johnson, Dorothy M., to Mel Ruder, December 26, 1956; January 3, 1957; April 7, 1959; and October 25, 1959.

Johnson, Dorothy M., to the *Montana Kaimin*, February 17, 1965, p. 2.

Johnson, Dorothy M., to Steward Richardson, December 30, 1968.

Johnson, Dorothy M., to *The Missoulian*, February 4, 1966, p. 4.

Johnson, Dorothy M., to *The Missoulian*, November 1, 1967, p. 6.

Johnson, Dorothy M., to *The Missoulian*, December 21, 1967, p. 6.

Johnson, Dorothy M., to *The Missoulian*, January 21, 1968, p. 6.

Johnson, Dorothy M., to *The Missoulian*, February 7, 1968, p. 6.

Johnson, Dorothy M., to *The Missoulian*, June 30, 1968, p. 6.

Johnson, Dorothy M., to *The Missoulian*, October 29, 1968, p. 6.

Lynde, Stan, syndicated cartoonist, to the author, December 12, 1968.

McLaughlin, Nancy, to the editor of *Montana, The Magazine of Western History*, XVIII, April, 1968, p. 94.

Myers, Mrs. Lena D., curator of the McGregor, Iowa, Historical Museum, to the author, October 6, 1968.

Owen, Charles N., to Dorothy M. Johnson, February 15, 1954.

Peterson, Helen M., publisher of the *Hardin* (Montana) *Tribune Herald*, to the author, January 7, 1969.

Pouliot, Gordon L., to Vivian A. Paladin, letter undated.

Sandberg, Paul, to Dorothy M. Johnson, February 2, 1965.

Stearns, Harold G., publisher of the *Harlowton* (Montana) *Times*, to the author, December 4, 1968.

Taggart, Mrs. Homer G., Dorothy Johnson's aunt, to the author, October 22, 1968.

Taylor, H.B., to Dorothy M. Johnson, November 23, 1953.

Other sources

"Beulah Bunny Isn't Dorothy Johnson," *Inside Information from the Saturday Evening Post*, March 16, 1945, p. 2.

Birch, James (pseudonym for Dorothy Johnson), *Printed Salesmanship Letter Problem No. 18*, October, 1934, p. 40.

Gurney Moss file on Whitefish and the Great Northern Railroad, available at the Whitefish Public Library.

Johnson, Dorothy M., "Books Can Get You Into Trouble as Well as Out of It," address reprinted in *The Idaho Librarian*, 19, July, 1967, pp. 75-81.

Johnson, Dorothy M., "My Goodness, All Those Books!" *Books Are Friends*, booklet published by the Montana State Library Association, 1962, pp. 6-8.

Johnson, Dorothy M., "The Use of Historical Material in Writing for Mass Media," address delivered May 20, 1967, at the Centennial Conference on the History of the Canadian West, Banff, Alberta, Canada, May 17-20, 1967.

Johnson, Marie, "The Moon Queen," *The Alforja* (1920 Whitefish High School yearbook), p. 29.

Johnson family baby book, now in Dorothy Johnson's possession.

Schaefer, Jack, foreword to *Indian Country* (New York: Ballantine Books, Inc., 1953).

"Short Life for Busy Boom Town," Warner Brothers Studio press release.